Following the Saints

THE CATHOLIC LAYMAN'S LIBRARY, Volume 6

John P. Bradley, *Editor*

Following the Saints

September 1st through December 31st

by Edmund Colledge, O.S.A.
and James Walsh, S.J.

GOOD WILL PUBLISHERS, INC.
Gastonia, North Carolina

Library of Congress Catalog Card Number:
74-92278

NIHIL OBSTAT
   Bernard L. Rosswog, O.S.B., S.T.D.
   Censor Librorum

IMPRIMATUR
   ☩ Edmund F. McCaffrey, O.S.B., Ph.D., D.D.
   Abbot-Ordinary, Diocese of Belmont Abbey Nullius

Art Editor: Kathrine B. Sanborn

ACKNOWLEDGMENTS

We wish to thank the following publishers for permission to use copyrighted material:

A. W. Sijthoff's Uitgeversmaatschappij N. V. for a quotation from *The Spiritual Espousals.*

Burns & Oates, Ltd. for a quotation from *Frances Xavier Cabrini: the Saint of the Emigrants.*

Charles Scribner's Sons for a quotation from "The Mirror of Holy Church" in *The Mediaeval Mystics of England.*

Oxford University Press and the British Academy for a quotation from *Archbishop Thomas Becket: a Character Study.*

The Catholic University Press of America for a quotation from "Clement of Alexandria" in Volume I of *Fathers of the Church.*

Contents

September

v

October

November   PAGE

December

Abbreviations

Gen.	Genesis		Gal.	Galatians
Ex.	Exodus		Eph.	Ephesians
Prov.	Proverbs		Phil.	Philippians
Is.	Isaiah		Col.	Colossians
Ezek.	Ezekiel		Thess.	Thessalonians
Matt.	Matthew		Tim.	Timothy
Acts	Acts of the Apostles		Heb.	Hebrews
Rom.	Romans		Pet.	Peter
Cor.	Corinthians		Rev.	Revelation

PG   *Patrologia graeca,* a collection of the writings of the Greek Fathers of the Church, edited by J. P. Migne.

PL   *Patrologia latina,* a collection of the writings of the Latin Fathers of the Church, edited by J. P. Migne.

AB   *Analecta Bollandiana,* a periodical published quarterly by the Society of the Bollandists; the first issue appeared in 1882.

BS   *Bibliotheca Sanctorum,* a reference work in dictionary form prepared by the Istituto Giovanni XXIII della Pontificia Universita Laterana in Rome.

DTC   *Dictionnaire de théologie catholique,* a dictionary of Catholic theology, 15 vols. (Paris, 1899–1950).

NCE   *New Catholic Encyclopedia,* Volumes 1–15, prepared by an editorial staff at the Catholic University of America, Washington, D.C., and published by the McGraw-Hill Book Company, New York, in 1966.

PES   *Pre-Reformation English Spirituality,* edited by James Walsh, S.J. (New York, 1965).

SC   *Spirituality Through the Centuries: Ascetics and Mystics of the Western Church,* edited by James Walsh, S.J. (New York, 1964).

Saints for September

If you would be perfect, sell your will and give it to the poor in spirit; come to Christ through meekness and humility; and follow Him to Calvary and the grave.

ST. JOHN OF THE CROSS
Spiritual Sentences and Maxims

Drithelm
Confessor

died about 700

OUR ONLY first-hand knowledge of St. Drithelm and of his visions is derived from Bede, who tells us that he lived in the first years of the eighth century, a layman farming in Northumberland who had lived with his family a most pious life. Then, stricken with sickness, he was thought to be dead for the whole of one night; but at dawn he sat up and spoke, to the terror of all the mourners, who fled, except for his wife, whose fear was overcome by her love for him.

He told her that he had been permitted to return again to the living, but that from now on his life would be changed. At once he shared all his possessions between her, his sons, and the poor. He then went to the abbey of Melrose, where the abbot accepted him, gave him the tonsure, and provided him with a dwelling apart, where he lived until the end of his days.

Bede says that even if Drithelm had remained silent, his life thereafter would have been witness enough to the visions of terror and delight which he had been granted. These visions, as he afterwards recounted them to Bede's informants, are of great historical interest. In part they are a witness to man's belief, older than Christianity itself, that the departed souls of those whom we have loved are not wholly beyond our help; the early Church was not slow to see in the pagan legend of Orpheus and Eurydice a "type" of the risen Christ invading Hell and leading out from it the souls of Adam and his progeny. Partly, too, what Drithelm saw corresponds to that ancient view, with its roots in pagan and Jewish traditions, of a life between death and judgment compounded of torment and suffering. When he has been led, as Dante was to be led by Virgil, through the nether world, his guide explains to him that the terrible valley of fire and cold, with despairing souls plunging themselves out of one insupportable affliction into another, is a place of expiation for those who have postponed repentance till the very moment of death—though prayers, alms, fastings, and Masses may all help them to escape this dread region even before the Day of Judgment.

Yet, as the vision proceeds, we come to an element rare among the horrific medieval accounts of the soul's purgations: the description of a place of peace and joy so wonderful that Drithelm himself is constrained to believe that this must be Paradise, until his guide instructs him better. In remarkable fashion Drithelm is anticipating the insights of a Catherine of Genoa (*see* September 15), and promising us that in Purgatory itself we shall "sleep the sleep of peace."

A Vision of Purgatory

"As my guide led me into the light of day, I saw in front of us an immense wall, extending so far in either direction and looming so high that it seemed boundless. I was amazed, and asked myself why we were going there, for it seemed to have no door or aperture or entrance. But when we arrived at the wall, we seemed at once to have surmounted it, how I do not know. And there we found a meadow, vast and filled with every delight, so perfumed by flowering, flourishing plants that all the evil odors of the dark furnace through which we had passed were dispelled. And the place was bathed in a light that seemed to surpass all the day's brightness and the splendors of the midday sun. And here in this field were countless groups of men clothed in white, and many others who sat there and rejoiced. And as he conducted me among all these happy citizens, I began to think that this perhaps might be the kingdom of heaven, of which I had so often heard men preach. But he replied to my thoughts: 'No, this is not what you think, it is not the kingdom of heaven.'"

Bede's narration of Drithelm's account of his vision of Purgatory

Bede: *Ecclesiastical History of the English Peoples.*

John Mary du Lau and Companions
Martyrs

died 1792

BLESSED JOHN DU LAU and his one hundred and ninety companions who perished with him during the "little Terror" in Paris represent here the many, from every walk of life, who died for the Catholic faith during the French Revolution. Our judgment today on these events must reflect present changes in thought on such topics as the right of the oppressed to fight against their misery and to resist tyranny, and the proper role of the Church in world politics. It is no longer possible for us, therefore, to regard the revolutionary forces in France as wholly evil. But the course of events which led to the Terrors illustrates too clearly what we have seen re-enacted in our own times: that the violent overthrow of tyranny leads to the substitution of other tyrannies, often worse.

The Revolution was bred out of the unspeakable degradation of the French workers and the impotence of the government to improve matters or to administer the country's affairs. It was inspired by the highest motives on the new American model; all men were to be free and equal, and events would show how this was to be achieved. The age of privilege was to end; and one of the most privileged classes was the clergy, possessed of great wealth and exempted from the ruinous taxation under which the country had groaned.

The clergy's privileges were abolished, their property was confiscated, and they in return were guaranteed a sufficient support, as servants of the State. This alone earned condemnation from Rome; but more was to come. A declaration of religious freedom was followed by the forcible closing of most religious houses, and then by a demand that all clerics take a civil oath to uphold the new constitution, enshrining such principles, which Pius VI had in 1791 solemnly condemned. Many took the oath, but others considered that to do so constituted apostasy; this opinion is most dramatically presented in the queen, Marie Antoinette, choosing to die on the scaffold without the sacraments, rather than accept the ministrations of a priest who had so sworn.

At first it seems to have been the intention that the clerics who did not take the oath should be expelled from France; but this was frustrated by events. In the summer of 1792 Austrian and Prussian armies invaded the country, and were pushing forward toward Paris, where panic and rule by the mob ensued. Clerics awaiting the journey into exile were rounded up and confined in the former Carmelite house and other places. There, self-constituted tribunals put the oath to them again, and, as they refused it, had them butchered out of hand.

Among them were John du Lau, archbishop of Arles, and two bishop brothers, the de la Rochfoucaulds, Francis Joseph, bishop of Beauvais, and Peter Louis, bishop of Saintes. With them died almost two hundred men representing many different orders and congregations (a notable number were former Jesuits who had persevered in the religious life after the dissolution of the Society), as well as the secular clergy. From the time of their death they were venerated as martyrs for the faith.

God's People Suffer Persecution

"Alas, why was I born to see my people ruined and the holy city despoiled, to live in it when it has been surrendered to its enemies? The holy places are in the hands of enemies, the Temple is like a man dishonored. The vessels which made it glorious are carried away, the old men are murdered in the streets and the young men have fallen to their enemies' swords. What nation has not seized and despoiled Jerusalem? Her adornments are taken away, and she who was born free is now a slave. Our sanctuary, our beauty, our glory are all destroyed, and strangers have defiled them. Why, then, should we live any longer?"

1 Maccabees 2:7–13

Acta Apostolicae Sedis, 1926, pp. 415-25.

Pius X
Pope

died 1914

BESIDES OUTSTANDING HOLINESS, St. Pius X and John XXIII have many other traits in common. They were each patriarch of Venice when they were elected pope; and, unlike most popes of modern times, they had had wide and long pastoral experience. But, unlike John, Pius worked all his life in Italy. After his ordination, he acted for nine years as assistant priest, eight as pastor, nine as spiritual director of a seminary and chancellor of a diocese, until, in 1884, he was made bishop of Mantua and, in 1893, cardinal patriarch of Venice.

He was compelled to accept these last two promotions despite his own extreme unwillingness; few electors can have faced the prospect of their own election to the papacy with more dread than he did. Yet, once elected, he showed a serene confidence that in accepting the divine will he would receive divine help.

It is easy to judge Pius X's pontificate by hindsight and to call him a reactionary. It is true that the cause of ecumenism (which, despite Leo XIII's encyclical letter declaring Anglican orders invalid, had made some progress under that pope) found little favor with Pius. It is also true that in the history of the development of doctrine he may chiefly be remembered for his campaign against modernism, and his condemnation in *Lamentabili* of many of the movement's propositions. But to read those propositions, to follow the later history of the modernist leaders who knew themselves to be condemned, is to realize how ill-judged their interventions were in that day and age, and what a danger much of their thought was, and would be in any era, to the faith of the Church. Pius was concerned, before all else, with the protection of the faith of the laity and the clergy. Some of the measures which he took to this end, and the "integralism" which he is said to have favored, are not for our times; but he believed that unrestricted freedom of utterance in theology could lead to the loss of many souls to the Church.

But it is false to claim that Pius, always protesting his own lack of learning, was himself either ignorant or an obscurantist enemy of scholarship. This would be proved alone by his success in establishing the Pontifical Biblical Institute, at a time when many with influence in such matters were convinced that modern techniques of biblical criticism were of their very nature aimed at undermining the inerrancy of Scripture.

When we read the evidence of those who knew him and worked with him concerning his own personal sanctity, his love of prayer, his consuming desire everywhere to promote peace, we perceive what an unending martyrdom his pontificate must have been to him; at its close was the outbreak of the First World War, which was truly the war that ended all peace. It is not too much to say that this cataclysm, and, above all, the spectacle of Catholic nations intent upon destroying one another, broke the old man's heart. He, to whom so many miracles of healing had been attributed during his life, thankfully accepted the death that was sent to him a few weeks after hostilities began.

When his personal possessions were collected, they were found to include an old purse containing his only ready money, a few lire, and the return half of the third class railway ticket with which he had made his last journey from Venice to Rome.

A Christian Attitude Toward Promotion to Authority

"After fifteen days of cruel agony, yesterday it was absolutely confirmed to me that the Holy Father wants me as bishop of Mantua. I had begged the Holy Father and begged him again to leave a poor wretch like me in his poverty, but my pleadings were unheard. My dear Monsignor—I, bishop of the diocese of Mantua, I to succeed holy and learned bishops like Monsignor Rota and Monsignor Berengo! Please pray for me to our good God, that he may pour a little balm in my wounds, may give me strength to carry this cross."

The future Pius X to the bishop of Padua, 13 September, 1884

H. Dal-Gal, trans. and ed. T. F. Murray: *Pius X* (Westminster, Md., 1953).
Nello Vian, ed.: *San Pio X, Lettere* (Rome, 1954).

Rose of Viterbo
Franciscan Tertiary

died 1252

TODAY, WHEN THE CHURCH's institutions are being so much criticized as formed by a paternalistic, male-dominated society such
as no longer exists in most Western countries, it is of great interest
to find, in former ages, women who could overcome opposition to
play a more active part in Christian living than tradition allowed
them. St. Rose of Viterbo, is, in medieval history, a most unusual
case, for the Holy Spirit moved her to proclaim in public the word
of God. For any woman to do this at that time branded her as a
heretic; but this was manifestly not true of her, for her whole
apostolate was directed against the heretics of her time and region.

The poverty of her parents seems to have been exaggerated by
the chroniclers. They were poor working people of Viterbo, but
since we know that they owned their house and a plot of land they
farmed, they cannot have been destitute. They lived in humble
obscurity, and so did their daughter until, two years before her
death, when she seems to have been about seventeen years old,
she received her first vision, of the souls and fates of many Viterbo
citizens long dead. Soon after, she was thought to be fatally ill,
but was cured, miraculously, it was considered, and on her recovery she was clothed as a Franciscan Tertiary.

She had already shown great love of poverty and a contempt
for earthly vanities and pleasure; and her spirituality was marked
by a profound and continuous meditation on Christ's Passion.
This was translated into action, as she went about Viterbo singing
"praises," calling men to the love of God and recollection of their
Savior's sufferings. Her biographers (the best authority is the

"First Life," a fragment only, but of the second half of the thirteenth century) hasten to assure us that this was no kind of preaching. But, although we can understand their anxiety to make the distinction, it is not perhaps so clear as they would have wished.

At this period a heresiarch called Peter of Lombardy was making many converts in Viterbo. He and his adherents seem to have enjoyed the support of the Ghibelline faction, who were aiming at the destruction, in favor of the emperor, Frederick II, of the Church's civil authority; and in return for Rose's vehement denunciation of them the heretics seem for a time to have contrived her expulsion from the city. But the death of Frederick caused great numbers of them to flee, and Rose was able to return. She then applied to the Poor Clares of Viterbo for admission, but she was refused, on a mere pretext, it is believed. Apparently, the nuns wanted no "evangelical preacheress" among them.

A year later she died; and this was followed by many miracles worked through her intercessions.

A Holy Woman's Role in the Church

"The bishop and clerics, the councillors and people of Viterbo desire that this light should not be hidden under a basket, but that it should shine out to show the truth for the instruction of the faithless, the increase of faith in believers. And they have been stirred by the signs and wonders to petition us to receive the fervent testimony of those who have faith in this new rose, in the merits of her life and the reports of miracles. . . wrought through the prayers of this holy intercessor for men at the throne of God."

Bull of Innocent IV, Sic in Sanctis, *November, 1252*

G. Abate: *S. Rosa da Viterbo, Terziaria Francescana* (Miscellanea Francescana, 52, 1952, pp. 113-278).

Lawrence Giustiniani
Patriarch of Venice

died 1455

St. Lawrence Giustiniani was born and died a Venetian, and he has ever since been held in special devotion by "the most serene city." At first he embraced a life of seclusion, in a company of secular canons regular who lived on one of the islands in the lagoon; presently they were constituted a congregation, which he served in many capacities, lastly, four times as their general.

In 1433 he was nominated bishop of Castello; and in 1451 Pope Nicholas V brought to an end a centuries-old dispute for pre-eminence between several sees constituting the Venetian archdiocese, by suppressing the diocese of Castello and the patriarchate of Gradi, and nominating Lawrence as archbishop and first patriarch of Venice. These changes, and Lawrence's taking possession of his new see, were strongly opposed, for political reasons, by the city's secular rulers, who, however, were in the course of time won over by the patriarch's personal qualities.

Singularly devoid of ambition, gentle and moderate in the exercise of authority, his attachment to his own poverty was equalled only by his liberality in alms-giving to the poor and distressed. He was a man of great holiness of life, a lover of prayer, an outstanding preacher and the writer of many spiritual works. These are filled with his love for Eternal Wisdom, the spirit of truth and understanding, transforming and divinizing men's lives, made known to them in the Word made flesh. A modern critic has said of his apostolate that it was "a diffusion of truth permeated by love."

66942

In recent times, the Venetian people have had few higher tributes to pay to his successors as patriarch, Pope St. Pius X (*see* September 3) and Pope John XXIII, than to recognize in them the traits of St. Lawrence Giustiniani.

The Grace to Accept the Message of Salvation

"When He who was the Wisdom of God, our Lord Jesus, came in flesh to us, He, the Lord of all, making Himself as it were common to every man, did everything to teach us to hate wickedness, to cultivate virtue, to recognize the truth and to hasten on the way that leads to eternal life. And yet not all the living received these words, but those only to whom this was given from on high. Such as were moved by an inward grace accepted the message of salvation, and were made members of the Body of Christ. The Lord knows who are His own, He knows who are predestined to life, whom in His own time He will justify. He spoke of them, solely and specially, when He said to the Father: 'I have made known your name to those whom you have given me out of the world.' Think carefully who those are to whom the only-begotten Son made known the Father's name: not indeed those whom the world counts wise, not those resplendent with the world's honors, not those demanding favors; but only those in whom the Father took delight, and whom He called, in His Son, before time began, to His own praise and glory."

Lawrence Giustiniani: Fasciculum Amoris, *XVIII*

Acta Sanctorum, January, vol. i.
G. Di Agresti, art.: "Lawrence Justinian, St." (NCE, 8, pp. 567–68).
Sancti Laurentii Justiniani Opera Omnia (2 vols., Venice, 1751).

Bertrand of Garrigues
Dominican Friar

died about 1230

BLESSED BERTRAND was born at Garrigues, near Alais in France. He was one of the first followers of Dominic (*see* August 4), from the year 1216 onwards often with him on his journeyings, and he was one of those who decided with him on the rule which the new Order of mendicants was to follow. They received the ready approval of the legate and the bishop to settle in Toulouse, recently reconquered from the Albigensian heretics, so that their house, its regular life, and the evangelical preaching campaigns organized from it, might give stability to the whole recently-converted region.

The Dominicans soon won a reputation for great learning, and came to occupy a place in the universities of Europe greater, perhaps, than their founder had foreseen; but Bertrand represents for us rather the saintly wisdom which inspired that learning. He had completely absorbed Dominic's own interior way of life; he had a reputation for relentless self-mortification, for his vigils and fasts, and he sought solitude whenever it could be won without depriving others. We may believe that it was only on a base like this that lives of such intense activity could be built and not founder.

Bertrand was the first provincial of Provence. He died with a reputation for great holiness, and twenty-three years after his burial his body was found still to be incorrupt.

Praying for the Dead

"Friar Bertrand used to offer his Mass almost every day for sinners. Friar Benedict, a holy and wise man, heard of this and asked him why he celebrated so often, not for the dead, but for sinners. He said: 'Because the dead for whom the Church prays are safe, and it is certain that they will come to salvation; but we sinners are in great danger, wavering on the brink.' The other friar said: 'Dearest Prior, if two beggars, equally poor, were here, but one was wholly sound in body, whereas the other was quite helpless, which of them would you aid first?' He answered: 'The one less able to help himself.' Then Friar Benedict said: 'The dead have no mouths with which to confess, no ears to hear with, no eyes to weep with, no hands to work with, no feet with which to go on pilgrimage; all they can plead for, all they can hope for is our help.'"

From Gerard de Francheto's Vitae Fratrum

Acta Sanctorum, October, vol. xiii.

Mark, Stephen, and Melchior
Martyrs

died 1619

IT IS PROBABLY TRUE to say that no other war of religion in Europe has ever equalled the Thirty Years' War in its accumulation of horror and of insane cruelty, displayed by all the contenders alike. As ever, it was the common people, the poor, the defenseless who suffered most. So long as history is read, men will be filled with disgust to read what, in those thirty years, was done in central Europe in the name of Christ. We know, of course, how mixed were the motives of those waging the war, how little religion entered into their true calculations; but, nonetheless, there were countless fanatics, on either side, who believed that their profession of one faith or another justified them in conduct so unspeakable that it is hard even to read of it.

Today three victims of that war are commemorated: Blessed Mark Crisin, a Croat, a canon of the archdiocese of Esztergom, and two Jesuits, Blessed Stephen Pongracz, a Hungarian, and Blessed Melchior Grodecz, a Czech. These men, of different nations and tongues, were all engaged in apostolic work in or about the city of Kosice in Slovakia, and were trapped in the city's siege by Calvinist troops. The authorities of the city, in surrendering it, were able to obtain unwonted clemency for its inhabitants, but these three priests were specifically excluded from the agreement to spare the Catholic population. It may be that they were chosen as scapegoats, to direct the fury of the soldiers away from the laity, who had to stand by and watch in helpless agony what was done to them.

They had been imprisoned in a place where they had a humble little oratory, and their lack of money, the poverty of their possessions and of the sacred vessels and furnishings, seems to have infuriated even further their captors, doubtless well conditioned by propaganda about the Church's untold wealth. They were subjected to prolonged and atrocious torture and butchery, the details of which it is not seemly to recount. All who were forced to witness the vile and shameful ways in which they were killed testified afterwards to their constancy, their patience, and to their unceasing prayer throughout their sufferings.

The First Christian Martyr

> "[Stephen said] 'Which of the prophets did your fathers not persecute? They killed those who foretold the coming of Jesus, whom you have betrayed and slain, you to whom angels delivered the Law which you have not kept.' When they heard this their hearts were full of rage, and they gnashed their teeth at him. But he was filled with the Holy Spirit, and looking up to heaven, he saw God's glory and Jesus standing at his right hand; and he said: 'Behold, I see the heavens opened and the Son of Man standing at the right hand of God!' But they raised a great shout, and would not listen to him, and all together rushed at him, and forced him out of the city, and stoned him."
>
> *Acts 7:52–58*

H. Leclercq: *Les martyrs*, 8, pp. 338–52 (Paris, 1908).

Sergius I
Pope

died 701

THE HISTORY OF Pope St. Sergius I evokes in us, more than anything, compassion for him and for any man called to rule in the See of Peter. In addition to his many other sorrows, it fell to his lot, though he was a Syrian born in Antioch, to assert the rights and privileges of the Church of Rome against Orientals, spiritual as well as lay rulers, who had no other end in view than the disruption of the Church's peace and unity.

His father, Tiberius, had been a Syrian merchant before the family emigrated to Sicily, where Sergius received his education, in Palermo. He showed, as a boy, outstanding musical ability; and he went to Rome for study, where he was ordained priest by Pope St. Leo II, that is, between 682 and 684, when, according to seventh-century custom, he would be about thirty years old.

In 687 Pope Conon died, and the scandalous contentions of the rivals for the succession threatened to divide the Church, as they did the city of Rome. Even before Conon was dead, his archdeacon, Paschal, had offered a handsome bribe to John Platyn, the representative at Ravenna of the emperor in Constantinople (Justinian II) to secure Paschal's election; and a factional college did name Paschal as pope. But another faction chose the archpriest of the Lateran, Theodore, and the rival "popes" and their supporters occupied different parts of the Lateran, refusing to budge until the Roman people drove them all out, and acclaimed and installed Sergius as pope.

In 692, under Justinian's aegis, was held in Constantinople

the "Council in Trullo" (called from the great hall in which it met), otherwise known as the "Quinisextum," the "Fifth-Sixth," because it claimed to draw up disciplinary canons to complete the work of the Fifth and Sixth General Councils. Two hundred and fifteen bishops attended, all of them Orientals, although one of them belonged to "the Roman patriarchate" and styled himself, evidently on no authority, "legate." The canons of this assembly, "this reprobate synod," as Bede was to call it, were intended to impose the discipline of Constantinople upon all the other churches, including Rome, especially in the matter of clerical marriage. When Sergius received these canons he said that he would die rather than confirm them; and when Justinian sent the leader of his guard to Rome to bring Sergius by force to Constantinople to submit, it was in the end Sergius who had to intervene to save the emperor's emissary from the fury of the Roman mob.

Sergius baptized Cadwalla, king of the West Saxons, a convert from paganism, and he did much to promote Willibrord's mission to the Frisians. He knew of the fame of Bede (*see* May 27), and asked his abbot to send him to Rome as a counsellor to the pope; but it is certain that Bede never went there.

We owe several features of our modern liturgy to Sergius, including the recitation of the Agnus Dei at Mass.

The Agnus Dei in the Liturgy of the Eucharist

"In ancient times there was mention by the Greeks of the 'Lamb of God' in the sacred liturgy, but not in the form of a prayer. In the Liturgy of St. James there is: 'Behold the Lamb of God, Son of the Father, who takes away the sins of the world'; and in the Liturgy of St. John Chrysostom, the priest, when he is about to divide the holy bread, says: 'The Lamb of God, the Son of the Father, is broken and divided' . . . It was Pope Sergius who decreed that in the Latin rite 'Have mercy on us' be said three times, but when later so many catastrophes befell the Church, as Innocent III says, or, perhaps, according to others, to pray for the end of schism, it was ruled that the third repetition should end with 'Grant us peace,' which rite is followed everywhere, except in the Lateran basilica, where the ancient form of saying 'Have mercy on us' three times is still followed.''

Cardinal Giovanni Bona

Acta Sanctorum, September, vol. iii.
Bede: *Ecclesiastical History of the English Peoples.*

Peter Claver
Jesuit Priest

died 1654

THERE IS PERHAPS no other saint in the Church's calendar whose vocation casts so vivid a light on one of the most excruciating dilemmas which face the Christian in the English-speaking world, particularly in the United States of America, as that of the Spanish Jesuit, St. Peter Claver. The root of the racial problem lies in the deep-seated remembrance of exploitation, injustice, and incredible cruelty on the one hand, and of unspeakable shame on the other. It is perhaps not too much to say that there is no other solution to the problem than the personal approach of a saint so assimilated to Christ that he can extend a compassion that is translucent in its complete absence of political motive, of superiority, or of guilt. So Peter Claver, without a trace of self-consciousness or arrogance, but in the deepest humility, named himself as "a slave of the slaves for ever"; one who can work for others with a sublime self-forgetfulness which breaks down every human barrier.

Peter Claver worked for over thirty years of his life at Cartagena, in what is now the republic of Colombia, the port which has been melodramatically described as "the scene of the most hideous traffic that ever disgraced the name of man and cried to heaven for vengeance." Almost every ship that docked there carried a dying freight of Negro slaves, rounded up in the interior of Africa, marched to the coast with much less ceremony and care than a herd of cattle, battened down into dark and airless holds, and shipped across the Atlantic. More than twelve thousand of them were landed yearly at Cartagena during the seventeenth century, to be sold in the slave-market for the plantations in the West Indies and the Southern states. Peter Claver's apostolate was simply to redeem, by his own personal efforts, man's inhumanity to man.

Peter was born at Verdu, near Barcelona, in 1580. He came into contact with the Jesuit Fathers at their college in Barcelona, where he was sent after his early schooling at Solsona; it was thought that he had a vocation to the secular priesthood. After receiving minor orders, he expressed his wish to enter the Society of Jesus, and was received as a novice at the age of 22.

He made his first profession in 1604. "I consecrate myself to God till death," he wrote at that time, "looking on myself henceforth as a slave whose whole office lies in being at the service of his master." He made such progress in his studies that he was immediately told to teach the subjects he was set to learn. It was at this time that he was sent to Majorca, where he came under the influence of the extraordinary lay-brother, Alphonsus Rodriguez (*see* October 30). Alphonsus seemed to know in advance the future apostolate of his disciple, and the perfection of charity which would be demanded of him.

Eventually in 1609 Peter set sail for the Indies before he had finished his studies for the priesthood. He was ordained in 1615. When he made his final profession as a Jesuit in 1622, he added a special vow of his own, "to devote myself for ever to the salvation of the Negroes."

Claver's apostolate, throughout the rest of his life, was simple in the extreme. Whenever a slave-ship was due, he was immediately alerted. He gradually organized a band of interpreters, through whom he could communicate with the new arrivals according to tribe or dialect. His was a truly social apostolate: he became doctor, protector, and lawyer to the slaves, as well as spiritual director. Gradually, it was taken for granted that a new batch of slaves would stay in Cartagena for an extended period, so that they might be tended physically as well as spiritually by Claver and his band of devoted helpers.

Not surprisingly, he was reverenced as a saint in the city long before his death. He was certainly a constant reproach to all those around him who were inclined to treat fellow human beings as less than human. His life and work should be a reminder, in terms of the Gospel for his feast, of the true meaning of the great commandment, "Thou shalt love thy neighbor as thyself," and the Lord's answer, in the story of the good Samaritan, to the question "And who is my neighbor?"

A Christian's Goal in Life

"To seek God in all things, and to try to find Him in all. . . . To seek nothing in this world but what our Lord sought there. As He came on earth to save souls and died for them on the Cross, we should try to gain them for Him, for this joyfully offering ourselves to any labor and to death itself."

From St. Peter Claver's Spiritual Note-book

A. Lunn: *A Saint in the Slave Trade* (London, 1935).
A. Rayex, art.: "Pietro Claver, Santo" (BS, X, coll. 818–21).

Nicholas of Tolentino
Augustinian Friar

died 1305

St. Nicholas could have enjoyed a prosperous career as a cleric, in an age when the Church offered rich prizes to the ambitious and successful; but as a young man, only in minor orders but already enjoying his first ample benefices, he saw that this was no life for him. He wanted to follow in every step the way that his poor Master had gone. He resigned his appointments and entered the Augustinian novitiate; and in that Order he spent his life.

Our chief sources of knowledge for him are the "Life" by his contemporary, Peter of Monte Rubiano, and the many references to him in the *Liber Vitasfratrum* by Jordan of Quedlinburg. This second source was not completed until half a century after Nicholas' death; but Jordan had been compiling it for many years, and, in writing of Nicholas and other wonder-working Augustinians, he had been guided by the directions in 1329, that all such alleged miracles were to be submitted for scrutiny of the evidence to future general chapters. At this time the process for Nicholas' canonization had already begun, and it may be that the regulations had this in mind; at all events, Jordan is to be considered as a serious historian, with a proper zeal to gain firsthand and reliable information.

It is in the *Vitasfratrum* that we read this beautiful tribute to Nicholas: "He was joy to the sorrowing, consolation to the afflicted, peace to the contending, rest to the laboring, help to the poor, a wonderful relief to captives and the sick. He had such compassion for sinners that he would pray, fast, offer Mass, and pour out tears for the many who came to confess to him, that the Lord might dispel the darkness in which they lived."

Nicholas' last thirty years were spent in Tolentino, where his concern with the city's moral laxity consumed his life, as he preached in the streets, and visited the people in their homes. From the accounts of his labors we gain an all too vivid picture of the life of the place, with its wealth and its slums, its quarrels and lawsuits and feuds.

Doubt has been expressed about the historicity of his appellation, "Patron of the Holy Souls," but both Peter of Monte Rubiano and Jordan of Quedlinburg testify that his devotion to the Holy Souls was well known while he was alive, and that many souls were said to have been released from the pains of Purgatory through his intercession.

Pope Eugene IV, himself an Augustinian and just the sort of simple, austere, generous, holy man to have devotion to Nicholas, was convinced that it was through his prayers in heaven that agreement, short-lived though it was, was reached between the Greeks and Latins at the Council of Florence; and it was he who accomplished Nicholas' delayed canonization.

Prayer for Church Unity

"Grant, we pray you, almighty God, through whose care for us, beyond all words, your Church has in these last ages been made to shine more bright by the great virtues and miracles of Blessed Nicholas, your Confessor, that through his merits and intercession the Church, all errors being purged away, may rejoice in endless peace and unity."

Original form, ascribed to Eugene IV, of the prayer for the feast of St. Nicholas

Acta Sanctorum, September, vol. iii.

Solemnia Canonizationis S. Nicolai de Tolentino. An. 1446 (Analecta Augustiniana, III, 1909–10, pp. 236–37).

R. Arbesmann and W. Hümpfner, edd.: *Jordani de Saxonia Liber Vitasfratrum* (New York, 1943).

Louis of Thuringia
Nobleman

died 1227

BLESSED LOUIS was the eldest son of Count Herman of Thuringia, and as a boy he was betrothed to Elizabeth (*see* November 19), the infant daughter of the king of Hungary. To our modern, Anglo-Saxon way of thinking, such arranged marriages offer little hope of the partners' happiness; but there are still, in other societies, those who think differently, saying that young peoples' families are better able than they to judge if a match is suitable and will turn out well. The marriage between Louis and Elizabeth was ideally happy, because it was an ideal Christian union, resting firmly on their Christlike way of life; and not only they but one of their children, Gertrude of Altenburg, also achieved formal recognition as a saint.

Louis was a great ruler, fearless in the defense of the rights of his people. War and politics often called him abroad, and then he could entrust the government of his land with perfect confidence to Elizabeth. He was wholly in support of her matchless compassion and generosity toward the poor, and she learned from him to be wise and prudent in the ordering of their affairs.

In the year 1227, still not yet thirty years of age, he volunteered to follow the emperor, Frederick II, on the Crusade, and embarked with him at Brindisi for the East, but he became violently ill, and had to be landed at Brindisi, where he died. When the news reached her Elizabeth could not be consoled, and said that life for her was over; but divine grace showed her the way to begin a new life, and to turn her sorrow into the joy of giving herself wholly to God.

The Upright Man

"The path of the upright man is straight; you smooth the way of the upright. Following the path of your judgments, we hoped in you, God; your name, your memory are all my soul desires. At night my soul longs for you and my spirit in me seeks for you; when your judgments appear on earth the inhabitants of the world learn the meaning of integrity."

Isaiah 26:7–9

C. Wenck, art: "Ludwig IV, der Heilige" (*Allgemeine Deutsche Biographie*, 19, Leipzig, 1884, pp. 594–97).

Victoria Fornari-Strata
Widow and Foundress of the Blue Nuns of Genoa

died 1617

BLESSED VICTORIA FORNARI was married at the age of seventeen to Angelo Strata, and only eight years later he died, leaving her ill provided for, with five small children, and about to give birth to a sixth. In her intense grief and bewilderment, all that she could do was to put herself and her children under the protection of the Blessed Virgin, and then set to work to bring up well her orphaned family. How well she succeeded in this is plain; of the five who survived childhood, the three sons became Minim friars, the two daughters canonesses regular. This itself speaks of the prayer and piety in which they had been reared, and also of Victoria's own love and longing for the religious life.

When she was first widowed she had taken a vow of perpetual chastity, and then resolved to eschew all worldly vanities. Our Lady had assured her that one day her hopes would be realized, after all her children had gone before her into religion, a plain mandate to Victoria to do her duty as a mother, and to wait patiently for God's good time.

At the beginning of her new life she had had some vague ideas of founding a new order of religious herself; and when at last she was free to follow the inclinations of her heart, her Order reflected the life which she had already lived for so long, a life lived under Mary's protection, dedicated to penance, filled with gratitude to God and charity to all God's creatures.

671

A Widow's Trust in Our Lady

" 'O, holy Virgin', Victoria then cried, 'you who were always filled with compassion, take to yourself these little children, adopt them as your own, for now they have no father, and they are truly orphaned, for I can no longer be of use to them as their mother.' 'Leave them to me,' the Virgin said, 'for I shall take special care of your home. What I ask of you is to place all your hopes in me, to concern yourself with one thing only, and that is to love God above all.' "

Agostino De Mari

A. De Mari: *Elogio della beata Vittoria M. Fornari-Strata, Matrona Genovese* (Genoa, 1829).

F. Dumortier: *La bienheureuse Marie-Victoire Fornari* (Langres, 1902).

Margaret Fontana
Dominican Tertiary

died 1513

OUR CHIEF SOURCE of knowledge of Blessed Margaret Fontana is the "Life" written by the Dominican, Desiderio Paloni, some seventy years after her death; but he quotes the testimony of people who had known her well in her lifetime, and it is clear, too, that her memory was still very much alive in her native city, Modena. What he tells us evokes the life of a small, crowded city, in which everyone knew everyone else, a life into the joys and sorrows of which Margaret had entered fully.

Paloni is somewhat snobbish in his insistence on the nobility of lineage of both Margaret's parents; but if we read with sympathy we discern the point that he is seeking to make, that the decision of a young girl so well born to turn her back on the world and its attractions must have been doubly pleasing to the Lord. She was strongly drawn to a life of simplicity, austerity, recollection, and she might have been expected to offer herself to some enclosed religious house. Instead, as many others did in Italy, she took a vow of perpetual virginity and joined a Third Order, in her case the Dominicans, so as to be free to move and work among the people.

Part of her fame rested on her wonderful charity to the poor and the sick. Her family told her that she was giving away so much of what they owned to relieve distress that they might well be in need of relief themselves. The stories of loaves turned into roses to avert her brother's anger, of wine-jars mysteriously never running dry, are doubtless merely the picturesque expression of the people's veneration of Margaret's care for them in their need.

But the people must also have known something of the intense inner life she lived. She would pass whole nights lying on the ground in prayer; but she was always careful to wait until her mother, whose room she shared, was asleep before she rose for this purpose. When she was reproached for the austere life she had chosen, she would answer: "It is not for a servant of God to be fastidious, but crucified and mortified for Christ." Her faith in Christ's Passion expressed itself in the resoluteness with which she drove away with the sign of the cross demonic visitors and visions. After her death she was considered an efficacious patron of those afflicted by such possession, and, in memory of her seemingly miraculous powers of healing, of women suffering in childbirth.

A Gentle Woman

"The Church militant on earth has made known with what fair decorum, with what holiness of life she wore the habit of St. Dominic, how in her own religious state she lived in recollection, and what has been the sweet fragrance of her fame. She passed all her days with never a quarrel, however just it might have been; her life was ever blameless, she was dear to all, praised by all, known to all and honored by all as a saint. She was meek and gentle as a lamb, full of love and pity, honorable and straightforward, simple and pure as a dove, sparing of her words, wise and direct in her replies, kind in her dealings and venerated for her every act."

Desiderio Paloni

Acta Sanctorum, September, vol. iv.

Notburga
Maidservant

died about 1313

THE CHURCH sets much store by the public fame and veneration of those who are proposed for inclusion in the roll of her saints. In Notburga's case, we can see how such veneration can compensate for lack of early and precise documentation. The very century in which she lived is disputed, and the information which we have comes to us from her ancient and persistent cult. When we have discarded elements in it which are plainly fabulous (the sickle suspended in the air when she refused to go on harvesting after the first Vespers of Sunday, the avaricious mistress who returned after death to haunt the pig-styes) she emerges as the model of a holy woman, content with her lowly station in life, finding in her work as a domestic servant perfect fulfillment of her vocation to love and serve God and His creatures, a very faithful follower of Martha.

We all know of Martha's complaint that Mary did not help her with the housework; but we tend to forget that when Jesus went to their house of mourning, it was the housekeeper, Martha, who went out to meet Him and made her wonderful profession of faith, "Yes, I believe that you are the anointed Son of God who was to come into the world." The story of Martha and Mary teaches us that the world needs both actives and contemplatives. St. Notburga, the domestic servant, in her active life of service to God and His creatures, achieved the outstanding holiness to which the Lord called her.

A Truly Christian Woman

"She did all her work while she prayed."

"She gave beggars the remains of the food, and taught compassion."

"While they used to spin, she fired their hearts with God's love."

"She fed and comforted prisoners, and turned them to God."

"She taught her master's children to pray and to fear God."

"She made peace between quarrelling brothers."

"She was drawn to her grave by two oxen, as she had asked."

Some of the legends concerning the life of St. Notburga

Acta Sanctorum, September, vol. iv.

Catherine of Genoa
Widow

died 1510

ST. CATHERINE was a visionary, not a writer; and we owe her "works" to a group of pious editors, who had recorded her vivid, spontaneous explanations to them of her spiritual insights, which, after her death, were written up in forms which often disguise her true qualities. But the famous "Treatise on Purgatory" seems to be closer to her own style, to contain less editorial matter, than the "Spiritual Dialogues."

The "Treatise" was produced by her confessor, and by one of her spiritual sons, at a time when Protestant attacks on the doctrine of purgatory had to be combatted; and it may be that some of the material, especially the insistence on man's folly in relying on divine love to help him to escape divine justice, reflects this, and is interpolated. Catherine's visions of the purgatorial state had been received in an age untroubled by such controversies, so that she could speak freely of her perceptions, a world removed from those medieval concepts which Dante, above all others, immortalized, of Purgatory as a way of being in which suffering and joy are indistinguishable.

It is abundantly clear that she was a frustrated religious, and that her family were much to blame in thwarting her early ambitions to take the veil. Instead, she was forced into a marriage of policy. She did her best to be a good wife to her husband, and to play the part convention demanded of her in the social life of a wealthy city. But it was all one long trial for her, until her husband's near-ruin, caused by his own folly and extravagance, brought her relief. Soon he was as devoted as she had always been to the care of the diseased and unfortunate, and they lived humbly, happily, and in continence, in the hospital where they worked.

One unusual feature of her spiritual life was its isolation. Experiencing visions and ecstasies, going for long periods without food or drink, she was for twenty-five years wholly without direction, relying solely on divine grace and inspiration. It was only after her husband's death, in the last years of her life, that she found a confessor who was able to guide and encourage her already remarkable life of contemplation. It would, indeed, be truer to say that her guides found and were guided by her.

The Peace and Joy of Purgatory

"The souls who are in Purgatory, so far as I have been able to understand it, cannot have any other will than to be in that place. This is ordained by God, and He has ordained it justly. They cannot now be absorbed with themselves, cannot say 'I committed these and those sins, and so I deserve to be here,' cannot say 'I wish that I had not committed that sin, so that I might now be in Paradise,' cannot say 'he there will get out of here faster than I' or 'I shall get out faster than he.' They cannot have any recollection of themselves or of others, not of good, not of ill, afflicting them more than they are afflicted. But they have an utter contentment to be at God's command, for Him to do all He wills and as He wills, so that in all their pain they cannot think of themselves, seeing nothing but the working of God's divine goodness."

"Treatise on Purgatory," chapter 1

Libro de la Vita mirabile e Dottrina santa de la beata Caterinetta da Genoa (Genoa, 1551).

H. Douglas Irvine and C. Balfour, trans.: *St. Catherine of Genoa: Treatise on Purgatory: The Dialogue* (London, 1946).

P. L. Hag, art.: "Catherine of Genoa, St." (NCE, 3, pp. 254–56).

F. von Hügel: *The Mystical Element in Religion*, 2 vols. (2d. ed., London, 1923).

Cyprian of Carthage
Bishop and Martyr

died 258

ST. CYPRIAN was a most powerful figure in the evolution of the doctrine and the discipline of the Church in Roman Africa; and, although his martyrdom left unresolved his famous and unfortunate dispute with Pope St. Stephen I, he was at all times an ardent supporter of the Church's peace and unity under the successors of Peter.

St. Jerome says that Cyprian was a native of Africa, and, like Augustine later, he was a teacher of rhetoric, and also practiced law. When in his middle years he was converted from paganism, he stripped himself at once of all his possessions, and devoted himself totally to prayer and study. He was very quickly ordained priest; and soon after this, he was, much against his will, named bishop of Carthage by popular acclamation.

Only a year later a new wave of persecution began, under the Emperor Decius; and Cyprian was much criticized, in Rome and at home, for going into hiding instead of staying at his post and accepting death. But he defended himself by stating that he was concerned, not for his own safety but for the well-being of his Church, and this is amply borne out by his later conduct.

The end of this persecution raised in an acute form the problem of how those who had apostatized through fear of death were to be treated. This was complicated by the case of an evil priest in Carthage, Novatus, who had been awaiting trial when the persecution broke out. In Cyprian's absence he had set himself up as a schismatic "bishop," and was pretending to reconcile the many apostates anxious to return to the sacraments but also to escape the rigorous penitential discipline of the African Church. Despite his own severe and authoritarian temper, Cyprian steered here a middle course between those who, like Novatus, asked little or no penance of apostates, and those others who held that the Church had no power whatever to reconcile them.

The later and greater quarrel in which Cyprian was involved concerned the validity of baptism conferred by heretics and schismatics. In Africa, where such abounded far more than in Italy, this question was a vexed one; and Cyprian held, wrongly, as events showed, that it was one not of faith but of discipline. A first North African synod confirmed his view that such baptisms were invalid, and referred its decision to Pope Stephen, who maintained the traditional teaching of the Church, and showed much severity toward Cyprian and those of his adherents who contested his ruling and continued to argue the matter. Wisely, however, Stephen refrained from anathemas against his opponents; and on Cyprian's side, intemperate though he showed himself in advancing his cause, his reverence and obedience to the Holy See was undiminished.

Cyprian's martyrdom in 258 ended the matter. How authentic are the "Proconsular Acts," which purport to record his two trials and his sufferings, is controverted; but even if they are, as many modern critics believe, a later, literary treatment of the facts, there is nothing in them discordant with what we know, from Cyprian's own genuine writings, of his unshakeable fidelity to the faith of the Church.

The Unity of the Church

"We ought all to hold fast to the Church's unity and defend it, and especially we bishops who have rule in the Church, so that we demonstrate that our episcopacy is one and indivisible. Let no one betray the brotherhood by lying, let no one corrupt the true faith with treacherous half-truths. The episcopacy is one . . . for the Church is one . . . just as the sun sends out many rays, but one light, just as a tree has many branches, but takes all its strength from its one firm root, just as from one source many streams flow off, so that they may seem to be diverse yet all are one in origin. You may screen off the rays of the sun, but you cannot divide light's single source. If you break off a branch from the tree, it cannot bear any fruit. Dam up a stream at its source, and its course will run dry. So the Church, illumined with the Lord's light, sends out its rays upon the whole earth; yet it is all one light, shed everywhere, nor is its unity divided. It stretches its branches with their rich fruit over all the land, its copious streams it sends far and wide; yet there is but one head, one source, one mother fruitful in offspring. We are born of her womb, we are fed by her milk, and from her spirit we take life."

From St. Cyprian's De Unitate Ecclesiae

S. Cypriani Opera, PL, 4.

The Stigmatization of Francis of Assisi

1224

ST. FRANCIS' dear companion in religion, Leo, has left us a record which the experts consider of incontestable authenticity. It reads: "The blessed Francis, two years before his death, kept a Lent in the hermitage of the Alverna in honor of the blessed Virgin Mary, Mother of God, and of blessed Michael the Archangel, from the feast of the Assumption of St. Mary the Virgin to the feast of St. Michael in September. And the hand of the Lord was laid upon him. After the vision . . . he had of a seraph, and the impression in his body of the stigmata of Christ, he made these praises which are written on the other side of this sheet, and with his own hand he wrote them out, giving thanks to God for the favor which had been conferred on him."

In the "First Life," written within four years of Francis' death, Thomas of Celano describes the appearance of these mysterious wounds: "His hands and his feet appeared pierced in the middle by nails, and the heads of the nails could be seen in the palms of his hands and the upper part of his feet, and on the other sides were their points."

Immediately after Francis had died, Brother Elias, announcing this miracle to the French provincial, wrote that nothing like this had been heard of since Christ's own Passion. In 1237 Pope Gregory IX, in his bull *Confessor Domini*, stated that Francis' wounds were imprinted by the divine power, but so far as Brother Elias' contention is concerned, modern scholars are inclined to tell us now that Francis was the greatest, but not the first, of those who have received the stigmata. The apostle Paul said: "I bear the marks of the Lord Jesus in my body" (Gal. 6:17); and although this is generally taken to refer to Paul's floggings and stonings, before the time of Francis an opinion was growing that it meant instead that Paul showed in his hands, feet, and side the wounds of the Passion. Opinions such as this were encouraged by the type of Passion devotion popularized by Bernard of Clairvaux and his followers; the great historian of such devotions and phenomena, Thurston, has collected much evidence on the subject.

What are the possible explanations of this strange manifestation of love of the Passion, of sympathetic participation in it? To begin with, we can leave aside the many frauds, however pious they may have been, in which such wounds were self-inflicted or otherwise simulated. Then, next, we must distinguish between cases such as that of Francis, where the wounds have been visible to others, and those like Catherine of Siena (*see* April 30) and Teresa of Avila (*see* October 15), where the subject alone could see them. It may be that, using the term in no derogatory sense, the causes have been hysteric. The Church has always been notably reluctant to pronounce on such matters.

But whether the causes be supernatural or not, what is beyond doubt is that in stigmatics who are genuine there has always been present an extraordinary love of the sufferings of the Lord, a sharing, granted to few, in the glorious agonies which accompanied His redemption of the human race.

Prayer to the Passion of Christ

"Soul of Christ, sanctify me.
Body of Christ, bless me.
Passion of Christ, strengthen me.
Blood of Christ, refresh me.
Water from the side of Christ, wash me.
Within thy wounds hide me.
Suffer me not to be separated from thee.
In the hour of my death call me,

And bid me come to thee,
That with thy saints I may praise thee
To all eternity."

Twelfth century hymn, Anima Christi

R. Balfour: *The Seraphic Keepsake* (London, 1905).
H. Thurston: *The Physical Phenomena of Mysticism* (London, 1952).

John Massias
Dominican Lay Brother

died 1645

BLESSED JOHN MASSIAS was born in Spain, of parents, if his early biographers can be trusted, who were both from good families that had come down in the world. But one can well believe that, despite their own modest means, they were known for their goodness to the poor. Though John, as life went on, grew wonderfully in grace, all that we learn of him suggests that he could build on that best of all foundations, a childhood spent in a happy, Christian home. His parents died when he was young. His elder sister was able to help him, and he, in his turn, looked after a younger sister for as long as she needed him. He worked as a shepherd lad, and, it would seem, was distinguished by nothing but his love of God and of holiness. Not even the stifling piety with which his early biographies are overlaid can conceal the traits of a youth constant in prayer and resolute against temptation.

When his family no longer needed him, he set out for South America, drawn there not by any hope of wealth, but because he knew already, vaguely, that this was God's will for him to achieve what he did not yet know. At Cheres in Spain the Dominicans, whose church he used to frequent, tried to keep him, but he pressed on, and after many false starts, in the end he arrived in Lima, Peru. John's biographers paint this for us as a city of saints; and it is true that in his time there were among its inhabitants: the archbishop, Toribio Alfonso Mogrovejo, Francis Solano, Rose (*see* August 30), and John's dear friend and mentor, Martin Porres (*see* November 3), all of whom are now, as well as he, venerated by the Church. But we know, especially from the lives of Rose and Martin Porres, that it was also a typical boom town, swarming with those willing to prey on the folly and weakness of others.

For a time John worked as superintendent for a rich merchant, who was highly satisfied with his upright integrity; but soon he was admitted as a postulant to one of the two Dominican friaries in Lima, and it was there that he found rest and happiness. His probationary year was spent in the lodge of the house's porter, a most holy brother in whose company he greatly advanced in prayer, from whom he learned to love Christ in His poor.

When he succeeded this man as porter, he had formed the habit of uninterrupted prayer, and a great love of solitude and silence, which, however, never made him less prompt and obedient to the claims of every man or woman on his time. He always knew how to cheer and encourage dejected young novices; and his insight into souls was extraordinary. He could refuse alms, saying that it was the price of sin, and agree to accept gifts only as loans, foretelling the day when the giver would be reduced to destitution.

He lived his life as he wished, a completely happy man in his obscurity. He cannot have known the veneration he inspired, a veneration which has not died three centuries and more after he went to God.

The House of God

"The very sparrow finds a house for herself,
The swallow a nest where she shelters her chicks,
At your altars, O Lord of armies,
My king and my God.
Blessed are those who live in your house, Lord,
They will praise you for ever and ever. . .
A day at your altars is more than a thousand days.
I have preferred to be of no account in the house of my God
Rather than to live in the fine dwellings of sinful men."

Psalm 84: 3–4, 10

G. Cipoletti: *Compendio della Vita del B. Giovanni Massias* (Rome, 1837).

Emily de Rodat
Foundress of the Congregation of the Holy Family of Villefranche

died 1852

St. Emily de Rodat was born into a family of landed gentry in southern France in 1787, the time of the outbreak of the Revolution; but her parents, and her grandmother, with whom she passed much of her childhood, were left more or less in peace, even though they shared the dangers then a necessary part of the practice of the Catholic faith. Emily, as a child, was much influenced by her grandmother, who seems to have been as shrewd and perceptive as she was pious, and also by a great-aunt, a Visitation nun driven out of her convent.

Outwardly, at least, Emily was a singularly normal child, with a strong attraction to society and pleasure; but while still a young girl she was aware of much conflict in her soul. At the age of seventeen she underwent a conversion, and five years later she entered one of the reopening religious houses. But she was at once overwhelmed there with depression and anxiety, and went for a time to live at her parents' home.

She then went through a period of much self-questioning and of search for her true vocation. One of the most urgent needs of the time was for proper education, religious and secular, for poor children; and it was to them that she decided to devote her life. Gathering around her three friends, of very different temperaments, in all of whom Emily discerned the right material, she rented a house, despite refusals of help and opposition on all sides. From the first, they pursued a double ideal: for their own inner lives, seclusion and contemplation, for their children, unremitting effort and care.

687

On the day that they opened their doors, thirty girls arrived. Later, Emily accepted fee-paying children too, but only on condition that the same standards of teaching were maintained in all the classes. They moved into a larger house, and seemed to prosper; but they had to overcome many hardships and trials, including the early death of two of the young founders. And at the same time Emily's own inner afflictions returned, seldom thereafter to leave her during her life; but she bore all these troubles, whatever their sources, with courage and cheerfulness.

We know little of what direction she received in forming herself and undertaking the foundation of a congregation and the devising of its rule. At first sight, she might seem to be self-taught; but the truth seems rather to be that she recognized and adopted those elements in older rules which corresponded to the needs of women like herself, wholly dedicating themselves to her two ideals.

Her spirituality is on the old model much disdained today; it is characterized by austerity, detachment, and an aloofness from human relations which, we are now told, is the antithesis of Christian living. But she found that if she was to serve Christ and His poor children as she wished, this was the regime she needed. It is not for us now to tell those who so conduct their lives that because this is not for everyone, it is therefore not for them.

A Letter to an Unsatisfactory Superior

"You should let Sister Vincent take care of you, and eat the agreeable dishes she asks you to; you would be doing it for the love of God. You send me many expressions of thanks in your letter, but that is not what I wanted. What we have is yours, so we do not need to be thanked. Just let me know that things have arrived. You are right to think that the sisters in Aubin should not have more than those here; on the contrary, they should all show true detachment in sharing what they have.... I had no intention of mortifying you when I said that if I were you, a downstairs kitchen would be a trial. I did not want to say that I have no authority in Aubin, but if you wish the kitchen to be there, and Father agrees, I shall trouble myself no further, being here; but if I were at Aubin, I should be troubled. That is all I meant when I wrote to you, and you can see that there is nothing in it to upset you. Good-bye, dear Mother. Think less about seeing me, find your consolation in our good Lord, and act so that the thorns of your office may be of great advantage and unite you closely with Him."

From a letter of St. Emily de Rodat

D. Burton: *Saint Emilie de Rodat* (London, 1951).
H. Marty, ed.: *Lettres de la vénérable Mère Emilie de Rodat* (Paris, 1888).

Francis de Posadas
Dominican Friar

died 1713

BLESSED FRANCIS was the son of a noble but impoverished family in Cordova. He was only a boy when his father died and his mother remarried. She was having him educated in the hope that he would enter religion; but he was very harshly used by his step-father, who forced him to leave school and learn a trade. This he did. He completely won over his master by his qualities of devotion and obedience, and it seems to have been with the master's encouragement and help that he was received as a novice by the Dominicans.

But his troubles were far from ended; it is sad to read of the unkind and contemptuous treatment he endured at the hands of the religious whom he had joined. But he suffered it all, humbly and patiently, and in time the community was brought to see how badly they had behaved.

His special patron was Vincent Ferrer (*see* April 5); and Francis too became a wonderful preacher, doing much to reform his native city. He steadfastly refused every office which was proferred to him, including, twice, a bishopric. His only love was his work among the poor; and he himself lived and died poor in all things, except in his heroic virtues.

Patience in Adversity

"He was ill used, but this was his own choice; and he did not open his mouth. He was led like a sheep to the slaughter, and like a lamb in the hands of its shearer he was dumb, and

690

uttered no cry. . . His soul's anguish over, he will look up and will be content. This just servant of mine will justify many, and he will bear their wrongdoings."

Isaiah 53:7, 11

R. Martínez-Vigil: *La Orden de Predicadores* (Madrid, 1884).
J. Procter, ed.: *Short Lives of the Dominican Saints* (London, 1901).

Matthew
Apostle and Evangelist

first century

THE PURPOSE of the gospel message, the good news proclaimed by Christ, and perennially by the Church at Christ's command, is to effect a radical change in men, to soften and to purify their hard and sinful hearts, and bring them within the ambit of Christ's loving and healing compassion. The Church, therefore, "embracing sinners in her bosom, is at the same time holy and always in need of purification and is always pursuing the path of penance and renewal" (Vatican II's *Constitution on the Church,* no. 8).

Perhaps the greatest patron of all those Christians who feel the need of this change of heart and of Christ's healing compassion (and who would dare to say that he does not?) is the apostle Matthew. For the righteous Jew, Matthew's profession of tax-collector or publican proclaimed his deep sinfulness. He had even taken a pagan (Greek) name, instead of his Hebrew name, Levi. The tax collector was one who was in such frequent contact with the pagan Roman that he could not possibly follow the strict requirements of the Law regarding the symbolic purification after "contamination" with the heathen. He was also a constant reminder of the Jewish subjection to the pagan foreigner, representing the worst form of collaboration, following a trade which typified injustice, oppression, and extortion.

By calling Matthew to be one of His closest followers, Christ vividly declared the universal nature of His mission; and Matthew's conversion proclaimed that hope and love were being offered to all, particularly to outcasts and sinners. In the summons of Matthew and in his unhesitating and immediate response to the divine vocation, Ezekiel's prophecy is seen to be fulfilled: "If a man turn from his sin and does what is lawful and right; if the wicked gives back what he has taken by robbery and walks according to the laws of life, he shall not die. None of the sins he has committed shall be remembered against him" (Ezek. 33:14 ff.).

So Christ never hesitated to give His friendship, to open His heart—which sitting down at table with another symbolized—to publicans and sinners, Matthew recalls Christ's friendship with publicans and sinners in his account of his own vocation: " 'Why does your Master sit down at table with publicans and sinners?' Jesus heard the question, and answered: 'It is not the healthy who need the physician, but the sick. Go and learn what the Scripture means, *It is mercy that I love, not sacrifices.* I have come to call not the just but sinners' " (Matt. 9:11–13). The beginning of holiness is the recognition of God's love given to us in the humble confession of our sins. "The publican would not even lift up his eyes to heaven, but beat his breast, saying, God be merciful to me a sinner. . . and he went home justified" (Luke 18:13-14).

Nothing is known for certain of Matthew's apostolate. Tradition has it that after his ministry in Judea, he made missionary journeys through Ethiopia and Persia.

Christ's Love and Forgiveness

"Jesus looked up and said to him: 'Zacchaeus, make haste and come down; for I must stay at your house to-day.' So he came down in haste and joyfully made him welcome. And when they saw it, they all murmured: 'He has gone to sit at the table of a man who is a sinner.' And Zacchaeus said to the Lord: 'See, Lord, I give half my goods to the poor; and if I have defrauded anyone, I restore it fourfold.' And Jesus said to him: 'Today salvation has come to this house.' "

Luke 19:5-9

Matthew 9:9-13.
J. Quinlan, art.: "Matthew, Gospel According to, St." (NCE, 9, pp. 493-502).

Thomas of Villanova
Augustinian Friar

died 1555

ST. THOMAS' life spans the close of the Middle Ages and the beginnings of modern times and of the New World. He was born in the reign of Ferdinand and Isabella, and saw the end of Moorish rule and the unification of Spain. While Augustinian provincial at Castile, he sent the first friars out to Mexico. He inherited an archdiocese which had been ruined by more than a century of the misrule which the medieval Church had, to its shame, so long countenanced; but he sent his brother bishops off to Trent with wise advice on the need for reform that the Second Vatican Council has reiterated.

He had studied the liberal arts at the newly-founded university at Alcala before he entered religion; and his whole career was marked by a broad outlook and a freedom from prejudice. He was in his thirtieth year when he joined the Augustinian Friars in Salamanca, the "Augustinian city." He had been with them only three years when he was made prior, and after this he continually held high office.

In 1544 he was compelled to accept the see of Valencia, which had not had a resident Ordinary since 1427. Its revenues were great, and during much of this time it had been treated as a family possession by the Borgias; the future popes, Callistus III, Alexander VI, and three of Alexander's sons, had all in turn been, in name, archbishops of Valencia. Thomas' conduct there, from the first, spoke for itself. He gave the money offered him to furnish his dilapidated palace for the repair of the hospital. He wore, and, when necessary, himself repaired the same old friar's habit; but he fed hundreds of the poor every day in his own house.

He did not attend the Council of Trent, perhaps, it is thought, because his own diocese was still in great need; but he impressed on the other bishops, before they left, how great was the Church's need to reform, not only the Reformers, but also her own self. He was no friend of coercion by anathema, preferring to rule by example and persuasion.

The "Life" written by his friend and fellow-Augustinian, John Muñatones, bishop of Segovia, pays especial tribute to his powers, as a preacher, of holding the minds and touching the hearts of his hearers; and it is today by his great sermons that he is chiefly remembered.

Worldly Christians

"This is what you profess; see for yourselves if you keep it. You have observed nothing of what you promised to God. You grasp at the pomps and riches of this earth as much as any . . . pagan. You live for the world, not for Christ; you spend most of your time in worldly business and pleasures; you profane and sully your bodies, which should be holy, in a thousand ways—the Holy Spirit is driven out, and you make yourselves the temple and the stable of devils. As soon as you were old enough to know what you were doing, you lost your baptismal innocence. The white garment that you should wear you stained, time after time, now with food, now with blood; you trampled on it and rent it in pieces. Your faith is dead, and you are without the light of love."

*Sermon preached by Thomas of Villanova to the court, 1527,
at the baptism of the future Philip II*

P. Jobit: *L'évêque des pauvres: Saint Thomas de Villeneuve* (Paris and Montreal, 1961).
E. Vidal, ed.: *S. Thomae a Villanova Opera Omnia*, 5 vols. (Salamanca, 1761).

Adamnan
Abbot

died 704

Sᴛ. Aᴅᴀᴍɴᴀɴ was the ninth abbot of Iona, where Columba (*see* June 9) had landed on Whitsun Eve, 563, to found among the Scottish isles a center of Irish holiness and learning second only to Armagh itself. And Adamnan's only peer, as saint and scholar, among the Iona monks was Columba. His chief claim to fame today is his *Life of St. Columba;* and as we read his pious, loving account of the deeds of his predecessor, he is unknowingly painting also his own picture: a man with infinite faith in the power of prayer, with boundless reverence for the Church of God as a humanizing, civilizing, divinizing influence on the lives of men.

Adamnan could through his family claim kinship with Columba. He was born in Ireland, about 624, in south-west Donegal; and at the age of fifty-five he was elected to rule over Iona. He seems to have known, if not to have taught, the young Aldfrid during his Irish exile; and soon after Aldfrid succeeded to the Northumbrian throne, in 685, Adamnan was sent on a mission to England, to redeem Irish captives carried off in the recent wars. In this he was successful. During his several stays among the English (when he visited Wearmouth, and was seen by the boy Bede) he became convinced that to adopt the newer Roman practice in such matters as the calculation of Easter and the form of the tonsure was not only expedient, as likely to promote peace between the English and Irish Churches, but right in itself.

He had much success in promoting this pacification in Ireland, but not in his own monastery, where conservative forces seem always to have been too strong for him; and though we cannot deduce from the evidence that he was hunted out of his abbey, he does seem to have spent much time during his last years outside Iona, in Ireland chiefly. There he was able to do much to promote the work of pacification which he regarded as the prime duty of servants of God. He seems to have been the chief influence at the Synod of Tara, where it was enacted that women should no longer bear arms in time of war, and that the ancient custom should be abolished whereby not only defeated warriors, but also their wives and children, should be put to the sword.

Not only Irish but also English historians pay tribute to Adamnan, as saint and scholar; we have for this the witness of Bede, of Ceolfrid, and of Alcuin. His work, *Of the Holy Places*, taken down from the narration of the Frankish pilgrim-bishop Arculf, became a classic, and is still today of great antiquarian value. His *Life of St. Columba* tells us almost all we need to know of the great qualities of the Celtic missionaries whose labors brought the love and knowledge of God to countless souls in western Christendom.

Peace and Charity

"The saint went to the church for the night vigil of Sunday; and as soon as this was over, he returned to his cell, and passed the rest of the night on his bed, where he had a flagstone for his mattress and a rock for his pillow, which stands to this day as a kind of monument beside his grave. While he was lying there, he gave his last charge to his brethren, in the hearing of his attendant alone, saying: 'These, my children, are the last words I address to you. Be at peace, and have unfeigned charity among yourselves; and if you thus follow the example of the holy fathers, God, the comforter of good men, will help you, and I, abiding with Him, will intercede for you; and He will give you not only enough to supply the wants of this present life, but will also bestow on you the good and everlasting rewards which are in store for those who keep His commandments.'"

From Adamnan's Life of St. Columba

Bede: *Ecclesiastical History of the English Peoples.*
W. Reeves, ed.: *Life of St. Columba* (Edinburgh, 1874).

Pacifico of San Severino
Observant Franciscan Friar

died 1721

PACIFICO is a saint for all on whom God lays the burden of great physical suffering and disability, from whom He seems to take away the ability to do their proper work. Pacifico was born in San Severino in 1653; while still a boy he lost both his parents, and was given into the care of an uncle, who used him harshly to the point of cruelty. He showed forbearance remarkable for his years in enduring this; and we may think that he learned early the lessons which stood him later in such good stead.

At the age of seventeen, he joined the Observant Franciscans. After ordination, he taught philosophy for a while, and then entered upon a life of work for which he seemed ideally suited: preaching, especially in remote Italian mountain villages, among the poor and abandoned, regaining many souls for the Lord. But at the height of his activity, when still only thirty-five years old, he was struck down by sickness, until in the end he was deaf, blind, and grievously crippled.

As an active man, he had already been marked out as one of exceptional holiness by his ecstasies, his powers of prophecy and healing, the gift of clairvoyance which he employed in the confessional. These qualities were only intensified during his long years of suffering, as he went on working as best he could, serving the house in San Severino as its head and administrator. It may well be that his great fortitude in bearing his afflictions drew even more people to God than did his preaching.

Fortitude Amid Afflictions

"In the last years of his [Pacifico's] life, when he had become blind, and deafness added to the heavy burden he must bear, he had to give up celebrating Mass. This was to him a grievous and unspeakable affliction, to which was joined that other of not being able in choir to read, blind as he was, nor, as a deaf man, to sing, when the others performed the divine Office. Yet never once was he heard to utter a word of irritation or complaint. But every day he gave thanks to the Almighty, and humbled himself before the Lord, saying that God's chastisements were far less than his faults deserved."

Luigi Maria di Vicenza

Luigi Maria di Vicenza: *Memorie Istoriche della Vita del B. Pacifico da Sanseverino* (Vicenza, 1787).

Herman the Cripple
Benedictine Monk

died 1054

THE STORY OF BLESSED HERMAN THE CRIPPLE can bring courage and hope to all who, because of physical disability, are unable to live a normal life. He could never stand upright or move without help, and even his speech organs were so deformed that his speech was intelligible only to his intimates. Yet he came to be counted among the most learned men of his age, and, far more than this, his life brought much love and joy to others.

At the age of seven this poor creature, deformed from birth, was sent to the monastery of Reichenau, on an island in Lake Constance. There, wise and gifted teachers must have discerned the fine mind and the beautiful soul hidden in his misshapen body. He grew to be what the French call a "universal genius," excelling in arithmetic, geometry, astronomy, history, poetry, and music. Professed in the monastery, he and his fellows devised aids, including a chair designed to hold him in a sitting position, so that he could read and write; and in this way he was able to produce, among other works, his brilliantly-conceived fraction-tables, and some of the Church's loveliest hymns (although *Salve Regina* is probably falsely attributed to him, he is certainly the author of, among others, *Alma Redemptoris Mater*).

Herman's friend and disciple, Berthold, continuing his chronicle in the year of his death, writes of him with deep emotion. He begins with a loving pun on his master's name, "Herimannus, qui et heros magnus," ("and also a great hero"); and he writes of his courage, patience, zeal, learning, his charity, obedience, and

700

faith, and, above all, of his happy, profitable life. He tells how Herman confided in him that in an ecstasy his coming death had been revealed to him, and then went on: "O, my dear soul, do not weep for me, but congratulate me, rather. And take my writing-tables, and whatever is unfinished in them first carefully correct, and then finish, if it seems worth while to you. And remember every day that you must die, make yourself ready for that journey, for you do not know the day or the hour when you must follow me, whom you have loved so much."

Hymn to Our Lady

"Mother of Christ, hear thou thy people's cry,
Star of the sea and portal of the sky!
Mother of him who thee from nothing made,
Sinking we strive, and call to thee for aid.
O, by that joy which Gabriel brought to thee,
Thou Virgin first and last, let us thy mercy see."

Alma Redemptoris Mater, *by Blessed Herman, trans. Edward
Caswall*

Herimanni Augiensis Chronicon, and *Lamberti Hersfeldensis Annales* (Monumenta Germaniae Historica, *Scriptores,* V).
H. Thurston: *Familiar Prayers* (London, 1953).

John de Brébeuf
Martyr

died 1649

SOME OF THE ARDORS and the glories of the first missionaries in "New France" have been described in the case of Margaret Bourgeoys (*see* January 19). St. John de Brébeuf has here been chosen to represent the eight North American martyrs, six of them Jesuits, two *donnés* or oblates, who died bringing Christianity to the Indian territories.

In the Jesuit seminary in Rouen, Brébeuf had been too sickly and weak to study regularly, let alone teach; and yet he developed a truly heroic fortitude of body and of soul. He was rightly acclaimed as the apostle of the Hurons, that branch of the great Algonquin family of nations which in his day occupied the territory between Georgian Bay on Lake Huron and Lake Simcoe. The more powerful and more wary Iroquois were the Hurons' inveterate enemies; and it was in the end as the Hurons' loyal friend and protector that Brébeuf met his death.

Most of our knowledge of him, his fellows, and their missions we owe to the Jesuit *Relations,* the enthralling annual accounts of the missions in New France sent home annually to France. The 1639 *Relation* estimates the total Huron population at around 20,000, living in scattered, small, ill-defended settlements. Brébeuf had first come to Quebec in 1615, and, after a first winter living among more accessible Algonquins to learn their language, he had entered Huron country, where he was soon left alone. The first annexation of Canada by Britain forced him and his other missionary companions to return home, but after Champlain had successfully contested in the London courts the legality of this action, he returned, in 1633. The Hurons invited him to return to them, and then robbed and abandoned him and his fellows on their journey; but no such set-back deterred Brébeuf.

Reading between the lines of his own despatches for the *Relations*, one can discern that perhaps the greatest trial he had to bear was the Hurons' own essential unloveableness; he found them deceitful, treacherous, abjectly superstitious, and, above all, insanely cruel. On one occasion Brébeuf thought it his duty to stay with an Iroquois prisoner, whom he had just baptized, while his captors tortured the poor wretch to death through the whole of one night. Brébeuf may well then have guessed that his own martyrdom, for which he now longed and prayed as a means perhaps efficacious in converting this intractable people, would also be of this sort.

The degraded lives the Hurons lived and the laxity of their marriage laws made the missionaries see that there was little hope for the young except by segregating them; and, accordingly, a seminary for Huron children was established in Quebec. Nonetheless, in 1637, Brébeuf could report to his general that in that year alone more than two hundred had received baptism. A fort at Ste. Marie was established as a center for missionaries and traders, and several smaller settlements grew up around it. It was in one of these, in 1649, that Brébeuf and Gabriel Lalement were captured, during a ferocious invasion of Huron territory by the Iroquois. Their converts begged them to leave them to their fate and flee; but the two priests remained to care as best they could for their spiritual children, and were put to death by their captors with excruciating torments, not fit for repetition. In all this Brébeuf displayed a rock-like endurance which amazed even his tormentors.

In all the later vicissitudes of French Canada, devotion to the North American martyrs never died; and their canonization was gained at last in 1930.

The Trials of a Missionary

"I shall pass over the long and wearisome silences to which a newcomer is reduced when there is no one with him who knows his language, and he does not know that of the savages. All such difficulties are shared by everyone coming to these lands. But on our journey we had others, less common. To begin with, we had to paddle all the time, neither less nor more than the savages, so much so that I never had time to say my Office, except when I lay down at night, when I used to need rest more than work. The other was that when we made portages we had to carry our packs, an experience as novel as it was hard, and more so for the others than for me, who had already learned a little of what fatigue is. At each portage I had to make at least four trips, and the others scarcely less. I had been among the Hurons once before, but I had never used an oar or carried packs, any more than the other religious who had passed this way. But on this trip we all had to begin like this, to carry the Cross which our Lord gives us for His honor and for the salvation of these poor barbarians. Sometimes, it is true, I was so weary that my body could not endure more. But my soul knew great content, for I knew that I suffered for God. No one knows this who has not experienced it; and not all of us were so richly paid."

Jesuit Relation *for 1635*

Relations des Jésuits dans la Nouvelle France (3 vols., Quebec, 1858).
F. Parkman: *The Jesuits in North America in the Seventeenth Century* (Boston, 1867).

Elzear and Delphina
Husband and Wife

died 1323, 1360

ST. ELZEAR was born in Provence, where, as also in Naples, he inherited great possessions at the age of twenty-three. He had been married, while still very young, to Blessed Delphina, an orphan heiress. Their biographers tell us the stories, so common in the lives of married saints in the Middle Ages, of how they agreed to live as brother and sister; but some of them shed further light on this matter, telling how Delphina, no more than a child, asked Elzear on her wedding night not to consummate the marriage, into which she had been forced, against her will, by her family. This may well have been the case also with her husband; indeed, one suspects that in either party there was a real religious vocation which had been suppressed in the interests of a dynastic union.

Nonetheless, it is plain that they were extremely happy together, and held their stations in the world as true Christians should. When they went to Naples to take over Elzear's estates, they found their tenants disaffected and defiant. Elzear was counselled to cow them by force, even by summary executions, but he was determined to win them over by mildness and justice, and in this he succeeded. In all his dealings he had his wife's support, and their home became proverbial for the decorum and good order with which it was conducted.

Elzear died in early middle age; Delphina survived him for thirty-seven years, not then entering religion, but living her last years in Provence as a recluse, living the solitary life which she came to prefer, once she had lost a husband whom she had loved so much.

A Saint's Rules for his Household

"Let everyone in our palace attend Mass every day, and not leave until it is ended.

Let everyone lead a pure and chaste life, free from every suspicion of grave sin; otherwise there is no place for him in our house.

Let none of the serving men and nobles, none of the women-folk go longer than a week unshriven or without approaching the banquet of the Lord.

Let all the women and girls spend the mornings in prayer and in holy works of mercy.

Let anyone who has told lies or blasphemed or used filthy language dine off bread and water, sitting on the ground.

Let all keep peace and friendship and harmony, and let anyone who has grieved another by word or deed seek pardon of him at once."

From St. Elzear's household ordinances

Rerum a S. Elzeario Comite Gestarum Commentarius (Ingolstadt, 1620).

Lioba
Abbess

died 782

THERE IS MUCH that is appealing and wholly recognizable in the first contacts of which we know between St. Lioba and the great St. Boniface, apostle of the Germans (*see* June 5). He was already a great fighter for the Church, pressing northwards on the European continent, extending the kingdom of Christ as he preached his word to the near kinsmen of the English, the Saxons and Frisians overseas; she was a shy young nun at home in the abbey of Wimborne in Dorset. Nonetheless she found the courage to write to him, to remind him that her dead father had been his close friend, that her mother, still alive and suffering much, was his kinswoman, and that she, her parents' only child, with no brothers of her own, would like to regard him in that light, to ask him for his prayers, and for help in her Latin studies. Her letter was indeed written in excellent style, and it ends with some modest, complimentary verses of her own composition:

> May the almighty Judge, He who alone made all things,
> And in the Father's kingdom shines ever resplendent,
> Where too the blazing glory of Christ eternally reigns,
> Keep you forever unharmed by His endless decree.

This letter first evoked, if we can judge by the evidence, an indulgent, noncommittal reply, prudently directed not only to Lioba but also to others of her sisters. Yet Boniface evidently did not forget this lover of Latin and of learning, or her artless confession to him that she learned her command of versification from her mistress at Wimborne, Eadburg, who was herself constantly composing holy Latin rhymes. Boniface was in need of such helpers. We have another letter from him to Eadburg, after she had become abbess of Thanet, asking for the copy of St. Peter's epistles which she is having illuminated for him; and we know from other sources that he asked the abbess of Wimborne for Lioba and many of her companions, to come out to him in Germany and help him there in his missionary work.

Lioba, her kinswoman Thecla, afterwards abbess of Kitzingen, and Walburga, later abbess of Heidenheim, and many others went in reply to his request; and they formed the abbey of Bischofsheim, with Lioba as their first head. Their learning, their religious observance, their piety, and their holy charm were a wonder in the new world to which they had gone. It is evident that Lioba herself, so far from thinking that in pagan mission territory less might be expected of them in the academic field, insisted on all the old Wimborne standards, and perhaps even more. She and her nuns became a model of what educated, Christian women might achieve, and her chief biographer tells us that as the new life brought by Boniface to Germany extended, a Bischofsheim-trained nun became a prerequisite in every new convent of nuns.

Even today, in the legends and the piety of Germany, a great tribute is paid to such apostles as Boniface and Lioba and Walburga: they are not thought of as English men and women, but rather as great Christians. That is as Lioba herself would have wished it.

A Great Woman's Contribution to Christianity

"At Bischofsheim a great number of God's handmaids assembled, who by the example of their blessed mother Lioba were formed in sacred science, and profited so much by her teaching that many of them afterwards became the instructors of others, so much so that there were hardly any convents of women in those parts who did not ask for nuns taught by Lioba. She was a woman of great force, so strong in what she had undertaken that she had no thought for her native land or for her kinsfolk . . . . She was always careful lest she should teach to others what she herself did not perform. In her demeanor there was neither arrogance nor pride; she was affable and kind to everyone, whoever it might be. Her countenance was angelic, her conversation cheerful, she was distinguished by her abilities, a wise counsellor, firm in the faith, enduring in hope, with love for everyone."

From the Life *by Rudolph of Fulda*

Vita Leobae abbatissae Biscofesheimensis (Monumenta Germaniae Historica, Scriptores, XVI, Hanover, 1887).

S. Bonifacii Epistolae (PL, 89, coll. 687-804).

W. Levison: *England and the Continent in the Eighth Century* (Oxford, 1946).

Charles of Blois
Duke of Britanny

died 1364

IN THE STORY of Blessed Charles of Blois we have an example of how a man, called to high office in the world, living a life of danger and anxiety, often of great hardship, can nonetheless preserve the peace of his own soul and a constant communion with God.

By his marriage with Joan of Britanny he laid claim to the duchy, and in this he was supported by the French king; but the rival claimant was backed by Edward III of England and his superior military forces. For some four years of warfare, Charles managed to hold his own, but was then defeated in battle, taken, a prisoner, to England, and held in close captivity in the Tower of London until his enormous ransom could be paid. Once released, he took up again the campaign; but after nine years of constant strife, he was killed at the battle of Auray.

One might expect that the Breton people, to whom his wars had brought such loss and harm, would have greeted his death with thankfulness; but instead they held him in veneration, as a most saintly man, and there ensued the remarkable spectacle of the popular demands of a people obtaining public investigation of his claims to sanctity, despite the opposition of their new ruler, his victorious rival.

In war and peace, in liberty and captivity, Charles had always shown himself a truly holy man, devoted to religion, merciful and just; and as such the Bretons have always venerated him and asked for his intercessions.

Preparing for Death

"He heard two Masses with his customary devotion, made his confession, and received Holy Communion before he went out to fight. He confessed again to his own confessor, before the battle, and during the battle itself he made a third confession to a priest who was one of his chaplains . . . . He was taken prisoner, and a little later one of his enemies struck him in the mouth with a dagger, so hard that it penetrated half a foot beyond his neck. Friar Geoffrey Rabin, a Dominican of Nantes, who was standing beside him, told him to think of God and of St. John the Baptist, for whom he had always had special devotion. The prince could say no more than "O, my Lord, my God!", and died at once. The English stripped him, and found, under his clothing, a coarse hair shirt, which they threw away in scorn; but the friar who had received his last words seized with holy greed upon this spoil, so precious, of one that he so revered."

G. A. Lobineau's account of Blessed Charles' death

G.A. Lobineau: *Les Vies des Saints de Bretagne* (Rennes, 1725).
F. Plaine: *Essai historique sur le culte du B. Charles de Blois* (Nantes, 1872).

Jerome
Doctor of the Church

died 419

"IGNORANCE OF THE SCRIPTURES IS IGNORANCE OF CHRIST," wrote St. Jerome in the prologue to his *Commentary on Isaiah*. No one man in the history of the Church has labored so hard, and with such efficiency, to dispel this ignorance as did St. Jerome himself. He remains the greatest translator of the Holy Scriptures that the Church has known. He was the first to realize the need to return to the original sources—the Hebrew—for a right understanding of the Old Testament. When he came to the revision of the Gospels at the order of Pope Damasus, Latin had been the liturgical langu-age of Rome for over a century and a half. There were several Latin versions of the Scriptures in use, many of them seriously defective. Jerome collected as many manuscripts as he could and collated them all, Greek and Latin. The result of Jerome's great labors was his version of the Bible known as the Latin Vulgate, which has served the Church so well in her preaching and her liturgy for a thousand years and more.

Jerome's lifelong labor to preach the word of God through the grinding monotony of continual study and writing was the material of his holiness. His biographers have often been at pains to catalogue his personal defects: his testiness, his over-sensitivity, the violence of his written attacks on those who im-pugned his work, his fond dependence on the devoted group of women—Marcella, Paula and her daughters Julia Eustochium and Blesilla—who sustained him and encouraged him in his immense task. But all these pale alongside his devotion to God's truth and his passionate attachment to the faith of the Church. His life was enlightened by the truth that the Scriptures reveal God in Christ.

Jerome was born in Stridon in north-eastern Italy about 345. At the age of 12, he went to Rome to begin that thorough education in grammar, rhetoric, and the liberal arts which was the firm foundation of all his later scholarship. Though born of pious Christian parents, according to the custom of the time he was not baptized in infancy. In the midst of his Roman studies, he enrolled as a catechumen, and received baptism at the age of nineteen.

About this time, he went to the court of the Emperor Valentinian at Trèves in Gaul, and made his first acquaintance with the monastic life; and having decided that this was his vocation, he began to study theology and received his first introduction to sacred Scripture through the *Commentary on the Psalms* of Hilary of Poitiers (*see* January 14). Soon he went to Antioch, where he began the serious study of the Bible which was to be his life's work. In spite of a long and debilitating illness, he determined to try to live the eremitical life, and joined a colony of monks living in caves near Aleppo. It was there that he met a monk who had been a Jew, and began his lessons in Hebrew, so exhausting and difficult that he was often tempted to give the whole thing up, but which were to bear such splendid fruit. Returning to Antioch, he was reluctantly prevailed upon to accept ordination to the priesthood, but on the understanding that he should be left free to study and to write.

In 382 he returned to Rome, where he remained for three years, working at his translations and commentaries under orders from Pope Damasus, and teaching Scripture to the group of women who gathered in the house of the widow Marcella. When eventually he left Rome, for Palestine, two of this group, Paula and her daughter Julia, left with him. Paula had two monasteries built at Bethlehem, one for monks, the other for nuns. There Jerome settled, and lived out his days. It was the most fruitful period of his life. There he made his great translations of the books of the Old Testament, and wrote his longer commentaries. Often he preached

at Bethlehem, and also kept up his correspondence; he was an
inveterate letter writer, and 117 of his letters are still extant.

Toward the end of his life, he was seriously involved in the
Pelagian controversy; and, with the bishop of Jerusalem siding
with Pelagius, life became hard for the double monastery at
Bethlehem. But, as Jerome wrote to his friend Apronius: "It
is better to have nothing but bread to eat than to lose the faith."
A few months later he died at the age of seventy-two, and was
buried, alongside Paula and Julia, next to the Basilica of the
Nativity.

True Faith

> "If I believed in God with real faith, I would purify my heart;
> for through this a man can see God. I would beat my breast
> and weep copious tears . . . I would throw myself at the feet
> of the Lord, I would cling to the tree of the Cross, and would
> never let go until I had received mercy. Instead of this, when
> I am at my prayers, often enough my mind is wandering. . . .
> I even catch myself thinking wicked thoughts. Where is my
> faith? Was it like this that Jonah prayed, or the three children
> in the fiery furnace?"
>
> *From St. Jerome's* Altercatio

J. Steinmann: *St. Jerome* (London, 1959).
F. X. Murphy, art.: "Jerome, St." (NCE, 7, pp. 872-74).

Saints for October

The saints reigning with Christ offer their prayers for men to God. It is good and useful to call upon them with supplication and, in order to obtain benefits from God through Jesus Christ, who alone is our Redeemer and Savior, to have recourse to their prayers, and aid.

COUNCIL OF TRENT
Session XXV

Remi
Bishop

died about 533

THOUGH IN THE CENTURIES after his death much edifying fiction was written about St. Remi, little of it is trustworthy; and most of the documents which might have furnished reliable evidence are now lost. The principal source which we can use with confidence is St. Gregory of Tours' history of the Franks; from this it appears that Remi did indeed play a great part in the establishment and the Christianization of the kingdom of the Franks.

King Clovis had inherited from his father, king of the Salian Franks, a small and uninfluential domain; but by the end of his long reign he had conquered and settled territory almost coterminous with modern France, and had made Paris his seat of government. This had only been achieved through much ruthlessness on his part, and he was almost constantly engaged in hostilities.

Clovis was born a pagan, but he had married a Burgundian Christian princess, Clotilda. The story appears to be authentic that before a great battle which he fought against a horde of the invading Alamanni, he asked for help from his wife's God, and that after the victory which he won—a turning point in the history of his country—he and some three thousand of his warriors received baptism at the hands of Remi, the bishop of Rheims.

Remi was the child of a noble house of Gaul which gave many other saints to the Church. He was chosen as bishop of Rheims when he was no more than twenty-two, so that he had to be dispensed from this impediment of age. He became a truly great bishop, learned, wise and holy, utterly devoted to his people and their care. He is said to have been a master of sacred eloquence, though none of his sermons have survived. All that we have from his pen is a few letters; but even these tell us much of the man, and especially of the saintly influence he exercised upon the king and on his subjects. So were laid the foundations of a Christian realm which has never since then failed to send its sons and daughters to the ends of the earth to proclaim the kingdom of Christ.

The Duties of a Ruler

"You should employ advisers who can add to your good reputation. You should be fair and honest in bestowing favor. You should show reverence toward your priests, and always seek their advice, for if you and they act in harmony, it will be the better for your whole realm. Help your subjects, relieve those in want, support widows, feed orphans, so that all may love and respect you. Let all your words be of justice. Do not oppress the poor or strangers, and refuse every gift they may offer you. Let it be known to all that no man ever leaves your hall of justice sorrowing."

St. Remi in a letter to King Clovis

Sancti Remigii Epistolae (PL, 65).
Gregory of Tours: *Historia Francorum* (PL, 71).

Gerard of Brogne
Abbot

died 959

ST. GERARD was born of the ruling house of the county of Namur, then still independent of the duchy of Burgundy. He inherited great estates and wealth, and as a young man served the ruler, his kinsman Count Berengarius. He was exceptionally well-liked by everyone for his placid and kind disposition, his unfailing courtesy, and his great goodness to the poor and unfortunate. But these were only the outward marks of a deep interior love of God; and in the midst of all his worldly occupations, he was much attracted by the life of prayer.

Sent on a diplomatic mission to Paris, he separated himself from those who accompanied him, and made a retreat in a monastery outside the city; he then formed the resolution to give up the world and enter religion. First he had to obtain the count of Namur's consent for this, and it was only given to him very reluctantly. But he was able to return to France, and to make there his religious profession as a Benedictine monk.

In religion he was as distinguished, and as popular, as he had formerly been; and in the course of time his abbot decided to establish a daughter-house on Gerard's own property at Brogne, and to make Gerard its head. He made a most successful abbot, sought after by many outside the house; but presently he found that his duties as administrator of the monastery and as host to many visitors were an intolerable distraction. Accordingly he built a cell, apart from the rest, and went to live there as a recluse.

However, he was not allowed to continue in this solitary life of

719

prayer for which he so longed. Instead, we find him being employed as visitor and reformer of many other religious houses, introducing or restoring the rule of St. Benedict, reproving laxity and suppressing corruption, and always with inimitable tact and charm and kindliness.

By now, he was an old man, quite worn out; and on his last visitation through France, the community of one house begged him to travel no further, to stay with them, to rest, and to continue to delight them with his holy words. But smilingly he told them that this could not be, that he would find his rest in his poor cell at Brogne which he so greatly loved. Returning there, he died a most holy death soon afterwards in his hermitage.

The Life of a Solitary

"O Hermit, didst thou flee away
Far from thy fellow men to stay!
   Moved by what fear!
What silent communing hast thou,
What visions crowd upon thee now,
   Encaverned here?

With the free spirit in her flight
Thou viewest all the realms of light,
   The eternal home;
No more thy converse might'st thou give
To mortals, but with God to live
   Art hither come".

Hymn for an anchorite's feast, from the Paris Breviary, *trans.*
D.T. Morgan

Acta Sanctorum, October, vol. ii.

Teresa of the Child Jesus
Carmelite Nun

died 1897

IN THE WHOLE HISTORY of the Church there have been few saints who have inspired such widespread devotion so rapidly as did "the Little Flower"; and there can have been few so misunderstood and misinterpreted as she. One difficulty, over which many intellectuals have stumbled, is that she was forced to employ the trashy language and imagery on which she had been reared, first in her intensely bourgeois, over-simply pious family home, thereafter in a Carmel little distinguished by its inmates' profundity. But we do not begin to grasp her message until we perceive that her trashy modes of expressing herself were employed to combat trashy ideas, which she will replace with a concept of the inner life of the spirit in God as heroic as it is simple.

It is of the essence of her famous "Little Way" that it must be ordinary, capable of imitation by ordinary people; and it is founded on her recognition of the endless humility with which God became man. "What helps and strengthens me is not all the rubbish we are told . . . [the Holy Family] lived the same life as ours." Most spiritual literature seemed to help her but little; she can talk of "the learned books which give me a splitting headache and a dried-up heart," and say that "all the sermons I have heard on Mary have left me cold." The one guide for her was "my spiritual director, Jesus," and her maxim was "if not by blood, then by love." Love for her was a sacrificial act, a very martyrdom.

She has been compared with Paul (not always approvingly) for her calm certainty of her reward; and even more than Paul, she has this certainty because of her knowledge of God's greatness and her own littleness: "I am a very little soul upon whom the good God has heaped graces." Many of her own religious community saw her only as a little soul; from them the graces were hidden. As she lay on her long deathbed, she heard one of them complaining how hard it was going to be to write the prescribed obituary notice for her. "She entered our convent, lived and died; there is really no more to say." But there were others more perceptive; and it was the much maligned prioress, Marie de Gonzague, with her stern treatment, who most helped her to love God alone. Her sisters and her father seem to have done their best, before and after her entry into religion, to ruin her with excessive affection and adulation.

Yet she received early intimations of the spiritual desolation in which so much of her short life was to be passed. As a child she could speak with knowledge of "night, dark night, utter dereliction, like death itself"; and she was to feel deep attraction to John of the Cross (*see* November 24), the supreme poet of "the Dark Night." That night was to be in Carmel her constant state. "I thank Jesus for letting me walk in darkness. Even as I do, I feel deep peace."

The history of her external afflictions, the conflicts, rivalries, and tensions which were the setting for her religious life, is too well known to need repetition. Those who are scandalized by it are closing their eyes to the real nature of religious life, part of the affliction and mortification of which will always be in putting oneself, under God, at the mercy of others, who will often themselves be experiencing yet greater suffering.

No one ever aspired less to be a doctor of the Church; but her keen insights often gave her almost prophetic powers. At a time when the dead hand of Jansenism still lay heavy on men's lives, she saw how much Holy Communion was needed by those weak and struggling souls whom God had come to save, as much as by the justified, and she could tranquilly remark: "When I am in heaven, the Church's practice concerning Holy Communion will change."

What was the "Little Way," as she herself followed it? In the first place, it demanded obedience to the letter of her Order's rule, often administered though it was by capricious and erratic superiors. (Those who today advocate "constructive disobedience" may consider this infantile and supine, if they will.) This obedience she practiced despite the contrary example of a whole convent. She sought and exercised love for the unloveable. She vowed herself to suffering, asking to be spared nothing, and, in a very genuine humility and simplicity, she sought and practiced a "spiritual childhood."

The Little Way of Love

"In the time of the law of fear, before the coming of our Lord, the prophet Isaiah, speaking in the name of the King of Heaven, could say 'Can a mother forget her child? Yet if she should forget, yet will I not forget you.' What ecstasy in that promise! Ah! and we who live under the law of love, how can we fail to put to profit the loving advances our Spouse makes to us? How can we fear one 'who lets himself be held by a hair of her neck'? So we must learn to hold Him prisoner, this God who makes Himself a mendicant for our love. In telling us that a hair can work so great a marvel, He is showing that the smallest actions done for love are the actions which win His heart. Ah! if we had to do great things, how much to be pitied we should be . . . but how fortunate we are, since Jesus lets Himself be held by the smallest!"

St. Teresa in a letter to her sister Léonie, July 12, 1896

A. Combes, trans. F.J. Sheed: *Collected Letters of St. Thérèse of Lisieux* (London, 1949).

A. Combes, trans. P. E. Hallett: *The Spirituality of St. Thérèse* (Dublin, 1950).

I. Görres, trans. R. and C. Winston: *The Hidden Face* (London, 1959).

H. Urs von Balthasar, trans. D. Nicholl: *Thérèse of Lisieux: the Story of a Mission* (New York, 1953).

Amoun of Nitria
Desert Monk

died about 350

THE PRINCIPAL SOURCE of our knowledge of St. Amoun is the "Lausiac History" of Palladius, a monk of Galatian origin, later a bishop in Bithynia, a work, primarily of edification, on the lives of the monks and solitaries of the Egyptian desert, which he wrote at the request of Lausus, grand chamberlain to the Emperor Theodosius II.

Amoun was an Egyptian Christian, who lived by growing balsam trees (as arduous an occupation, Palladius tells us, as cultivating vines) and manufacturing from them medicinal balm. He was orphaned as a boy, and the uncle who was his guardian forced him into a marriage with a girl, a Christian, but, seemingly, with little knowledge of the faith. Amoun suffered the wedding ceremony and the attendant festivities; but on their wedding night he explained to his wife his desire to live chastely for the love of God. He first suggested that they should separate, but, at her request, they lived under one roof, but as brother and sister.

This continued for eighteen years, during which time Amoun kept a strict regime of unremitting labor, a sparse diet, and many bodily mortifications. When his wife suggested to him that he ought to make public profession of his way of life he went to Nitria, while she turned their house into what we today would call a convent for religious women. Twice a year Amoun used to visit them and give them religious instruction.

Palladius visited Nitria fifty years after Amoun had lived there, and says that the many ascetics and penitents who went to it chose it because life there was even harder than in the desert. St. Jerome calls it "the city of the Lord." On the mountain above the poisonous marsh Amoun settled, and collected around him a number of anchorites. At first they seem to have lived solitary lives, until St. Anthony the Abbot (*see* January 17), who became Amoun's dear friend, advised them to adopt some more communal form of life.

Amoun is typical of all that we know of the lives of the Desert Fathers: their love of solitude and silence in which to pray, and the cruel treatment to which they subjected their bodies so as to subdue their every passion. Palladius leaves us in no doubt that Amoun and his wife loved one another dearly; but even that chaste love became something separating them from the love of Christ, and therefore that, too, was willingly sacrificed to God.

Amoun and his Wife Separate

"Amoun's prayers had their effect; and in the end his wife said to him: 'I have something to say to you, sir; and if you will listen to me, I shall believe that you love me in God.' He said to her: 'Say what you wish.' She said to him: 'It would be right for us to live apart, for you are a man living righteously, and I have done all that I can to follow the same way as you; and I think it strange that you should live in chastity with me, and so conceal from men your great virtue.' And when he had given thanks to God, he said to her: 'Very good: you shall have this house, and, as for me, I shall find another dwelling.' And leaving her, he went into the remotest part of the mountain of Nitria."

From Palladius' "Lausiac History," book viii

Acta Sanctorum, October, vol. ii.
A. Lucot, ed. and trans.: *Palladius: Histoire Lausiaque* (Paris, 1912).

Raymund of Capua
Dominican Friar

died 1399

BLESSED RAYMUND was the son of a distinguished family of Capua. While studying at Bologna he entered the Dominican Order, and by the age of thirty-five was prior of their house, the Minerva, in Rome; later he lectured to their students in Florence and in Siena.

It was there that he encountered the great St. Catherine (*see* April 30). Raymund was no "enthusiast," lacking both her force and her eccentricity; but he seems early to have recognized her saintliness, and in many ways to have smoothed her path for her. When he became her confessor, he at once permitted her to receive Holy Communion daily if she wished; the lack of this permission had till then been a source of trouble to her.

Together they cared for the victims of a terrible outbreak of plague in the city; Raymund himself contracted the disease and was thought to be dying; but Catherine's prayers for his recovery were granted, and thereafter he was her right hand man.

He acted as her secretary and biographer, and has recorded for us much of her activities and correspondence, such as the famous letter she sent, at the outbreak of the Great Schism, to the cardinals leagued against Urban VI, the one beginning: "What are you doing, you great hinges of the heavenly gates, you noblest chamberlains of the palace of God, you most illustrious princes of the angelic mansion?" Urban sent him to France, to preach there against his rival, the anti-pope Clement VII; but Raymund submitted, much to Catherine's chagrin, to being roughly turned back at the border.

Soon after this, on the day of Catherine's death, Raymund was convinced that he heard her promising him her prayers and help in heaven; and at this time he became unofficial head of her bereaved "family," and was also elected master general of the Urbanist Dominicans. It is characteristic of him that he seems at once to have attempted an appeasement with his precursor in the office, Elias of Toulouse, who, as a Frenchman, adhered to Clement and had been deposed and excommunicated by Urban; but these efforts (if they were made – the archives of the Bologna chapter which elected Raymund are lost) met with no response.

In Rome, he was as tireless as Catherine had been on behalf of the pope, who said that Raymund was "his head, his eyes, his mouth, his hands and his feet." Perhaps the source of the strength which he showed in supporting a man whom he must have known unworthy of the papacy was his unquestioning application of the principles of religious obedience; and this also characterized his reforms in the Order. In these there was nothing new, nothing of his own, but, always, an appeal to St. Dominic and to the Order's constitutions. Not himself an especially forceful character, Raymund found his motive-power in religion, in obedience, and, above all, in prayer.

A Promise of Protection

"On the morning when the virgin [Catherine] died [in Rome], I went down into our church [in Genoa], because it was the feast of Blessed Peter Martyr, and there, unworthy as I am, I celebrated Mass; and after that I went back to the dormitory to get my travelling bag ready. Passing a painting of the glorious Virgin, I said the Angelic Salutation to myself, as is the friars' custom, and stood still there for a little while. Suddenly I heard a voice – and yet it had no sound – uttering words – yet audible not to my ears but to my mind – and I grasped their meaning – and yet better than if any earthly voice had spoken them to me . . . 'Do not be afraid, I am here on your behalf. I shall protect, I shall defend. Be assured, fear nothing, I am standing here for you.' And when I had understood this in my mind, I suffered greatly, to tell the truth, wondering what could be this consolation and this promise of safety."

From Raymund's Life of St. Catherine

F. J. P. Bliemetzrieder: *Raimund von Capua und Caterina von Siena* (Historisches Jahrbuch, 30, 1909, pp. 231–73).

D. A. Mortier: *Histoire des maîtres-généraux de l'ordre des frères prêcheurs,* vol. iii (Paris, 1907).

Bruno
Founder of the Carthusian Order

died 1101

ST. BRUNO was a Rhinelander, born at Cologne about 1030; but he was educated at the Rheims cathedral school. He had a long and successful career as a teacher of theology; Anselm of Laon, St. Hugh, bishop of Grenoble, and the future Blessed Urban II were all his pupils. This culminated, in 1075, in his appointment as chancellor of Rheims.

The archbishop there was Manasses, a notorious simoniac and a relative of the French royal house. In obedience to Pope Gregory VII, Bruno denounced Manasses before the Council of Autun as unfit for office; and in return, the archbishop despoiled him of all his possessions and drove him out of Rheims.

In the end the pope prevailed, and the Rheims chapter was on the point of electing Bruno to the see when he, who several years before had taken a private vow to leave the world so soon as circumstances would permit, left the city with some friends. After some first attempts at the eremitical life, they asked Bruno's old pupil, the bishop of Grenoble, for a place well suited to a life of solitude.

So it was that they began to live, at Chartreuse, that rigorous existence, singular among all western monastic rules for the solitude in which its followers spend their lives, wholly devoted to prayer and contemplation, which distinguished and still distinguishes the Carthusians.

Guigo I, Bruno's fourth successor, was the first to draw up their constitutions; but it is evident from other accounts, notably that of Guibert of Nogent, that the whole life of the Grande Chartreuse bore the imprint of Bruno's character and habits. But this solitary and awesome place was not destined to be his last earthly home. In 1090, in obedience to his other former pupil, Pope Urban II, he went to Rome. He was followed on the way by his faithful disciples, but he sent them back to their monastery.

In Rome, where he served faithfully as a counsellor to Urban, he lived as a hermit; but later he obtained the pope's permission, not, as he wished, to return to the Grande Chartreuse, but to withdraw from the city and to live the life he had devised and practiced. He died in 1101, in one of the Carthusian foundations he had made in Calabria.

The austerity of the Carthusian life makes it the more wonderful that the Order spread everywhere in the West so rapidly. One of its greatest glories, the finest tribute to the spirit of its founder, was the saintly heroism of some of its members at the time of the Reformation, in the face of persecution and cruel death.

The Austerity of the Carthusian Life

"Each of them has his own private cell set around the cloister, and in these they work, sleep and eat. On Sundays they receive bread from the distributor of food, and vegetables, out of which each one in his cell cooks the same kind of broth. They have water which they draw from a channel which runs around the whole cloister and is piped into each cell. On Sundays and great feasts they eat fish and cheese—not that they buy fish, but they will accept it from good men's charity. But they will take gold or silver or ornaments for their church from no one, except for a silver chalice. They do not assemble in the church at what we would consider the usual hour, but at times of their own. Unless I am mistaken, they do hear Mass on Sundays and feast days. They hardly ever speak, but if it is necessary to ask for something, that is done by a sign. When they do drink wine it is so sour that it gives them neither strength nor pleasure. Next their bodies they wear hair shirts, and the rest of their clothing is very skimpy . . . .

Though they deprive themselves of everything else, they have assembled a very sumptuous library."

Guibert of Nogent, About my Life, *written some 20 years after Bruno's death*

Acta Sanctorum, October, vol. vi.
PL, 156.
Y. Gourdel, art.: "Chartreux" (Dictionnaire de spiritualité, ii, coll. 705–76).

Artaldus
Carthusian Monk and Bishop

died 1206

St. Artaldus was the son of a noble family in Savoy, and as a young man he was at court, evidently with the intention of making a career in politics for himself; but these plans were soon given up, and instead he entered the Carthusian monastery at Portes. There he became known as a model religious, and for many years his life was passed in useful, prayerful obscurity. Then he was given the heavy charge of founding a new monastery at Arveyres in the Savoy, a place near to his own home, wild and desolate, scrubland in summer, snowbound in winter, haunted by bears and other wild beasts, significantly known to the dwellers of that region as "the Grave." He and his community experienced many reversals of fortune, including the destruction by fire of their new buildings; but they prospered, and their house became famous for the holiness of their lives.

But Artaldus was often called from this solitude to serve the Holy See with his counsel, as the founder of his Order, Bruno (*see* October 6), had done before him. He was over eighty years old when it was made known that it was the will of the clergy and the people of the diocese of Belley that this saintly old man should be their new bishop. He protested that his age and his calling unfitted him for this, but in vain; in 1185 he went to Belley, but after only two years as bishop, to his great thankfulness he was released, to return to Arveyres, there, he must have hoped, soon to end his life. But he lived on for another twenty years; and we know from the story of the visit to him by St. Hugh of

732

Lincoln how much he must have been revered in his Order as a father in God.

Like Bruno before him, Artaldus was not permitted to live his whole life in the solitude to which it seemed that the Lord had called him; both of them offer an example of the rewards which can come to those who will generously sacrifice even their own spiritual aspirations in obedience to the needs of the people of God.

Conversation in the Cloister

"When St. Hugh, the bishop of Lincoln, was returning to England from the Grande Chartreuse, the house of his profession, in the year 1200, he made a special visit to Artaldus' monastery, even though he had to go out of his way to this mountainous place, so difficult of access. Blessed Artaldus, once a bishop, now again a simple monk in his cell, had for long yearned to see his brother bishop . . . . When they were talking with the brethren, the former bishop of Belley asked the bishop of Lincoln to tell them all the terms of the peace which had been made between the kings of France and England, for he knew that Hugh had been involved in this matter. But Hugh, so zealous for the spirit of their Order, was not a little grieved to be asked this, and he said, gently and as if in jest: 'O, my lord and father, even if it is permitted for bishops to listen to gossip and pass it on, it is not good for monks. Rumors should not enter cells and cloisters; those who have fled from towns should not carry news into the desert.' And at once he turned the conversation to matters of spiritual edification."

Charles Le Couteulx

Acta Sanctorum, October, vol. iv.
C. Le Couteulx: *Annales Ordinis Cartusiensis*, vols. 2 and 3 (Montreuil, 1888).

Bridget of Sweden
Foundress of the Order of the Most Holy Savior

died 1373

IT MAY BE DIFFICULT for us today to understand and sympathize with the immense veneration accorded to St. Bridget in her own lifetime, and in the century and a half after her death. But if we place her in her times, if we observe what the forces were against which she was fighting, we begin to see how much she was a woman of our own epoch, how generous and pure was her vision of what the Church could and should be, and that in a century when the Church's fortunes and reputation were at their lowest ebb.

She was the daughter and wife of great landowners in Sweden, and her character and her training fitted her to command, as she did to the end of her days. She served for a while at court as a lady in waiting, but there and in her own home all her efforts were exerted in the interests of religion, and it is evident that she was always strongly drawn to the enclosed, contemplative life. Enclosure as such she was never to know, and this is not the place to ask how much of a contemplative she can be considered to have been; but an ecstatic and a visionary she undoubtedly was, and she founded one of the greatest of contemplative Orders.

The "Babylonian Captivity," the long residence of the popes in Avignon, was to her, as to most Christians of her age who had not to cope with the practical difficulties of maintaining the government of the Holy See in Rome, a scandal and a grief. And it was notorious that in the security and ease of Avignon, the popes' courts, their courtiers, and sometimes their own persons gave cause for grave criticism. Bridget believed that she was called by God to set this right. In the year 1347 or 1348 she had already sent emissaries to Avignon to tell Clement VI that Christ had bid her say "I constituted Peter the shepherd and servant of my sheep, but you scatter and worry them; for you are worse than Lucifer."

By this time her husband had ended his life in monastic seclusion in a Cistercian house which they had founded, and she was projecting a rule which she herself might follow. In 1349 she went to Rome for the next year's jubilee; and she never returned to her native land. In the City, she surrounded herself with a cosmopolitan group of devotees, all of them convinced of the authenticity of her visions and of the necessity, for the well-being of the Church, that the pope should return to Rome. Her own labors were vast; they are all recorded for us in the huge volume of "Revelations," recorded as they were dictated by her, and after her death edited by her spiritual family.

In November, 1371, she went on pilgrimage to Jerusalem. Less than two years later she died in Rome, in the house in which she and her intimates had kept the rule which had not yet received papal approbation, a house still standing, hard by that hospice for pilgrims from England which was to become the present English College.

She had never ceased to urge upon the popes that they must leave Avignon; and it is evident that her efforts, and those of St. Catherine of Siena (*see* April 30) to this end, were one of the factors in finally persuading Gregory XI to return to Rome. But his death, and the election of his successor, the notorious Urban VI, divided western Christendom in a schism more grievous than it had ever known. In the events which followed, her family, including her daughter Katherine, herself to be canonized in the next century, threw all their weight behind Urban VI, and that included the great prestige of Bridget's name and writings. Though the issue was in many ways a clear-cut political one (France appointed and supported the anti-pope, therefore England supported the pope in Rome, therefore Scotland sided with

France, and so on), great theological issues were also at stake, particularly that issue which is still alive today: the powers and duties, vis-á-vis one another, of popes and ecumenical councils. The *moderni* would have subjected the pope to a council; and, as late as Basle, Bridget and her "Revelations" were a rallying-point for the *antiqui*, led by Torquemada.

But if we identify Bridget with what has come to be known as "Ultramontanism," we are in error. Centuries before her time, she had been given to see that popes should rule, not over territories with armies, but with holy wisdom over the people of God. With amazing prescience, she had written: "I saw in Rome as it were a space, stretching from St. Peter's to the Castle of St. Angelo, and from the castle to the House of the Holy Spirit, and from there to St. Peter's, surrounded by a strong wall . . . and I heard a voice saying: 'That pope who loves his Bride with that same love as I and my dear ones have loved her with, he will possess this place with his assistants, so that he may the more freely and peacefully summon his counsellors.'" It was God's inscrutable will that half Christendom should be lost to the Church before her vision should come true.

Distilling Every Goodness

"Rose distilling every goodness,
Star that guides us with your brightness,
Bridget, vessel of God's grace!
Drop the heavenly dew of pity,
Instil your own chaste ways within us,
Here amid this vale of woe.

Christ who leads us, that sweet teacher,
He chose you, to love and guide you
From your earliest childhood days,
You, His vine, so tender, growing,
Shooting, springing ever higher
Till you towered above the stars.

Love made you in faith so steadfast,
Pure in thought—love bound and led you
Forward on your holy way.

Seemliest and noblest woman,
Christ you loved, Christ you entreated
On every day of your great life."

Rosa rorans bonitatem, *hymn for St. Bridget's Office, composed by Nicholas of Linköping* (see *July 24*)

Revelationes (Lübeck, 1492).

E. Colledge: *Epistola solitarii ad reges: Alphonse of Pecha as Organizer of Birgittine and Urbanist Propaganda* (Mediaeval Studies, 18, 1956, pp. 19–49).

I. G. A. Collijn, ed.: *Acta et processus canonizacionis B. Birgittae* (2 vols., Uppsala, 1924–31).

H. Redpath: *God's Ambassadress* (Milwaukee, 1947).

Louis Bertrand
Dominican Friar

died 1581

WE ARE WELL INFORMED about St. Louis Bertrand's life, since the *Acta Sanctorum* prints a Latin version of the Spanish *Life* written by Vinant Justinian Antist, who was his close friend and disciple; this is supplemented by a still longer biography published in 1623 by Avinoñe, who was familiar with the evidence given in the process of beatification.

Louis was born in Valencia, of the same family as St. Vincent Ferrer (*see* April 5); like him, he joined the Dominicans, and he was ordained priest by St. Thomas of Villanova (*see* September 22). For long years he served the Order as novice master, and in this office he gained a reputation for great severity. He had no special intellectual gifts or charm of manner, but he was outstanding for immense and intense self-dedication. St. Teresa (*see* October 15) thought so highly of him that she sought and obtained from him encouragement for the reform she planned, and he then prophesied the success and fame which would soon be granted to her enterprise.

When he was forty years old, he was sent on the mission to the Americas, and helped to evangelize Colombia, Panama, and the Leeward, Virgin, and Windward Isles. During his six years there, the enormous numbers of converts he baptized recall the stories told of St. Francis Xavier's labors in the East. Needless to say, both saints have been charged with irresponsibility, in making Christians of so many thousands whose subsequent instruction and Christian living they could not guarantee; but they worked

738

and acted in faith, and, surely, the later histories of their mission territories has been their justification.

In the Americas, Louis was greatly troubled by what he saw of Spanish cruelty to Indian natives and to imported Negroes, and of his countrymen's active opposition to their subjects' evangelization. In the stories told of his relations with these oppressed peoples, we see the man's true compassion. Antist tells us that already in Spain Louis' mind had been turned toward the West Indies when a native of the islands, masquerading as a Dominican student, obtained by this ruse hospitality at their house in Valencia, where Louis and Antist were both living. Louis and his fellows detected the fraud, but when even their provincial wanted the culprit punished, he begged with tears that the Indian be spared, saying that if anyone had sinned it was he, Louis. The meaning of his words is not hard to seek: he was acknowledging the heavy moral responsibility of every conquering race toward those they conquer. Later, when the Indian told Louis of how those who preached the faith in his land were often killed, and sometimes eaten, Louis decided that that was the place for him.

The Gospel Denied to Colored People

"On one occasion when Louis was preaching to a great number of Indians, a government official burst into the church and drove them all out with a club, shouting 'Outside, all you darkies, and get back to your work.' And since they were not only unarmed but defenseless too, naked as they were, as is the custom in some of those parts, they had to flee at once, and leave their preacher alone in his pulpit."

Vinant Justinian Antist

Acta Sanctorum, October, vol. v.

Francis Borgia
Jesuit Priest

died 1572

IN 1528, YOUNG FRANCIS BORGIA, heir to the duchy of Gandia, great-grandson of the notorious Pope Alexander VI, grand-nephew of Cesare and Lucrezia Borgia, was riding through Alcalá on his way to the court of the Spanish king, Charles V, when his cortege met a group of guards with a shabby prisoner. When Francis enquired who he was, he was told that the prisoner was a Basque, called Ignatius Loyola (*see* July 31), being dragged to trial by the Inquisition for heresy. It was twenty years later that Ignatius obtained leave from the pope for a certain layman, who would remain anonymous, to be professed as a Jesuit and remain in secular life for three more years to wind up his business affairs. When the three years were completed, Borgia received the imperial permission to abdicate his duchy. He had been studying theology for several years, so that he was quite ready for ordination in the following year, 1551.

Though he was only forty years old, the ex-duke had led an extraordinarily full and varied life in the courtly and martial world of a Spanish grandee. With his "royal" background and fortune, he had the entree to every court in Europe. When he joined Charles V at Valladolid he was only seventeen; but he immediately became the intimate confidant of the twenty-seven year old emperor. A marriage was soon arranged for him with Eleanora, the empress' favorite maid of honor; and the marriage was blessed with children. The young couple enjoyed the unique favor of the empress at court for ten years.

When the empress died in 1539, life began to change for Francis. He was immediately appointed viceroy of Catalonia, and worked hard at administration for three years. During this time he built a harbor in the province's capital, Barcelona, remodelled its fortifications, and began to build up a fleet. He reformed the prisons, took steps to control lawlessness and brigandage, and tried to form a foreign legion, for service in Algeria, out of ex-prisoners.

In 1543, on the death of his father, Francis resigned as governor, and began to administer his own duchy of Gandia. By this time he was in frequent correspondence with Loyola, general of the Jesuits. When his wife died in 1546 (a holy death bed, on which the duchess received the last sacraments and then asked for the Lord's Passion to be read to her), Borgia at once decided to prepare for withdrawal from secular life.

After ordination, Ignatius Loyola left Francis free to conduct his own apostolate in northern Spain, where he preached and taught to such effect that within six months he was known as "the apostle of the Basques." But it was impossible for him to lead the private life of a religious. He was compelled to visit the Portuguese king at Lisbon and transact official business; and in 1554 the Borgias became involved in a vendetta with the de la Casta family. Francis was afraid to go to Rome, as Pope Julius III was anxious to make him a cardinal; it seemed to Julius grotesque that a Spanish nobleman should beg in the streets, live in hospitals, and go about in shabby black. Great pressure was put on Francis, but he resisted it, made his solemn profession as a Jesuit in 1554, and was able afterwards to refuse other such pressing solicitations.

In this same year Ignatius made Francis commissary-general of the four Spanish Jesuit provinces. He made it his business during the next few years to establish proper novitiates. It remained impossible for him to live a normal religious life. "People look at me," he said, "as if I were some strange animal. Well, if God had not chained me up in a cage of religion, I would be a wild beast. So let them stare."

In these years he was still involved in affairs of state. He found himself, with the consent of Ignatius, helping Juana, regent of

Portugal, with the government of the country, and consoling the Spanish emperor Charles after his abdication. These relationships, of course, made enemies for him. He was accused of heterodoxy by the Inquisition, and eventually had to leave Spain. He spent the rest of his life in Rome.

There he was soon appointed vicar-general of the Society of Jesus, becoming the friend and director of Charles Borromeo (*see* November 4); and eventually, in 1565, he was elected general. The last seven years of his life, spent chained to his desk, were most distasteful to him. He repeatedly prayed: "May God take me, or help me to govern aright, or remove this cross." He was particularly successful in developing the mission in Africa, and creating those in the Americas. During the short years of his generalate, sixty-six members of the Society suffered martyrdom.

It may be said of St. Francis Borgia that his life consisted in repeated attempts to leave behind the worldly grandeur of his past, in order to devote himself more completely to the Lord's work. But God also showed him how natural talents — hereditary gifts for government and for leadership — can eventually be harnessed to God's will and so lead to sanctification.

A Prayer to the Blessed Trinity

"I gave thanks for the holiness of the Father, the Son and the Holy Spirit . . . . I gave thanks for the glory of the Father, the Son and the Holy Spirit. I offered myself, I asked to do everything for their greater glory . . . . I gave thanks for the immensity of Father, Son and Holy Spirit. I asked an unlimited love, part of their infinite love. I gave thanks for the all-power of Father, Son and Holy Spirit. I asked to be all-powerful in them. 'I can do all things in him who strengthens me.'"

From the Spiritual Diary *of Francis Borgia*

C. C. Martindale: *In God's Army: II, Captains of Christ* (London, 1917).

Mary Soledad
Foundress of the Handmaids of Mary Serving the Sick

died 1887

WE ALL EXPECT the opposition of the world as we try to do the will of God; but sometimes it comes to us as a rude shock when we see such opposition coming from those whose own Christian profession should make them most sympathetic toward new enterprises undertaken for the love of Christ. Yet this need not surprise us. Christ found, not only among the Pharisees, but from His own, incomprehension and even betrayal; and one of the lessons of His life for us should surely be to meet such trials with His own loving fortitude and forgiveness.

Blessed Mary Soledad is greatly to be revered for the charitable work which she undertook; but we should venerate her just as much for the patient and trustful spirit in which she accepted the many crosses which came to her because she wanted to work for Christ's afflicted ones. She was the child of humble shop-keepers in Madrid; and it was through a parish priest of the city, a Servite tertiary, that she was drawn into an undertaking, much needed and close to this priest's heart: the nursing of the neglected and poor sick in their own homes. He directed her and six others into such work, and they elected to live in community.

From this humble start the Handmaids of Mary grew; their leader, Emanuela Torres-Acosta, took for her religious name "Mary Soledad," the Blessed Mother "sorrowing alone." When the parish priest was withdrawn from them, they received further encouragement and help from Augustinian friars, and in the great cholera epidemic of 1865 they became famous for their heroic labors. Yet, within their community, there were many dissensions and defections; Mary Soledad was cruelly and baselessly calumniated, and suffered the humiliation of being deposed. She endured this with patience and charity. In the end she had the reward of reinstatement, and, even more, of seeing her congregation prosper, so that in 1875 it could send its first pioneers overseas, to found a much-needed daughter house in Santiago in Cuba.

She whom the Dominican nuns had once rejected as too young and too delicate, when as a girl she had offered herself to them, lived a life full of toil for the Lord, richly blessed. Her dying words were the fruit of her religious experience: "Children, live together in peace and unity."

Compassion for the Sorrowing Mother of God

"Now sinks the sun behind the wood apace;
I sorrow, Mary, for thy lovely face.
Now sinks the sun behind the tree;
I sorrow, Mary, for thy Son and thee."

English, anon., 12th century

Acta Apostolicae Sedis, 1950, pp. 182–87.
J. A. Zugasti: *La Madre Soledad Torres y Acosta* (2 vols., Madrid, 1916).

Wilfrid of York
Benedictine, Bishop

died 709

ST. WILFRID was born in 634, only thirty-seven years after the arrival in England of the mission led by Augustine of Canterbury (*see* May 28); and it is certain that his grandparents, if not his parents, were converts from paganism. As a youth, he entered the monastery of Lindisfarne. He was evidently talented and personable, and quick to gain royal and papal favor. Yet, despite all his great successes, he was very far from being a careerist. On his first visit to Rome he asked for the grace to teach the gospel to the nations, and later he was to convert pagans, both in the remoter parts of England and in Frisia.

The first time that he went abroad, he spent several years in Lyons and in Rome; and he was present at the murder (if it was not martyrdom) of his patron, Archbishop Annemund. He volunteered to share the archbishop's fate, but was spared.

On his return to England, he was well received by the king of Northumbria, who was anxious to introduce Roman ways and discipline into his kingdom, still much influenced by the forms of Celtic Christianity. Wilfrid was made abbot of Ripon, and in this capacity he was present at the famous synod of Whitby, decisive for the future of the Church in England, where he was a powerful advocate of the Roman system of reckoning the Easter date. As a result of the synod, Colman (*see* February 18) and his adherents withdrew from Northumbria, and Wilfrid succeeded Colman as archbishop of York.

He went to Gaul for consecration, only to find on his return that in his absence the see had been bestowed by the king on Chad (*see* March 1), who, though an Englishman, favored Celtic ways. Wilfrid withdrew to Ripon, but frequently exercised his episcopal functions in the kingdoms of Mercia and Kent, until Archbishop Theodore of Canterbury restored him to York, where he regularized Chad's orders and made him bishop of Lichfield. The dispute thus settled had been conducted, on Chad's side, with mildness and humility, on Wildfrid's with a fierce determination to fight for what he knew to be his rights.

Once reinstated at York, he went on as he had begun: a great builder and legislator, devoted to his rule and his Order, a great acquirer of land and wealth for the Church and the Benedictines, surrounding his office and his person with the splendor which had so beguiled him in Rome. His riches and his magnificence aroused royal envy, and he was again deposed; he returned to Rome to appeal. Of the legality of his title to his see there could be no question, and after the Holy See had made searching investigations he was sent back with a favorable decision; but there is criticism of his conduct in the see implicit in his instructions to consecrate co-adjutors to help him in his work. The king of Northumbria, unappeased, imprisoned him, and on his release he went into exile again, and helped to evangelize the still unconverted parts of Suffolk.

A new king of Northumbria recalled and reinstated him, but it was not long before there was fresh trouble, caused, significantly, by the king's alienation of Church property and determination to create suffragan sees in his kingdom. Yet another visit and appeal to Rome followed; and Wilfrid's life ended in Ripon, with his star very much in descent.

We know of his life from the biography by Stephen, "Eddius Stephanus," who, according to Bede, was brought by Wilfrid from Kent to teach singing in Northumbria. Some of Stephen's evidence is first-hand; it is plain that he was with Wilfrid on the last journey to Rome. The *Life* is partisan, credulous, lively, loving. Today, we may find it difficult to feel affection for Wilfrid, and we may identify him wholly with that "triumphalism" which we now so much deplore. But in asserting the Church's rights, spiritual as well as temporal, and in his gallant defiance of royal masters who thought that the Church was theirs to command, Wilfrid was one of the first witnesses in England to the principle that Christ and His vicars alone have rule over men's souls. Sometimes he may remind us of his successor in the see of York, Thomas Wolsey; but there was also in him the same brave and fearless willingness to fight for Christ's Church and, if need had been, to die for it, which animated St. Thomas of Canterbury and the Reformation martyrs.

Ready to Die and Be with Christ

"The nobles, filled with malice, summoned Bishop Annemund to appear before them, and he, quite unafraid, knowing what was in store for him, went to the place where he was to suffer; and though he forbade this, Wilfrid, God's servant, went with him, saying with joy 'What better could happen to us than to die, father and son together, and to be with Christ?' And so the holy bishop received his martyr's crown; but when the nobles saw blessed Wilfrid standing, stripped and undaunted, ready too for the palm of martyrdom, they asked 'Who is this handsome youth, making ready for death?' When they were told that he was from over the sea, and an Englishman from Britain, they ordered him not to be touched, but spared; and so our saintly Wilfrid was made a confessor of the faith."

From Stephen's biography of St. Wilfrid, chapter 6

B. Colgrave, ed. and trans.: *The Life of Bishop Wilfrid by Eddius Stephanus* (Cambridge, England, 1927).

J. F. Webb, ed. and trans.: *Lives of the Saints* (London, 1965).

Magdalen Panattieri
Dominican Tertiary

died 1503

THE TEACHING of the Second Vatican Council has encouraged all the faithful to reconsider the role of the Church in the world, and to ask for apostolic work from those whose vocation it is to remain in the world. Such lay apostles have precursors and intercessors in the many who, from the later Middle Ages onwards, worked for Christ as laymen, and yet satisfied their needs for a religious association by belonging to one of the Third Orders, notably those of the Franciscans and Dominicans.

Today, when so many gifted and spiritually-minded women are asking if the Church has hitherto permitted them to do all that they might for her children, we do well to remember those women of times past whose apostolate was not narrowly confined by tradition. Some of them, like Bridget of Sweden (*see* October 8) and Catherine of Siena (*see* April 30) were drawn into the great world of ecclesiastical politics and became prophetic counsellors to kings. Blessed Magdalen Panattieri was not called on to play any such role in the world; but the very obscurity of her humble life makes her work as a public preacher of the word the more remarkable.

Her whole life was lived out in Trino-Vercellese in Montferrat. It might have been a placid and uneventful existence, but one circumstance militated against this, her fiery and all-absorbing love of the Redeemer and His Redemption. As a young girl she joined the Dominican Third Order of Penitents, remaining at home and dedicating herself to self-mortification and charitable works. She is said to have enjoyed frequent visions and ecstasies, as well as gifts of healing and prevision. But her greatest gift was that of calling sinners to repentance.

The local Dominicans took no offense, and did as she counselled, when she called them to a stricter observance of their Rule; and it was with their encouragement and that of the other clerics of Trino that she began to give conferences, first for women and children, but, in the end, much frequented by men, including priests.

What would St. Paul have said of this? Was this the sort of conduct which he deprecated in apostolic Corinth? We do not know, because we were not there; but it does not seem to have been a problem to Magdalen and her directors.

A Woman's Apostolate

"In the spiritual colloquies which she used to hold with those whom she strove to draw away from the banquet of their sins to a sound diet, she preached with such force and such sweetness that even though her discourses lasted four or five hours, hardly a moment seemed to have passed; and her hearers were so kindled with the love of God and of virtue that they were ready to suffer everything, rather than once to offend God's divine majesty. Her devotion to the name of Jesus and to the most holy Sacrament it is hardly possible to describe . . . . She received Holy Communion every day; and that, in these wretched, frigid times, seemed itself a miracle."

Marchese in his Sagro Diario Domenicano

J. A. Iricus: *Rerum Patriae Tridinensis Libri Tres* (Milan, 1745).
Marchese: *Sagro Diario Domenicano* (a Latin version in *Acta Sanctorum*, October, vi).

Angadrisma
Abbess

died about 695

ST. ANGADRISMA is regarded as the patron and protectress of Beauvais, near which the abbey she ruled was located. Her help was often invoked during the city's many times of peril during the Hundred Years' War. When Beauvais seemed likely to be taken by the Burgundians in 1472, the saint's relics were paraded on the ramparts before the besieging army, which was then routed by the citizens, after a local girl, Jeanne Hachette, had captured one of the Burgundian standards.

Angadrisma was the daughter of Count Robert of Renty, an officer of the court of Clotaire III, king of Neustria. Her father had promised her in marriage, but she was determined to become a nun; and the legend tells how she prayed to be visited by some hideously disfiguring disease, and that her prayer was granted until the day of her clothing in the religious habit, when her former beauty was restored.

She was abbess of a house of Benedictine nuns near Beauvais, and, though she was in her fifties when appointed there, she governed it for thirty years. We are told that she won the love of her every subject by her just and kind regime; and yet when she was dying she had the community assembled, so that she might ask them all very humbly for forgiveness for any fault she had committed against them.

Angadrisma lived in a violent, lawless age, but all that we know of her speaks of peace and justice. In Merovingian society, especially, women of high station often showed themselves as daring and ruthless as their menfolk in politics and in war; but Angadrisma gave herself instead to God, to help to bring on earth the kingdom of righteousness.

In the Service of Christ

"All for His dear service
Life's bright bloom you gave;
Nor the joys of sense could tempt you
Nor the world enslave.
Christ the Virgin-born for each one
Wreathed a spotless crown,
And in heavenly places made you
With Himself sit down."

Virgines Egregiae, *hymn for the feast of a Virgin, trans. D. T. Morgan*

Acta Sanctorum, October, vol. vi.

Teresa of Avila
Carmelite and Mystic

died 1582

THE HISTORY of Christian spirituality is remarkably rich and varied; but one topic, one controversy we might almost say, which is rehearsed with monotonous regularity, century after century, concerns the relationship between the active and contemplative lives. It is generally held that the heights of contemplative prayer are reserved to those who have withdrawn into a physical and mental fastness in which silence and solitude reign uninterruptedly. Yet over and again in the history of the Church, God has raised up saints to confound our theoretical divisions and distinctions. St. Paul (*see* January 25 and June 30) was an outstanding example in the early Church. Nearer to our own times, no one has so united the heights and depths of the perfect love of God in contemplative prayer and extraordinary physical energy and activity as has St. Teresa of Avila, often called "the great St. Teresa" to distinguish her from her fellow Carmelite, Thérèse of Lisieux, the "Little Flower" (*see* October 3).

Teresa was born at Avila in Castile in 1515. She tells us herself in her *Autobiography* that she was one of twelve children, all well-favored by nature and grace. Her mother died when she was young, and as a child she was much in the company of her favorite brother, Rodrigo, with whom she devoured the lives of the saints, as well as books of chivalric romance. It was with him, at the age of seven, that she tried to run away to seek martyrdom at the hands of Moors, "not for any love that I bore God, but to enjoy without delay the great riches of heaven."

When she was twenty, in spite of family opposition, she entered the Carmelite convent of the Incarnation at Avila. She writes with great poignancy of this separation from her family: "I do not think that my feelings will be any more painful when I die." For nearly thirty years she remained in obscurity in Carmel, suffering from constant ill health, and in a sort of no man's land between the perfect love of God, for which she was being purified, and the love of family and friends.

At last the time came when she was ready for the Lord's work: the reform of the Order of Carmel. The Carmelites, whose origins are uncertain, were still dwelling in Palestine in the twelfth century. But when they migrated to Europe, far from being hermits, they became mendicant friars, which involved a series of mitigations of their primitive observance to suit a more active life.

Teresa, particularly after her "conversion," began to desire a more strict way of life: silence, solitude, absolute enclosure, more prayer and fasting; in fact, to return to the primitive Carmelite rule. Though the bishop of Avila was of the opinion that such a reform was a foolish idea, he supported her; and the first reformed convent was dedicated, with a community of four poor orphan girls, in 1562. After living the reform for five years, she began to travel the country founding convents of the reform, and, very soon, for men as well as for women. Her great friend and ally, as well as spiritual director of the Reform Convents, was St. John of the Cross (*see* November 24).

Teresa's *Book of Foundations* contains vivid accounts of her experiences while travelling, and of the physical labor involved, in extremes of cold and heat. Perhaps her most important work was the reform of her own old Carmel of the Incarnation in Avila: the story is the perfect example of the only successful way to carry out spiritual reform. Altogether, in these twenty years she founded personally thirty-two religious houses, as well as supporting and directing John of the Cross, her most valued helper.

In between times, she was writing abundantly; there were always letters and more letters, not only to her immediate friends and

assistants, such as Fr. John and Fr. Gracian, but also to her benefactors and creditors, others to her brother, Lorenzo, about the
proper care and upbringing of his family, and, not least, to her
nuns, her spiritual daughters in every sense. It was for them that
she wrote her great mystical treatises, *The Interior Castle*,
with its seven stages or "mansions" of mystical prayer, and,
expecially, her *Way of Perfection*, for the most part a spiritual
commentary on the "Our Father," which has served so many
generations of devout Christians in every walk of life.

Though much of her writing deals with her own mystical experiences, visions, locutions and the like, she laid as much stress
as did John of the Cross on the necessity for the renunciation of
self if truly loving union with God is to be a reality and not an
illusion.

When viaticum was brought to her on her death-bed, she cried
out: "O my Lord, now is the time for us to see each other!" She
was canonized forty years after her death, with three other great
Spaniards, Isidore (*see* April 4), Ignatius Loyola (*see* July 31),
and Francis Xavier (*see* December 3).

The Love of God

"O Beauty that doth far transcend
All other beauty! Thou dost deign
Without a wound our hearts to pain,
Without a pang our wills to bend,
To hold all love for creatures vain.

O mystic love-knot that dost bind
Two beings of such diverse kind!
How canst thou, then, e'er severed be?
For bound, such strength we gain from thee,
We take for joys the griefs we find."

    A hymn of St. Teresa

E. Allison Peers: *Studies of the Spanish Mystics* (London, 1927), vol. i, pp.
134–225.

Gerard Majella
Redemptorist Brother

died 1755

ST. GERARD MAJELLA'S history is that of a short lifetime full of cruel troubles, each of which seemed only to bring him even closer to God. From his earliest years there seems to have been no veil between him and the world of eternity: we are told of his miraculous receptions of Holy Communion, of angelic visitations, and of apparitions of the Infant Jesus.

He was the youngest child of a poor tailor in Muro, in southern Italy; he was twelve years old when the father died, and he was apprenticed to another tailor, so that he might learn to carry on the family business. The foreman of this business hated Gerard's piety and gentleness, and gave him most brutal treatment, which he bore with patience and equable fortitude. Then he was taken into the household of a bishop whose temper was so notoriously bad that he could not keep servants. Here Gerard endured three years of slavery and unkindness, but he stayed at his post till the bishop died, because, as he mildly observed, if he did not look after the bishop no one else would.

Gerard then returned to Muro, where he prospered as a tailor, partly because of his reputation for honesty. It was said of him that he would not charge a customer for a piece of thread if he had not used it on his coat. All his spare money and all his free time were devoted to prayer and pious works; and he practiced most severe penances and self-mortifications. Some of these were strange indeed: in reparation for Pilate's soldiers' mockery of Christ, an incident in the Passion which greatly afflicted him, he feigned mental derangement so as to attract to himself the townspeople's scorn and ill-usage. When his confessor learned of this, he told him, with good sense, we may think, to stop it.

Twice he offered himself to the Capuchins, who would not have him; his appearance was already that of one much enfeebled. He attemped a hermit's life, but that did not last long, because, once again, his confessor intervened. Then a Redemptorist mission in Muro clinched matters; he forced himself upon the fathers, wearing down their determination to reject him, showing them how useful he could be to them, till at last they gave in, and he was despatched to one of their houses with the celebrated letter: "I am sending you another brother, but so far as work goes, he will be useless." Far from this being true, he is today put forward to all Redemptorist brothers as their pattern. Manual work was their vocation, and Gerard could turn his hand to anything, in any part of the house. It would be good to be able to relate that now his troubles were at an end, but this was not so; even in his convent he experienced the persecutions of an unkind and unjust superior.

Soon it became apparent that he could not be confined to the traditional life of a brother. His informal discourses to lay people and to nuns, during some of which he was in ecstasy, were never forgotten. He was endowed with that disconcerting gift, the discernment of spirits; and visitors and retreatants at his monastery were often called to account, with gentle authority, for concealed and unconfessed sins. Redemptorist priests going out on missions were frequently asked to bring Gerard with them; and toward the end of his brief life he was keeping several of them busy hearing the confessions of those who came to him for counsel. He was twenty-nine when he died, "consumed more by love than by disease."

No one could have been more ready than Gerard to acquiesce in any superior's opinion of his abilities; but his own life shows the essentially apostolic nature of the brothers' vocation, and how dear it is to God.

Gentleness in our Dealings with Others

"One always gains more by mildness than by harshness, which leads to distress, temptation, gloom, and discouragement. On the other hand, gentleness is followed by peace and tranquillity, and animates the soul to the love of God. If all superiors would follow these rules, all subjects would become saints."

St. Gerard's advice to a prioress

J. Carr: *Saint Gerard Majella* (Dublin, 1959).
A. M. Tannoja, ed. F. W. Faber: *The Lives of the Companions of St. Alphonso Liguori* (London, 1849).

Margaret Mary Alacoque
Visitation Nun

died 1690

MARGARET MARY, Claud de la Colombière, and John Eudes (*see* August 19) are known as "the saints of the Sacred Heart." In fact, none of them innovated but all three helped powerfully to revive this devotion. The very fact that Margaret Mary's insights seemed to her contemporaries so outlandish and new-fangled indicates the damage done to the spiritual development of the life of the people by the schisms of the Renaissance, and by the undue insistence, after Trent, upon the merely intellectual elements in the soul's drawing near to Christ.

St. Margaret Mary was the child of a royal notary in France; and orphanage and sickness made her and her mother painfully dependent, for long, on other members of their family, who did not use them well. During these years of unhappy retirement she devoted herself to contemplative prayer, and developed a strong attraction to the vocation of suffering.

She was in her middle twenties when she gained her way and entered the convent of the Visitation nuns at Paray-le-Monial. A few years after her reception the famous revelations began, in which, she averred, Christ commanded her to spread devotion to His Sacred Heart, to encourage frequent Communion and to institute a Holy Hour in reparation for men's injuries to that Heart, and to promote a special feast to the Sacred Heart's honor. What some of her own sisters in religion rejected as brain-sick fantasies has now become a constant element of the devotional life of the whole Latin Church.

In this she was greatly helped by Blessed Claud de la Colombière. When he came to her convent as extraordinary confessor, she knew that her troubles were over. Their time together was very brief, for he was soon sent to England to serve as chaplain to the duchess of York, one of the foreign Catholic princesses who were permitted the Mass and the sacraments in their own chapels. Claud died at Paray-le-Monial in 1681.

It was her love for Christ and for His sufferings which sustained Margaret Mary. There was "no beauty in her"; she was gauche, inept, blundering, tactless; yet when she was made mistress of novices, the professed nuns asked permission to attend her conferences. She had been truly a suffering handmaid, and in suffering she found what was so often on her lips and in her letters, "the peace of the adorable heart of Jesus."

Mankind's Response to Jesus' Love

"This is the Heart that has loved men so much that it spared itself nothing, wearing itself out, devouring itself to show its love to them; and from most of them by way of recompense, I receive nothing but ingratitude, scorn, irreverence, sacrilege and coldness towards me in this sacrament of love. But what repulses me even more is that this is all from hearts consecrated to me."

Jesus speaks to St. Margaret Mary—from Blessed Claud de la Colombière's notes of his retreat, made in London in 1677

Vie de la bienheureuse Marguerite-Marie Alacoque, écrite par elle-même (Paray-le-Monial, 1918).

F. L. Gauthey, ed. and trans., C. A. Herbst: *The Letters of Saint Margaret Mary Alacoque* (Chicago, 1954).

V. Kerns, trans.: *The Autobiography of St. Margaret Mary* (Westminster, Md., 1961).

A Ravier, ed.: *Bienheureux Claud La Colombière: écrits spirituels* (Bruges, 1962).

Luke
Evangelist

first century

Sᴛ. Lᴜᴋᴇ is named by Paul as the "beloved physician" (Col. 4:14), and he was with Paul during his imprisonment in Rome (2 Tim. 4:11; Philemon 24). Tradition has it that he was a native of Antioch in Syria; and many scholars still accept the suggestion of Origen and of St. Jerome (*see* September 30) that he and Titus (*see* February 7), another favored companion of Paul, were actually brothers; "we have also sent with Titus," says Paul to the church at Corinth, "the brother whose fame is in all the churches for his preaching of the gospel" (2 Cor. 8:18).

It is as the author of the third Gospel and of the Acts of the Apostles that we honor St. Luke. His authorship, which has never been seriously contested, is first mentioned indirectly by Justin Martyr (*see* April 14) at the beginning of the second century, and directly by Irenaeus (*see* June 28) some sixty or seventy years later.

Luke tells us himself of the nature and purpose of his Gospel: "to set in order a narrative of the things accomplished among us, just as they were handed on to us by those who were eye-witnesses and ministers of the word from the beginning" (Luke 1:1–4). And the Acts of the Apostles forms a sort of appendix to the Gospel (alluded to by Luke as his "first book"), which "dealt with all that Jesus began to do and teach, until the day when he was taken up," and is addressed to the same person, a certain Theophilus. It has been suggested, and the suggestion has been given a certain amount of credence, that Luke wrote both books with a specific Gentile audience in mind, the Roman nobility. At any rate, he goes out of his way to give his Gospel a certain Roman flavor (e.g., Luke 2:1; 3:1-2); and the various Roman officials in Acts are usually presented in quite a favorable light (e.g., Acts 25:10-11; 26:32).

His Gospel is noteworthy for its universality: from the beginning Christ is presented as "the salvation prepared for all people . . . a light for revelation to the Gentiles" (Luke 2:30-32). But what is really special about the Gospel of Luke is its concern to show Father and Son as filled with loving compassion for the outcast and the sinner. It is Luke who records the story of the woman who was a sinner: "Her sins, which are many, must have been forgiven, or she would not have shown such great love" (Luke 7:47). He also wishes to show our Lord's concern for the Samaritans, whom the Jews have ostracized (see Luke 9:51-56); and in one of the greatest parables of love and mercy, that is, of true neighborliness, the Samaritan is the hero (Luke 10:29-37).

It is in Luke that the contrast is drawn between the righteousness of the Pharisee and the humility of the publican, the tax-collector whose trade and name are synonymous with sinfulness (Luke 18:9-14). It is Luke who tells the parable about the love of God the Father for His sinful and wayward children (Luke 15:11-32), the story which explains what Christ meant when He first announced His message: "The Spirit of the Lord is upon me; he has anointed me to preach the good news to the poor; he has sent me to proclaim freedom for captives, to give sight to the blind, and to relieve those who are oppressed" (Luke 4:18). It is Luke also who shows us the reality of Christ's acceptance of human nature with its sinfulness and pathetic weakness; he alone records the sweat of blood during the agony in Gethsemane (Luke 22:44).

Nothing is known of St. Luke's last years, or whether he was martyred or not; there are conflicting traditions. Underlying them, however, is the truth about Luke's witness to Christ, whether it was unto blood or not: "May St. Luke, your evangelist, intercede for us, O Lord; for he carried about continually in his body the sufferings of the Cross, for the honor of your name."

A Father's Love and Compassion for his Son

"And when the son was still a long way off, his father saw him and was filled with compassion; he ran to him, threw his arms around him and kissed him. And his son said to him: 'Father, I have sinned against heaven and before you. I am no longer worthy to be called your son.' And the father said to his servants: 'Quickly, bring out the best robe and put it on him; and bring a ring for his finger and shoes for his feet. Bring out the fatted calf and kill it. Let us eat and make merry; for this my son was dead, and has come to life again; he was lost, and is found.' "

Luke 15:20–24

V. Taylor, art.: "Luke, Gospel of" (*Interpreter's Dictionary of the Bible*, vol. 3, pp. 180-88, New York, 1962).

Peter Alcantara
Observant Franciscan Friar

died 1562

PETER GARAVITA was born at Alcantara in Spain, in 1499. After studying at Salamanca University, he entered, in Manjaretes, a convent of the Observant Franciscans, one of the several movements in Renaissance times which sought, especially among the orders of mendicant friars, to restore their primitive rules, to repress all laxities, and to attain a still stricter observance of their first ideals.

St. Peter, as an Observant, was distinguished by his deep knowledge and understanding of spiritual matters, so deep that it can only have been a gift of the Holy Spirit, and the reward of a life wholly devoted to prayer. It was at their house of Lapa that he wrote his famous *Treatise on Prayer*, which saints like St. Teresa of Avila and St. Francis de Sales were to acclaim as a masterpiece.

He was one of those who were privileged to guide and encourage St. Teresa (*see* October 15). His own spiritual insights helped him to value hers, and his experience of the trials that beset souls enabled him to show her how to throw off the scruples and anxieties which beset her. He was able to assure her that her visions and her modes of prayer were gifts of God, and that she was on the right road.

He finally succeeded in establishing among the Observants a further reform, which his superiors thought too strict, but Pope Julius III approved, and this was the genesis of the Alcantarine Reform which lasted until the general reunion of all Observants in 1897. Peter is one of the outstanding figures of the late medieval reforming movements within the Church; and his own Franciscan Observants were the only representatives of that reform in England. Their firmness and bravery in resisting Henry VIII and the Royal Supremacy tends to be forgotten, partly because so many of them who died under persecution are still unknown. Their house at Greenwich was one of the few monasteries restored by Queen Mary Tudor, who had great devotion to them for their loyal support of her mother in the days of her affliction and abandonment. When she was succeeded by Elizabeth I, they went into exile again; and later English fugitives from Protestant England became Alcantarines. One of them was Giles Willoughby, the translator into English of Peter's great treatise.

Distractions in Prayer

"Against the temptation of importunate and unprofitable thoughts, which often vex those who pray, disquieting and much disturbing them, this is the remedy: to resist them manfully, provided always that the resistance be not too violent or anxious. This exercise depends not so much on our strength as on God Almighty's grace and our deep humility. So when anyone is attacked with these temptations, let him confidently turn to God, with no scruples or anxieties (for this is not a fault, or only a very small one), but with great submission and devotion of heart, saying: 'Look, Lord, look at what I am. What else can be expected from this carrion but such foul stinks, what else can grow in this earth, which you cursed at the beginning of the world, but thorns and thistles?' "

From the Golden Treatise *of St. Peter Alcantara*

Acta Sanctorum, October, vol. viii.
A Golden Treatise of Mentall Praier, trans. G(iles) W(illoughby), Brussels, 1632.

Philip Howard
Martyr

died 1595

THERE WERE MANY DISTINGUISHED MEN who suffered for the faith in the persecutions under Elizabeth I of England, but none so high in rank as Blessed Philip Howard, earl of Arundel and Surrey and premier earl of England. It may also be said that no martyr's death was so dolorous as his. When first imprisoned in the Tower of London, he was only twenty-eight years old. He died there ten years later, a gaunt and wasted figure. And during the whole of this decade he saw neither wife nor family, nor any of his close friends. His only form of communication with the outside world was by infrequent letter. Much of the *Epistle of Comfort* of Robert Southwell (*see* February 21) was originally written in the form of letters to Philip Howard. For a time the two men were fellow-prisoners in the Tower; but they never met. Philip was neither able to hear Mass, nor have his confession heard; all the consolations of the religion for which he died were denied him.

What was surprising in him, during this long and solitary confinement, was his constancy and cheerfulness. He had great confidence in the mercy and goodness of God. As he wrote to a friend: "I assure you I prepare myself as much as my weakness and frailty will permit, and I had rather perform more than come short of what I promise, especially wherein my frailty and unworthiness and infinite sins may justly make me doubt of the performance. But I know God's mercy is above all, and I am sure He will never suffer me to be tempted above my strength; and upon this I build with all assurance and comfort."

765

Philip's father, Thomas, was executed in 1572, convicted of treason. He had thought to marry Mary, Queen of Scots, and had conspired for her escape from prison. At this time, Philip was at Cambridge, where he took his degree in 1576. At once he devoted himself to cultivating Elizabeth's favor; no courtier spent so extravagantly upon his queen as did Philip. And during this time he so shamefully neglected his wife that she went off to live in his grandfather's house at Arundel.

The first change in a life given over to pleasure and entertainment occurred when his grandfather died. Philip took his seat at once in the House of Lords, and began to take a serious interest in politics. He was also reunited with his wife, who had at this time been reconciled to the Church. Philip himself was present when Edmund Campion (*see* December 1), recently captured, had to defend the faith publicly against Protestant divines. It was the beginning of his conversion.

For some time he debated within himself the cost of returning to the old religion, an act of treason punishable by death. He was already in disfavor with the queen, who had imprisoned his wife. But once he had decided, he acted with resolution, and arranged a meeting with the only Jesuit then in England, Fr. William Weston. Philip told him that he wanted to practice his faith fully; to do this he would have to leave England, itself a crime in the circumstances. Letters of his to Cardinal Allen were intercepted, and a plot was arranged whereby Philip should be captured as soon as he left England for Douai.

So he was taken, tried for being reconciled to the Church, fined ten thousand pounds, and committed to the Tower at the queen's pleasure. She left him there, perhaps with the hope that he might recant, more probably out of malice. In 1589, after the defeat of the Spanish Armada, he was brought to trial and condemned, on false witness, for having prayed for the success of the Spanish invasion. But again, as he lived in daily expectation of death, he was left literally to rot in his prison cell. It was at this time that he chipped into the wall of his cell an inscription still to be seen there: "The more suffering we endure in this world, the greater our glory in the next."

A Martyr's Profession of Faith

"I do most firmly, resolutely and unmoveably hold and believe this One, Holy, Catholic and Apostolic Faith. And as I will die in the same, so am I most ready at all times, if need be, to yield my life for the defense thereof . . . for as Christ is life unto me, so account I death a most happy and glorious gain unto me, being in defense of His Faith and for His Holy Name."

Letter of Philip Howard to Robert Southwell

J. H. Pollen: *Ven. Philip Howard, Earl of Arundel* (Catholic Record Society, 21, London, 1919).
M. Waugh: *Blessed Philip Howard* (London, 1961).

John of Bridlington
Augustinian Canon Regular

died 1379

St. John, who was born about 1320 at Thwing near Bridlington in East Yorkshire, entered Bridlington's great house of canons regular, studied at Oxford, and for the seventeen years before his death served as prior. Some of the buildings of his priory are still standing, including the monastic church; its austere beauty, flooded with light, leading the eye and the mind aloft, is a fitting memorial to the man.

But, although it is a commonplace that the records of misdemeanours punished and laxities reproved in the visitations of bishops and other superiors can give us a one-sided and distorted view of medieval religious life, since good and faithful observance usually goes unrecorded, still it seems that for many years before John's election his wealthy house had been characterized by the worldly ways of many of its officials. So much the better for his brethren, who had insisted, despite his reluctance, that John accept office as prior.

The virtues for which his contemporary or near-contemporary biographers praise him were not common in all religious houses. Though fine private apartments were provided for the priors, John never used them unless he had guests to entertain, eating and sleeping instead as did all the other canons. His clothing was seemly, but coarse and cheap. Sedulous in his attendance at choir, he was also devoted to private prayer; usually he was the first in and the last out of church. He dealt with his subjects with patience, peacefulness, and humility; and he used the riches of the monastery to help the poor and to support scholars.

He lived in the same age as that other Yorkshireman, Richard Rolle of Hampole; but he was, it seems, no friend of the religious "enthusiasm" which Rolle and his school promoted. It is told of him that once he visited a recluse near Richmond in Yorkshire when he was in those parts on business, hoping for spiritual consolation from her. But when she told him of her "vision" of an eagle bearing in its beak a scroll written with "Jesus is my love" (a device beloved of many such enthusiasts), and explained that John himself was the eagle, he cut the conversation short, saying that he had come there to talk with her of the grace and the goodness of God; and with that he left abruptly. The recluse said later that she had "hardly ever seen anyone who so quickly fled from incautious praise"; such flattery was evidently her stock in trade.

The Devil

"The venerable William Sleghtholm, a secular priest, once put this question to that most holy father: 'It puzzles me greatly why that wily serpent is no longer seen by men today as he was in ancient times'; and John's fatherly wisdom quickly resolved the problem thus posed. 'The hearts of the ancient fathers,' he said, 'were not filled with longing for the glory of empty subtleties. God filled them with the light of heavenly grace, they recognized the devil's deceitful wiles, and like invincible fighters they drove him off as he lay hidden to prey on them. So he had to join battle with them, tempting them to fall into sin by openly attacking them in some monstrous appearance. But nowadays, when we are more than ready to concede him his every wish, he can conquer us with the weapons of secret temptations; he has no need of any frightening disguise.' "

John Capgrave's Life

John of Tynemouth: *Nova Legenda Angliae*, ed. C. Horstman (2 vols. Oxford, 1901).
P. Grosjean: *De S. Iohanne Bridlingtoniensi Collectanea* (AB, 53, 1935, pp. 101–29).
J. S. Purvis: *St. John of Bridlington* (Bridlington, 1924).

Philip
Bishop and Martyr

died 304

ONE OF THE FIERCEST AND BLOODIEST PERSECUTIONS the Church in her long history has endured was that directed by the Roman Emperor Diocletian at the end of the second century. We shall never know how many Christians testified to the love of Christ in their hearts by their imitation of Him in death. Among the many records handed down to us telling of the sufferings of some of these martyrs, it is inevitable that legend has become inextricably mixed with fact. Fortunately, however, devoted historical work, especially on the part of the Bollandists, has given us several well-attested accounts of martyrdom under Diocletian. Among these is the story of the sufferings of St. Philip, bishop of Heraclea, the metropolis of Thrace, of Severus his priest, and Hermes, his deacon and a former magistrate of the city, who suffered with him.

When the edicts against the Christians were published in Heraclea, Philip's friends advised him to leave the city; but he merely said: "Let heaven's decree be fulfilled," and began to prepare his people by instruction in prayer and the virtue of heavenly patience. He was preaching in this vein on the feast of the Epiphany when the town officers arrived, with instructions to seal up the church. Philip declared that the omnipotent God dwells in men's hearts rather than within stone walls, and continued to encourage his people while the guards began their search for the sacred books and vessels.

The next day, he was brought before the governor's tribunal, and cheerfully admitted to the charge that he was the teacher of the Christians in Heraclea. He refused to reveal the whereabouts of the sacred Scriptures, and was put to the torture. Meantime, the hiding place of the Scriptures and vessels was discovered. The Scriptures were burned, and the vessels distributed among the soldiery.

Next, Philip and Hermes, who had revealed himself by coming to his bishop's defense in court, were dragged off to the market place, and ordered to offer sacrifice before the statue of Heracles, patron god of the city. Steadfast in their refusal, they were taken to prison, where, during a long incarceration, they were able to continue the work of giving instruction to both Christians and the catechumens.

Once more they were brought before the tribunal, and again commanded to sacrifice. Philip's reply was: "I am a Christian bishop, and cannot do what you command. You can torture me, but you will not conquer me. No power can induce me to offer sacrifice." It was at this time that the priest Severus, who had successfully hidden from the prosecutors, was moved by the Holy Spirit to present himself before the tribunal. And at last Philip and Hermes, after being removed to Adrianople and kept in prison there for three months, were condemned to be burned at the stake. As they walked to the place of execution, Philip was so weak that in the end he had to be carried. Hermes said to him: "Most sweet teacher, let us run to the Lord; we need not be concerned any more about our limbs—we have no further use for them." Severus, who was kept apart from them, prayed so fervently for martyrdom that he too was condemned to the same punishment, and suffered on the following day.

A Prayer for Martyrdom

"Father of our Lord and Savior Jesus Christ, light unconquerable, you have given me the sign of the Cross of Christ. Do not judge me unworthy, Lord, of enduring the same passion as my companions. Give me a share in their crown, that I may be one with them in glory, even as I was one with them in prison. May I share your rest with them, even as I confessed your glorious name with them in the face of savage torture."

Severus' prayer for a share in his companions' martyrdom

Acta Sanctorum, October, vol. ix.

John Buoni
Founder of the Boniti Penitents

died 1249

THE BONITI PENITENTS were one of the numerous movements of the time which formed communities of those who wished to live in mendicancy and devote themselves to evangelization. The chief of these was the Friars Hermits of Tuscany; and, seven years after Blessed John's death, they, the Boniti, and several other such congregations were united to form the Order of Augustinian Friars.

John died with a great reputation for sanctity, and we have the depositions of many witnesses at the processes for his cause held in 1251, 1252, and 1254, who had known and lived with him.

He was born in Mantua, and, on his father's death, he left home and became a professional entertainer, earning his living in the houses of the rich. This was in itself reprehensible enough; but his mother feared even more for his soul because of the wandering life he led, lest he should take up with some of the many heretical sects with which Italy then abounded. That does not seem to have happened, but his biographers tell us that he led a "licentious and debauched life," until sickness and the fear of death brought him to repentance. Thereafter, his life followed a classical order. First he went off to live a solitary life and do penance. Then this way of life attracted to him like-minded men. Presently they were given the Rule of St. Augustine by Pope Innocent IV, and set to work to care for others as well as for their own souls.

In John we have an example of "the uses of adversity." So

long as he prospered in the entertainment world, he lived a sinful life; the sickness which visited him was by God's mercy, to bring him to a proper sense of whither his own soul was bound.

A Miracle to Strengthen Faith

"When Blessed John had called us to him, he said: 'Stand beside that fountain,' for there was one close to his cell. And taking a clean cup, he came to us and prostrated himself in prayer by the fountain, filled the cup with water, placed it on the fountain's rim, prayed again and made the sign of the Cross over the water in the cup. Then he took it and offered it to Brother Nasinbeno, saying: 'Brother, accept this gift of God, for all things are possible to Him; and do not not believe that I have done this, but He who can do all things.' And Nasinbeno and the rest of us tasted it, and it was good wine, sweet-tasting and smelling, of a golden color. And he said to Brother Nasinbeno: 'See, my brother, and believe that just as the Lord has made wine of this water, so out of bread and wine He can make His body and blood, whenever it is pleasing to Him.' "

From the testimony of James, a lay brother, at the 1251 process
in Mantua

Acta Sanctorum, October, vol. ix.

Anthony Mary Claret
Founder of the Missionary Sons of the Immaculate Heart of Mary

died 1870

ANTHONY CLARET was born in Spain in 1807. He was the son of a weaver, and himself as a youth worked in the Barcelona mills; and it was from these early years that he derived that knowledge and understanding of the lot and the needs of working people which he never lost. In his late twenties he was ordained priest, and he became one of Spain's most popular preachers, especially noted for his devotion to the Eucharist and to the Immaculate Heart of Mary, to which devotion he dedicated his "Missionary Sons."

In 1850 he was appointed archbishop of Cuba, a territory which had been much neglected, and which he at once set about restoring and reforming. He was shocked by the evil ways into which many of the clergy had fallen, and by the general disregard by the people of the sacrament of matrimony. But it was not only against concubinage and illegitimacy which he campaigned. He saw that one of the greatest enemies of Christian family life in Cuba was poverty, and he threw all his force behind the introduction of sound farming methods and the establishment of credit unions.

In 1857 he was recalled to Spain to accept an appointment as confessor to Isabella II; but he spent as little time as possible at court, and occupied himself, as he had always done, with ameliorating the spiritual and social lot of the people. Greatly exercised over problems of communications, he founded societies to publish and distribute Catholic literature. His own output of sermons and pamphlets was enormous.

For his pains, he was constantly traduced and misrepresented in the radical press, and in the 1868 revolution he was forced to flee Spain. He was present at the First Vatican Council, where he was a defender of papal infallibility. This was his last intervention in public affairs; a few months later he died in a Cistercian monastery in France.

His own first attraction, after his ordination, had been to the religious life; he had considered the Carthusians and tried his vocation with the Jesuits. But it was God's will that he and his Congregation should remain in the thick of events in the world. In these present anxious days in Cuba, when the material and spiritual wellbeing of its citizens are in such jeopardy, he will be a powerful intercessor for a people who were so much his concern here on earth.

Social Justice

"Human institutions, both private and public, must labor to minister to the dignity and purpose of man. At the same time let them put up a stubborn fight against any kind of slavery, whether social or political, and safeguard the basic rights of man under every political system."

The Second Vatican Council's Constitution on the Church in the Modern World (no. 29)

M. Aguilar: Vida admirable del P.A.M. Claret (2 vols. Madrid, 1894).

Richard Gwyn
Schoolmaster and Martyr

died 1584

WHEN BLESSED RICHARD GWYN, the first Welshman to suffer martyrdom under Queen Elizabeth I of England, had been condemned to die for his faith, his prosecutors brought his wife, with their youngest child in her arms, into court, in the hope of shaking his constancy. But, as the contemporary account of his trial and death records, "Mr. Gwyn's wife said unto him [the judge], 'If you lack blood, you may take my life as well as my husband's; and if you will give the witnesses a little bribe, you may call them — they will bear evidence against me as well as they did against him.'"

On the morning of Richard's execution, the jailer's wife was unable to control herself at the thought of this good man's punishment and death; so Richard turned to his own wife, who was with him, saying: "I pray thee, Catherine, go and comfort her."

The strength of the faith in Wales, even after the dissolution of the monasteries, is epitomized by the Gwyn family. He was born in Llandidloes in Montgomeryshire, and studied at St. John's College, Cambridge, until, on the accession of Elizabeth, his friend and patron George Bullock, master of the college, had to resign his fellowship and all academic honors for conscience's sake. Gwyn then returned to his native North Wales, and began his teaching career at Overton in Flintshire. "His moderation and temperance were such," says the old account, "that his enemies to this day could never charge him with any fault other than the following of his faith and conscience — which nowadays is accounted madness."

During this time he married, and his wife Catherine bore him six children, three of whom died in infancy. For a while, he yielded to the persuasion of his friends to attend the Protestant church; but on one occasion, coming out of church, he was pursued by a flock of crows and hawks, which filled him with fear and led him to believe that his soul also was in danger. After this he refused to participate in Protestant worship.

For Richard the years which followed were filled with petty persecution. He was constantly being driven from one town to another for his refusal to conform, and he was imprisoned at least twice. In 1579 he was denounced and arrested, but escaped before he could be brought to trial. But in 1580 the Privy Council directed the Protestant bishops to be more vigilant in dealing with obdurate Catholics, and especially schoolmasters. Richard was soon taken, and sent to Ruthin Assizes to be tried. The trial was inconclusive, and he spent the next year in Wrexham jail. Tried again in May, 1581, his judges attempted to make him retract so far as to hear a Protestant sermon, and they had him forcibly carried into church and stood in irons under the pulpit. But he shook his irons so loudly that the preacher could not be heard. On this occasion he was fined for brawling in church.

He remained a prisoner and was subjected to inconclusive trials for another three years, occasionally being put to torture. In 1584 he was indicted for the eighth time, at Wrexham Assizes. Gwyn, who had a ready tongue, and has left many poems in his native Welsh, exasperated his judges by his bold speech and his propensity to Latin puns. Eventually he was condemned to be hanged, drawn and quartered, on false evidence, for trying to reconcile certain persons to the Church of Rome, and for maintaining the pope's supremacy.

Cut down before he was dead, he was subjected to unbelievable butchery, and was eventually despatched by beheading, even as he said "Jesus, have mercy on me."

This Life Compared with Eternity

"My dear countrymen, I beseech you for God's sake to have regard upon your souls, and to reconcile yourselves with the

Catholic Church, for I fear you are led astray unto everlasting damnation, except you take heed betimes. Remember your souls, and lose them not for this vile transitory muck which Christ hath so dearly bought. This is but one hour's pain to me, and what is that in respect of the torments of hell, which shall never have an end?"

Blessed Richard Gwyn's advice, given from the scaffold, to his Welsh countrymen

Anon.: *A True Report of the Life and Martyrdom of Mr. Richard Gwyn* (published from a contemporary manuscript, London, 1961).

Bonaventure of Potenza
Franciscan Friar

died 1711

BLESSED BONAVENTURE was born at Potenza in Naples, and joined the Conventual Friars Minor at Nocera. He worked with great profit in Amalfi, where he was exceptionally happy in the company and direction of his superior, Fr. Dominic Girardelli, and became known to the people as a devoted shepherd of souls, with extraordinary spiritual gifts. At a time when religious decadence in Naples was extreme, his mere presence and bearing were sufficient to recall men to Christian ideals of purity. In an outbreak of cholera in the Vomero district of the city of Naples, he did truly wonderful work in caring for the souls and bodies of the stricken people.

He had great devotion to the doctrine of the Immaculate Conception, a doctrine that would not be defined until more than a century later; and his religious life and his apostolate were marked by his gifts of ecstasy, divination, and prophecy. In his lifetime many miracles of healing were attributed to his intercessions, and before he died he was venerated by many as one of God's saints.

Simple Obedience

"On one occasion Bonaventure had collected a quantity of ice for the use of the brethren, and when he asked where he should put it, the guardian said: 'In the sacristy cupboard.' This was meant as a jesting reply to a stupid question, since everyone knew where the ice should be kept. But Bonaventure took it seriously, and put the ice in the cupboard. And at dinner time, when he was asked for ice, he said that he had done his superior's bidding and put it in the cupboard in the sacristy. Those who heard him were first surprised, then alarmed lest the sacred vestments should have been stained with dirty water. But though it was the height of a very hot summer, enough of the ice had remained to hold the water, and the vestments had come to no harm."

From the Life *compiled from earlier sources by Rugilo and*
Rossi

Acta Sanctorum, October, vol. xii.

Contardo Ferrini
Jurist

died 1902

THERE MAY BE MEN STILL ALIVE who were taught by Blessed Contardo Ferrini in the Italian universities; many of the witnesses at the process for his beatification, including the future Pope Pius XI, had been his colleagues and friends. He belonged to that uneasy and difficult epoch when the Church, recently dispossessed of its territorial goods, was still finding the way to peaceful relations with newly-evolved and often hostile secular states. Ferrini's career reflects these difficulties. As a post-graduate student in Berlin he had seen an educated Catholic laity learning to take their place in daily life after decades of silence and repression. And in Italy, though he taught in many of the country's secular universities, he refused to do so in Rome itself, where his presence in the university would, he feared, be interpreted as a sign of his disloyalty to the Holy See.

Both he and his father seem to have lived under the thumb of his domineering and not very perceptive mother; but their home, for all that, was a happy and a deeply Christian one. Even at the time of Contardo's first Communion, we can discern in him a settled if precocious spirituality, much influenced by the Scriptures and by Augustine's *Confessions*. He could not help displaying the symptoms of an abnormal sensitivity, and he was always to find the world hard and hostile. At school and at university he seems to have impressed most of his fellows as a prig, but inwardly he was suffering greatly through his refusal to truckle to the demands upon him of those who took his own high standards, especially of purity, as criticism of themselves. Then, as later, his friendships were few but intense, and they were all with young men. He could be very firm, not to say cutting, both with his own mother and with her match-making friends; marriage was not for him, but he was equally sure that he had no religious or priestly vocation.

His years in Berlin came as a welcome escape from the pervading anti-clericalism of the Italian universities, and there, as later in Milan, he worked for the Society of St. Vincent de Paul. Though of wide intellectual interests (his knowledge of Oriental languages was to be of great profit to him in his own studies in the Scriptures), he had already decided to specialize in Greek and Roman law; and in 1883 the University of Pavia created a special chair for him. He seems to have been a prolific and perhaps profound scholar, though not a specially painstaking or accurate one, and he was an inspired and inspiring teacher, if very demanding of his pupils. But the supremacy which he gained in the field of study of Roman Christian law in the East never tempted him to retire into a professor's ivory tower. Catholic Action attracted and engaged him, and he served on the Milan City Council at a time when this was to invite denunciation from both rearguard Catholics and rationalists.

His own interior life was marked, above all, by a great devotion to the Mass, and by his assiduity in searching the Scriptures. He was an able and lively apologist, much influenced by Newman, in an age and country where positivism was the fashion. His life, difficult, restricted, and lonely though it was, still was very much of one piece. Even in sport (like his friend Achille Ratti—later Pius XI—he was an ardent mountaineer) he saw God's glory and found a way of glorifying Him.

The Rule of God's Justice

"This is the covenant which I shall make with the house of Israel in those days, says the Lord . . . I shall plant my law in their innermost being, and I shall write it in their hearts; and I shall be their God, and they shall be my people. And then no man shall teach his neighbor or his brother, saying 'Know the Lord'; for they will all know me, from the least of them to the greatest."

Jeremiah 31:33-34

Opere di Contardo Ferrini (Milan, 1929–).
B. Jarrett: *Contardo Ferrini* (London, 1933).

Simon and Jude
Apostles

first century

AMONG THE TWELVE APOSTLES, Saints Simon and Jude are perhaps the most obscure figures. The New Testament gives us very little information about them beyond listing them at the end of the catalogue of the twelve, just before Judas Iscariot. Simon is called "the Zealot" in the Gospel of Luke, and some have taken the title to mean that he belonged to a political group fanatically opposed to the Roman occupation of Palestine. We find him identified in early church history with Simeon, son of Cleopas, who succeeded St. James (*see* May 1) as bishop of Jerusalem. The strongest tradition is that perpetuated in the Roman liturgy: Simon, after preaching in Egypt, went with Jude to evangelize Persia, and with him suffered martyrdom at Suanir.

What we know of St. Jude, also called Thaddeus, in spite of his considerable popularity as the patron of lost causes, is also minimal. It is not certain whether he can be identified as the brother of James, son of Alpheus, and thus a relative of our Lord. And there is no evidence to prove that he is the author of the epistle which bears his name.

It was Jude, however, who addressed to our Lord at the Last Supper the question which prompted the profoundest teaching on the blessed Trinity and on the participation of the Christian in God's own life. It is for this consoling doctrine in particular that we should venerate the memory of Jude and the other apostle whose name is linked with his in the New Testament and in the tradition of the Church.

In his Gospel, John relates that after the Last Supper, Jesus spoke of the intimate relationship between the Father, Himself, and His apostles: "I am in my Father, and you in me, and I in you." And He promised that the time would come when He would show Himself to every man who truly loves Him. It was then that Jude put his question: "Lord, how is it that you will show yourself to us, and not to the world?" Jesus answered him: "If any man loves me, he will keep my word. And my Father will love him, and we shall come to him and make our home with him. He who does not love me does not keep my word" (John 14:22–24).

The "world," then, as used by our Lord in John's Gospel, refers to those who, either through ignorance or malice, do not seek to discover and fulfill the will, the word, of the Father, which is that of the Son. But those who seek God through His Word, which is Christ—and all that is revealed of the Father and the Son through the Holy Spirit, who speaks in the Church—will have God dwelling in them in the most intimate way possible. So St. Paul says to his Christians at Corinth, when he is rebuking them for their sinfulness: "Do you not know that you are God's temple, and that the Holy Spirit has his dwelling in you?" (1 Cor. 3:16). It is to Jude, and to his companion-apostle, Simon, that we may most appropriately pray for a deeper understanding of the mysterious truth which lies at the heart of the Christian life.

The Apostles

"The eternal gifts of Christ the King,
The apostles' glory, let us sing;
And all with hearts of gladness raise
Due hymns of thankful love and praise.

For they the Church's princes are,
Triumphant leaders in the war,
In heavenly courts a warrior band,
True lights to lighten every land.

In them the Father's glory shone,
In them the will of God the Son,
In them exults the Holy Ghost,
Through them rejoice the heavenly host.

To Thee, Reedeemer, now we cry
That Thou wouldst join to them on high
Thy servants who this grace implore
For ever and for ever more"

"Hymn to the Apostles" in Hymns Ancient and Modern

John 14:22-23; Luke 6:15; Mark 3:18, Matthew 10:4; Acts 1:13.

Dorothea of Montau
Wife and Mother

died 1394

BLESSED DOROTHEA is remarkable on several counts. She was one whose cause for canonization came to a halt almost as soon as it was begun; but such was the strength of popular devotion to her that her cult spread from her native Prussia to Poland, Lithuania, and Bohemia, and she is still regarded by the people as patroness of Prussia. Doubtless her official process was deferred because of exaggerations in the account of her visions and revelations written by her director, and especially the allegation that the Lord revealed to her that His Mother was conceived in original sin. But far more important than these is the manifest holiness of her life at every stage.

Born at Montau (Marienburg) in Prussia of peasant stock, Dorothea was married at the age of seventeen. She bore her husband nine children, but none survived childhood except the youngest, who later became a Benedictine nun. Dorothea's husband Adalbert was an extremely difficult person, morose and overbearing by turns. And it says much for Dorothea's Christian love and fortitude that after nearly twenty years of married life, Adalbert began to take his religion seriously.

His wife had long exhibited signs of a special proclivity to contemplative prayer, and she began to feel that normal relations with her husband were becoming an obstacle to her dedication to God. Adalbert gradually became convinced that his wife's desires were genuinely inspired by the Holy Spirit, and after the birth of their ninth child, they agreed to live as brother and sister. Adalbert began to share his wife's spiritual life, and they made several pilgrimages together before he died. It was later revealed to Dorothea that her husband was in heaven.

After his death in 1390, Dorothea, on the advice of her confessor, went to consult a certain John, canon of the cathedral in Marienwerder. After a short time under his direction, she asked if she could be given an anchorhold in the church of the Teutonic Knights. John made a careful investigation into her whole life, and tested her over a period of eighteen months. Finally, with the approval of the bishop and his chapter, she was walled up in her cell in 1393. She maintained that Christ Himself had revealed the manner of her life as a recluse: "After you enter your anchorhold, you must live after the manner of a saint. You must not even stretch your hand out of your cell without the permission of your confessor. If ever you do so, you must always confess it, and receive salutary penance. Receive no gift from anyone; I myself will reward you."

During the short time in which she lived in her cell, with one of its windows looking out on to the altar of the church, Dorothea was able to be continually in the presence of the Blessed Sacrament, for which she had a special devotion. She was said to have the gift of prophecy and of reading men's hearts. Many, from her own country and elsewhere, came to consult her in times of trouble and distress, and went away comforted.

A Prayer for the Wisdom and Strength to Live a Good Life

"Most merciful Lord Jesus Christ, you gave to your servant Dorothea, widow and anchoress, a new heart for her heart of flesh, often wounding this heart with the arrows of your love. You espoused her to yourself by the bond of your infinite love; you filled her with the joy of the Holy Spirit, and revealed to her those secrets of yours which are hidden from the wise of this world. Hear our prayer through her intercession; mercifully grant to us, wretched sinners, a contrite heart, renewed in humility, so that we may understand what your will is, and in that understanding faithfully carry it out in right conduct and holy living. Amen."

Prayer for the help to love God as Blessed Dorothea loved Him

Acta Sanctorum, October, vol. xiii.

Alphonsus Rodriguez
Jesuit Brother

died 1617

NOWADAYS, when the traditional understanding of religious obedience is frequently challenged, it may be helpful to reflect on the example of the Spanish lay brother, St. Alphonsus Rodriguez, who found in the practice of literal and absolute obedience a high road to sanctity and to extraordinary graces in prayer.

As a boy of ten, he had been prepared for his first Holy Communion by Blessed Peter Favre (*see* August 11), and it would appear that in these early years he felt the promptings of a religious vocation. But when he was only fourteen years old, and had just begun his studies at the Jesuit College, at Alcalá, his father, a prosperous clothier of Segovia, died suddenly; and it was decided that Alphonsus must help his mother to carry on the family business. Ten years later his mother retired, leaving Alphonsus in complete charge, and in due course he married and had a daughter. But within the space of three years his little daughter died, then his mother, and finally his wife, giving birth to a son who did not live. His business also failed.

Alphonsus had always been an extremely devout Catholic; and now, in his misfortunes, his thoughts turned toward the religious life. He presented himself for admission to the Society of Jesus in his native town of Segovia, but he was rejected because he was reckoned too old for priestly studies, and too weak in health for the brotherhood. But Alphonsus persevered in his attempts to give himself wholly to God. After a somewhat disastrous experiment in living as a hermit, he applied once more to join the Jesuits, this time with the enthusiastic support of his Jesuit confessor. He was admitted, after a good deal of hesitation, because of his reputation for holiness.

Soon after he began his novitiate in January, 1571, he was transferred to Palma in Majorca. There he remained for the rest of his life, confounding those critics who had wished to reject him on the score of poor health, for he reached the advanced age of eighty-four.

His life, externally, was one of utter monotony and complete obscurity. During his forty-six years as a religious he never held any other post than that of doorkeeper or receptionist, and at the age of sixty-one he was relegated to the position of doorkeeper's assistant, merely tolerated as a chronically sick person who needed something with which to occupy himself.

Yet this external monotony was simply a cover for a rich and dynamic inner life. As he wrote himself, "holiness has to be won at the cost of many great labors, in the interior battle to uproot vices from the heart and to implant there the virtues in which holiness consists: and all this with the grace of God."

His great fear was of being deluded in his union with God; and all the prophecies, visions, and miracles with which he was credited constantly filled him with the dread of being deceived, to such an extent that for six long years he was victim of the most agonizing of spiritual trials, scruples. Even on his deathbed he found himself the prey of fierce temptations; but these he expected, because "death must be the greatest labor there is in this world."

He achieved the closest conformity with the will of God, simply by fulfilling, to the letter and without question, his superior's every command and request. But this obedience was no automatic, servile or infantile response. It flowed from virtue, which he explains thus: "Virtue is a grace and communication of God in the superior part of the soul."

When his contemporaries ridiculed him for his foolishness ("the obedience of a donkey," they called it, and indeed it often did appear so, as when he made vigorous attempts to comply when ordered at dinner to "eat up his plate"), he had one reply which silenced them all. Those who have not penetrated the mystery of virtue, the divine communication in the soul, are like those who watch others dancing, but without hearing the music. They see only strange gyrations, movements without apparent sense or purpose. But the dancer who hears the music can appreciate the pattern and the beauty of the actions he performs. Alphonsus saw obedience as a "being with" God, of accomplishing with Him a work which He wants done. For him, obedience was rooted in love. Four years before his death he said that his chief prayer was to ask insistently for four loves: "love of God, love of Jesus, love of the Virgin Mary our Lady, and love of my neighbor." And he was accustomed to describe the love which filled him as a great martyrdom.

The Virtue of Resignation

"In the exercise of the acts of this virtue of resignation, the soul lifts itself up to its God. and sees itself in God . . . . There in its God it sees how He gives it labors as gifts, not using any instrument for His purpose, but Himself giving them . . . . There the soul looks in mind and spirit at its God, joyfully accepting from Him all that He does to it and gives it as He exercises it with labors. There with its God, the soul is greatly delighted that its Lord does what He likes with it."

Alphonsus Rodriguez: Autobiography

W. Yeomans, trans.: *The Autobiography of Alphonsus Rodriguez* (London, 1965).

Wolfgang
Bishop

died 994

AS A YOUNG MAN ST. WOLFGANG was a considerable figure in the international world of learning which was one of the Church's greatest gifts to the Middle Ages; he was a talented teacher in several cathedral schools, the centers of higher learning out of which the universities of Europe would presently grow. He might well have devoted all his life to teaching and study; instead, he became a great bishop, a true father in God.

A Swabian by birth, he was first educated at the abbey of Reichenau, already a famous school, which in the next century was so wonderfully to foster the gifts of Herman the Cripple (*see* September 25). Then he was drawn, first to the new school in Würzburg, then, under the patronage of its young archbishop, to Trier. But when after eight years the archbishop died, Wolfgang left Trier, and entered another abbey, the house at Einsiedeln, in what is now the Swiss canton of Schwyz, then not long founded. Here he became a Benedictine monk, and soon was put in charge of the monastic school, which prospered under him in the first years of its great history as a house of scholars.

Yet the enclosed academic life was not enough for Wolfgang, and, after his ordination to the priesthood he and some of his brethren went, with his abbot's permission, to preach the faith to the pagan Hungarians. This venture seems not to have prospered, and, returning to German-speaking territories, he was made bishop of Ratisbon in 972.

Here he succeeded to a vast diocese, in which he could have lived, had he wished, at his ease, like a prince. But that was no part of his intention. Instead, he refused to discard his monastic habit, and lived his former life of austerity and penance. With great gifts of prayer, he became a preacher of exceptional powers, and for the rest of his life he devoted himself wholly to his pastoral duties.

He found in his territories many abuses and corruptions which he set about reforming; and it is typical of him that one of his earliest reforms concerned the abbey of St. Emmeramus at Ratisbon, which, by tradition, never had an abbot, his duties being performed by a deputy while the bishop enjoyed much of the abbey's revenues. This, the so-called *in commendam* system, one of the medieval Church's greatest abuses, always produced harmful effects, and Wolfgang was prompt to abolish it at St. Emmeramus, forgo this part of his income, and give the house a proper head. And, later, he voluntarily gave up a large share of his territories, so that it could be made into the new archdiocese of Prague; thus his Bohemian subjects could have prelates of their own race and tongue.

In his own lifetime he was given great veneration as one who walked constantly with God. He was canonized less than sixty years after his death, and the German lands have ever since then kept alive his memory.

Preaching the Gospel Effectively

"This gentle father wanted in all things to be good and useful for his people, and so in preaching the kingdom of heaven to them, he made no use of confusing, sophisticated arguments, but governed his sweet eloquence with a wonderful austerity, so that it could be seen how he touched the secret places of each man's heart with his simple, holy words, moving many of his hearers to tears. Such was the grace given to him by the Holy Spirit, that it was seldom or never that those who came to his sermons and listened to them attentively left the church without weeping."

From Othlo's biography of St. Wolfgang

Acta Sanctorum, November, vol. ii.

Saints for November

Holiness consists not in doing uncommon things, but in doing all common things with an uncommon fervor.

CARDINAL MANNING
The Eternal Priesthood

All Saints

THE HEART of the Second Vatican Council's *Constitution on the Church* is the fifth chapter, "The Call of the Whole Church to Holiness." There it is taught that the people of God, the followers of Christ, are really made holy according to God's grace, because they are redeemed by our Lord, and through their baptism, sought by faith, they truly become children of God and sharers of the divine nature.

From very early times, the Church has celebrated the glory, in Christ, of all those who have lived "in a way that becomes saints" (Eph. 5:3), who have shown in the simple details of their lives "the heart of mercy, kindness, humility, meekness, and patience," so that they were recognized by God, if not necessarily by their fellow-men, "as God's chosen ones, holy and well beloved" (Col. 3:12).

A saint is one who has given supreme witness to the truth of Christ, either by showing that greatest love in death, the death of the martyr, or by the daily death to self which the perfection of charity demands. "You shall love the Lord your God with your whole heart, with your whole soul, with all your mind and all your strength; and you shall love your neighbor as yourself."

The first saints to be honored in the Church were the martyrs of the Roman persecutions. But the vast numbers of Christians martyred during the fierce persecutions under the Emperor Diocletian made it impossible for each one to be commemorated separately, even if the supreme witness of every individual were known. So it was that in Rome at the beginning of the seventh

799

century, Pope St. Boniface turned the Pantheon, a temple built by Marcus Agrippa in honor of all the gods known and worshipped by Romans, into a Christian basilica dedicated to Our Lady and All Martyrs. We know from a sermon of St. John Chrysostom (*see* January 27) that the Eastern Churches kept (as they still keep) a feast of All Saints on Trinity Sunday. His sermon is entitled "A panegyric of all the martyrs who have suffered all over the world." In Ireland, by the beginning of the ninth century, there was a feast of "All Saints and Virgins of Ireland and Britain and the whole of Europe."

On November 1st, then, we, the Church on earth, celebrate the memory of our brethren, the Church in heaven. We reaffirm our belief in the Communion of Saints. Out of our own sinfulness we acknowledge the truth that the Church is holy, because she offers to us all the means of holiness, and is furthermore distinguished by the eminent holiness of so many thousands of her children, who "have come out of great tribulations, whose garments are washed clean in the blood of the Lamb. Therefore those are before the throne of God, in his sheltering presence, night and day. They no longer hunger and thirst . . . and God will wipe away every tear from their eyes" (Rev. 7:14–17). They are for us the living evidence that God's promise comes true: if we endure with Him, then we shall be glorified with Him.

The Vision of God

> " 'Blessed are the pure in heart, for they shall see God'. How stupid then are they who seek God with their bodily eyes, when He can be seen only by the heart. So it says in another place: 'Seek him in simplicity of heart'. To have a pure heart means to have a heart that is lightsome. And just as the light cannot be seen except with eyes that are free from blemish, in the same way God is not seen, unless that by which He is seen is free from blemish."
>
> *Augustine:* Homily on the Sermon on the Mount

Vatican II's *Constitution on the Church* (nos. 39–42; 48–51).

Thomas Netter of Walden
Carmelite Friar

died 1430

LIKE JULIAN OF NORWICH (*see* May 14) Thomas Netter has no cultus formally approved by the Holy See; but there is ample evidence that devotion to him did flourish in England after his death, especially within his own Order.

He was born at Saffron Walden in Essex about the year 1375, and joined the Carmelites in London at a time when their intellectual and political influence was great. He studied theology at Oxford, and later was a theological expert in the English delegations to the Councils of Pisa (1409) and Constance (1414-18).

It was at Constance that the teachings of Wycliffe and Hus were formally condemned. Thomas was well able to speak against them, for, as he himself in his writings admits, though he was never attracted by Wycliffe's social or theological teachings, as a young man at Oxford, Wycliffe's logic had swept him off his feet. "Then after a while I consulted the sacred books, and it was not long before I discovered him to be an open falsifier of the Scriptures, distorting them into a sense opposing that of all the Fathers, and making what was plain seem difficult." It was revelation which saved Thomas from error; and he shrewdly observes that Wycliffe would reduce revelation by half, appealing, when it suits him, to Scripture, but ignoring the common faith of the Church.

In the field of Wycliffe's teaching on "necessary contingents," so brilliant and seductive, it was Netter who was able to demonstrate, as he has been formulated by a modern scholar, that "all divine foreknowledge is necessary, but the future remains either necessary or contingent; and the contingent future is neither more nor less necessary for being foreknown." Of his great anti-Wycliffe tract, the *Doctrinale,* another recent scholar has described it as a demonstration so authoritative "that no reply to it was even so much as attempted."

Netter's relations with the royal house were close. He seems to have had a part in the upbringing of the Prince of Wales, and later, when he had become Henry V, Netter was his confessor, accompanying him on his last campaign to France, where the king died in his arms. He had been tutor to his son, and was with the young king, Henry VI, in Rouen in 1430, when he died. He had served his Order as prior provincial, and his part in the orthodox religious life of the times seems to have been mild and pacific. In consort with the Franciscans, he forbade disedifying public controversy on such vexed topics as the historic claims to extreme antiquity of the Carmelite and Augustinian friars, "absolute poverty," and the doctrine of the Immaculate Conception. All who had dealings with him speak of his deep personal sanctity.

Today, we may deplore the part he played in the repression of the Lollard heresy. He acted as a theological expert and assessor at the trials of John Badby, the second Lollard martyr, burned at the stake, of Sir John Oldcastle, whose daring escape from prison only saved him from a similar fate, and of the priest William Taylor, degraded and also burned to death. But this is a judgment of the twentieth, not of the fifteenth century. However mistakenly, the men of the time believed that their duty to the Church and its faith justified such savagery.

Prayer for Understanding

"Great God, your prophecies are immeasurable, your foreknowledge is infinite. You hide your mysteries from the wise and prudent, and make them plain to little ones. Let me so understand and write of your foreknowledge that no slip-shod thinking, no affirmation of what is not true will make me stumble, or, through me, any of your children who believe in you. I confess to you: I would rather have a mill-stone tied round my neck and be thrown into the deep sea, than ever once to assert that you can err, that what you foreknow can be mistaken, that your preordaining can be changed, your fore-knowledge be variable or uncertain."

From Thomas Netter's Doctrinale

A. B. Emden: *A Biographical Register of the University of Oxford to A. D. 1500,* vol. 2 (Oxford, 1958).

D. Knowles: *The Religious Orders in England,* vol. 2 (2d ed., Cambridge, England, 1958).

J. A. Robson: *Wyclif and the Oxford Schools* (Cambridge, England, 1961).

Martin Porres
Dominican Brother

died 1639

WITHOUT DOUBT, ST. MARTIN PORRES owes some of his world-wide popularity to his color; he was the illegitimate son of a Spanish father and a freed Negro slave from Panama; and the great increase of devotion to him in modern times, especially among colored people in the Americas, gave powerful impetus to his cause, until he was at last canonized in 1962. Whatever his race and ancestry had been, he would have been a dear and efficacious servant of God; the unhappy circumstances of his birth, the contempt in which he and those like him were held in the white society of Peru in his days, only served to deepen his own Christ-like humility. He delighted to call himself what others, some of his own Dominican brethren included, had called him: "mulatto dog."

He was born in 1579 in Lima, where later he was to become an intimate of Rose (*see* August 30) and John Massias (*see* September 18). He inherited his mother's dark beauty and coloring, and so at first was repudiated by his father, who, later, accepted responsibility for his upbringing. He became a barber, a trade which, in those days, included pharmacy and surgery, so laying the foundation of his natural but divinely-aided skills in healing. Already as a boy he showed devotion and compassion to those poorer than himself.

Martin was fifteen or sixteen when he went to the Dominicans of the city, and was enrolled as a lay helper of the Third Order, wearing a form of the habit, living in and supported by the community, but without vows. Characteristically, his father thought this not good enough for his son, and pressed to have him admitted as a full lay brother, but this Martin himself refused. From his earliest days in religion, he showed supernatural patience and humility, especially in his work in the infirmary. He had immense devotion to the Blessed Sacrament and to the Rosary; and he began a lifetime of severe mortifications, for his own soul's good and in reparation for the sins of others.

After nine years of lay status he was professed as a brother; and by this time his sanctity was generally known, in and out of the monastery. He never felt that he was doing enough for God, and he had a great longing, never satisfied, for mission work in the Far East. His miraculous appearances in China and Japan, and in other far-off lands, were often averred.

His counsel, in spiritual and temporal matters, was sought by many, from the viceroy downwards, and he revealed a knowledge of the classical texts of theology quite astonishing in a largely uneducated man.

He was gifted with prescience, including foreknowledge of his own death, and this was accompanied by many ecstasies. All that Archbishop Felician de Vega, whom Martin was to have accompanied to Mexico, could say after his death was "Brethren, let us learn from Brother Martin how to die."

St. Martin is a saint for all of us who need to learn to be humble and to do God's will unquestioningly, as he is for all the wretched and oppressed of this world.

The Joy of God's Humble Servants

"God our protector, look upon us, regard the face of your
  anointed one.
For a day in your courts is better than a thousand other days.
I have chosen to be of no account in the house of my God,
Rather than to dwell in the mansions of sinners.
For God loves mercifulness and truth,

And the Lord gives grace and glory.
He will deny no good thing to those who walk in innocence,
Lord of all powers, blessed is the man who trusts in you."

A passage from Psalm 84, a psalm constantly recited by St.
Martin

G. Cavallini, trans. Caroline Holland: *St. Martin de Porres* (St. Louis, 1963).

Charles Borromeo
Cardinal Archbishop

died 1584

ORSENIGO, IN HIS perceptive if somewhat wordy biography, written before the very beginnings of the Second Vatican Council, shows us how clearly the Council of Trent understood what were the needs of the Church in its time, how well Charles Borromeo understood and obeyed the enactments of Trent, and how the Church's needs today are little different from what they then were.

At the outset of his career St. Charles Borromeo was marked by his probity and ability; but he gave few other signs of the remarkable and holy character he was to become. His father was the head of a princely Milanese family, his mother the sister of the future Pope Pius IV. From the first, Charles, as a younger son, was intended to succeed to the many Church benefices which the family possessed; and when in 1559 his uncle was elected pope, he, already a cleric and a doctor in civil and canon law, was summoned to Rome, there to become the "Cardinal Nephew." He seems to have been anything but indifferent to such worldly honors; but he took his new duties very earnestly, and at once set about the serious study of theology, as well as applying himself assiduously to his work as the pope's chief adviser, and, in effect, secretary of state.

In 1563 he was ordained priest and consecrated bishop, and was promoted to the see of Milan, which, it was expected, he would hold as an absentee. But a striking change in his character and life was appearing, accelerated, perhaps, by the early death of his beloved elder brother. Soon Pius IV reconvened Trent and brought the Council to a successful end; and Charles began to apply its resolutions to his own case. It urged upon all who held pastoral office their responsibility for preaching God's word to their people; Cardinal Borromeo began to preach in his titular church in Rome, an unheard of thing.

Trent decreed that all diocesan bishops should reside in their dioceses, and in 1565 Charles at last gained permission to leave Rome and live in Milan. By its legislation Trent had shown great concern to raise the standard of education for the priesthood; before he took possession of his see, Charles had begun to implement this, setting up one great seminary in the city, and minor colleges in the remoter parts of his vast diocese. A month after his solemn entry, he had summoned his fifteen suffragan bishops to a provincial council, and he continued to convoke provincial councils despite the active opposition of some of them. Nor was he deterred by seeing some of his own proposals laid before such councils absolutely rejected; the council was there to discuss and to legislate, not merely to agree with higher authority.

In his twenty years of residence in Milan he held eleven diocesan synods, conducted on similar lines; and he was a devoted visitor to all, even the most distant and inaccessible parts of his archdiocese, sharing there the frugality of the pastors' lives, showing his devotion to the teaching and encouragement of the people. His Sunday schools, "Schools of Christian Doctrine," and his parish catechetical classes greatly raised the level of knowledge of the faith and of its practice among his people; and he promoted everywhere the confraternities of penance and of the Blessed Sacrament.

It need not be supposed that all these reforms and innovations went through smoothly, or were everywhere welcomed; opposition to him reached its culmination when the Humiliati, a strange quasi-religious congregation which he sought to reform, attempted his assassination.

We are well informed about Charles Borromeo's public life, and the documents which illustrate it, even though much of it is yet unpublished. His *Transactions of the Church of Milan* can still serve as a model for the conduct of a busy diocese; and in the Ambrosian Library in his cathedral city there are two hundred volumes of manuscript letters received or sent by him during the course of twenty-five years. Of the inner, spiritual life of this saint we know less, partly because he was always at such care to conceal wherever possible his mortifications and his communings with God. By our standards Charles' life was not long; he chose to wear out, not to rust away, and his life, pre-eminently, was lived for others, never for himself.

The Spiritual Life

"So, my children, let us acknowledge the Lord God before men, imitating His life as it behooves us, despising this world and its riches, giving ourselves as we are called to serve Him, as our duty, but yet with joyful hearts, our lives mortified, poor, wretched, abject; loving prayer, welcoming scorn and humiliations, at one with the divine will, always peaceful, joyful, calm. So we shall acknowledge our duty to the Lord God before mankind, we shall show ourselves His disciples and His servants, and we shall be known as such upon the Last Day."

Saint Charles' Sermon for the Feast of Saints Gervase and Protase

Sermoni Familiari di S. Carlo Borromeo (Padua, 1720).
C. Orsenigo, trans. Rudolph Kraus: *Life of St. Charles Borromeo* (St. Louis, 1947).

Gomidas Keumurgian
Martyr

died 1707

BLESSED GOMIDAS KEUMURGIAN was a martyr to the cause of ecumenism. His life and death are sad testimony of how persecution, though it can bring constancy and patriotism, also results, too often, in narrowness and bitter hatred.

To understand his strange story, we must know something of the history, tragic as it is complex, of the Armenian people and their faith. Today they occupy territory in north-eastern Turkey, and also the Armenian Soviet Socialist Republic; and there are scattered Armenian communities in the Ukraine, in France and the Balkans, in South America and in the United States. Their record is one of wanderings, exile, and oppression.

In the late third century they were converted to Christianity through the missionary efforts of Gregory "the Illuminator." They were then already under the suzerainty of the Byzantine emperors, and their clerics were prevented from attending the Councils of Ephesus in 431 and Chalcedon in 451, so that they rejected the decrees of these Councils as heretical innovations. Thus they became, nominally at least, Monophysites, teaching, that is, that in Christ there is one nature only, in which the human and divine are fused.

When in the twelfth century the Armenians who were settled in Cilicia (now in modern Turkey) came in contact with the Crusaders, a reunion with the Latin Church took place which endured for almost two centuries. But there were many internal dissensions that led to the setting up of rival patriarchates, which persist today. There had always been an occasional Catholicos (patriarch) united with Rome, but after 1375 there was no stable Catholic Armenian Chruch, until one of their bishops, Abraham Ardzivian, elected Catholicos of Sis, went to Rome and was confirmed in his see by Pope Benedict XIV in 1742. Unable, because of this submission, to return to Sis and oust a rival claimant, Abraham transferred his seat to Kraim in Lebanon; and it is this Catholic Patriarchate, now at Beirut, over which Gregory Peter XV Agaganian ruled from 1937 to 1962.

The real issue between the schismatic Armenians and the Latin Church has always been that of submission to the Chair of Peter. Monophysitism always seems to have meant little more to them than "Filioque" has meant to the Greeks: a rallying-sign and a mark of difference in which they take otherwise little interest. In 1964, at Aarhus in Denmark, an Orthodox-Monophysite conference reached an agreement on the decrees of Chalcedon which makes Monophysitism merely nominal. In the Latin Church there has never been any questioning of the validity of Armenian orders and of their other sacraments; and in dealings between the two Churches there seems always to have been recognized what the Second Vatican Council made explicit, that Oriental discipline, including the marriage of their clergy, was a matter for Orientals only.

This, then, was the situation in Gomidas' time. He was born in Constantinople in 1656, the son of a schismatic Armenian priest, and he himself worked as an assistant priest in the great Armenian parish of St. George in south Constantinople, a married man and a father.

The Armenians under the rule of the Ottoman empire were living in ghettoes such as even modern times have not known. They had no legal rights whatever; it has been said that life itself was regarded as a favor granted them. They were subject to degrading sumptuary and residential laws, they were cruelly taxed, and excluded from most occupations. Yet, like the Jews under similar conditions, they contrived to survive and even to prosper, and there was bred in them a strong, militant determination not to be extinguished.

It was partly under the influence of the famous Abbot Mekhitar, partly through his own researches in the Fathers and Church history, that Gomidas with his family came to be reconciled with the Roman Church. All that seems to have been asked of him was juridical submission to the Holy See, and, thereafter, he was permitted to continue living with his family and ministering in his parish. But soon some of his brother priests followed his example; the dissident Armenians, alarmed, denounced them to the Turkish authorities, and it was judged wise to send Mekhitar to Venice, Gomidas to Jerusalem.

Gomidas lived there in the Armenian monastery of St. James, where he found the community divided in its allegiance. He earned the enmity of the leading schismatic in the monastery, James the Syrian. When it was deemed safe for Gomidas to return to Constantinople, he was soon followed by James, who was, first, vicar-general and then patriarch. Twice at his instance Gomidas was arrested and charged as a "Frank"; and, although he could properly deny this, since the term meant specifically a Roman Catholic, he refused to conceal his submission to the pope, to abjure, apostatize or even compromise. In the end, though the Turks were reluctant to do this, they were urged by the schismatic Armenians to condemn him to death. According to one account, the grand vizier said to them: "His blood be on your head," and they replied: "Let it be rather on the Jesuits who perverted him."

Attwater, who writes of Gomidas with the special authority with which he treats of all matters concerning the Oriental Churches, remarks that he was "possibly the first recorded priest-martyr since the days of the early persecutions who was followed to the place of execution by his wife and children." He had spent his last imprisonment in fasting and prayer; the tranquil bravery with which he bore himself moved all witnesses, and his death led to the reconciliation of many Armenians and other Eastern rite schismatics.

A Prayer for Mercy

"All-merciful Lord, have mercy on all those who believe in you; on those who belong to me, and those who are strangers to me, on those whom I know and those whom I know not; on the living and on the dead; and forgive my enemies, and those who hate me, the trespasses they have committed against me; and turn them from the malice they bear against me, that they may be worthy of your mercy."

From the Prayers *of the Armenian Patriarch Nerses IV Shnor-hali* (A.D. *1102–72*)

Preces Sancti Nersetis Clajensis (Venice, 1862).
J. Kaftandjian, art.: "Armenian Rite" (NCE, 1, pp. 834-37).
H.Riondel: *Une page tragique de l'histoire religieuse du Levant* (Paris, 1929).
Vaham Inglesian: *Der Diener Gottes Mechitar von Sebaste* (Vienna, 1929).

Joan Mary de Maillé
Franciscan Tertiary

died 1414

WE ARE WELL INFORMED of the facts in the case of Blessed Joan Mary de Maillé, for we possess a *Life* written by her confessor of her last years; were this not so, we might wonder if hers were not the traditional riches-to-rags story so beloved of the romancers of her age. She was born in Touraine in 1331, of noble descent on either side, and when she was still a child, her father's death left her sole heir of his considerable possessions. Her grandfather therefore judged it prudent to espouse her to a boy who had been her childhood companion, Robert, heir of the baron of Sillé; and although Mary had already decided to vow her virginity to God, in obedience to her grandfather she went through a form of marriage. But she and Robert lived in continence, though it is plain that there was a deep love between them.

Their home was an example of Christian order and piety; idleness and gambling, in particular, were forbidden to their household, and they became famous for their hospitality and charity toward the distressed and afflicted.

Robert was called by the king of France to the defense of the country against the invading and marauding English, in the disastrous years after the battle of Crécy; and he fought at the battle of Poitiers, an equally serious defeat for the French, in which the king lost his life, and Robert was gravely wounded. Soon after that, though their own countryside had been overrun by the English and their castle captured, Mary had to raise an enormous sum for her husband's ransom. A famine followed, during which they almost beggared themselves to help the needy; shortly after this Robert died.

To Mary's grief at the loss of a young husband whom she had loved very much was added the afflictions she suffered at the hands of his family, who turned her out of her home, heaping reproaches on her for the generosity to others which had so reduced the estate. One such misfortune followed another, till she was compelled to seek refuge in her mother's house, where her own family lost no time in arranging to marry off again this still young and lovely and well-born woman.

But by this time Mary, devoted as she had always been to a life of virginity, seems to have come to see that God's hand was in her sorrows, and that she had a vocation also for a life of poverty. She joined the Franciscan Tertiaries, living in great austerity and zeal in a humble dwelling in Tours, where she was free to give all her time to charity and prayer. Often she lived by begging. Many thought her mad, and her family said that she was their disgrace. She made sporadic attempts to live in community; but in the hospital which she entered to do all the vilest and most painful work, she encountered such jealousy and unkindness from the others that she was driven out again.

She lived to be an old woman, roaming from place to place, sometimes in a hermitage, sometimes haunting a church in Tours and sleeping by night there on a bench. The destitution which had first been forced on her, the solitude which came from others' aversion to her, had become dear to her for the sake of Christ. She was granted supernatural favors and insights into divine providence; and so she died, sharing to the end the hidden, lonely life of the Poor Man of Galilee.

Tolerance

"I know that it is not possible to live among men without tolerance; for it is rare for a man to be at peace within himself for so long as a day. Some ill mood will overtake him, from where he does not know. To refuse to forgive others is the way devils behave; but to love enemies and to return them good for ill is the distinguishing mark of the children of God."

From the household ordinances of Robert of Sillé

Acta Sanctorum, March, vol. iii.
Père Frédéric: *Vie de la bienheureuse Jeanne-Marie de Maillé* (Bordeaux, 1817).

Willibrord
Bishop

died 739

ST. WILLIBRORD, who was born in northern England, was brought up from early childhood by the monks of Ripon, and became a professed member of their community. He was about twenty years of age when he went to study in Ireland. He remained there some twelve years, during which time he was ordained priest, and he did missionary work among the Irish.

He was thirty-three when he was chosen to head a mission to the Frisians, the people who today inhabit the coastal districts and islands of northern Holland and Germany, and whose language is very closely related to English. Their leader at this time was Radbod, who lived and died an enemy of Christianity; but recently he had been defeated by the Franks under Pepin II, son of the founder of the Carolingian dynasty and "mayor of the palace" (in effect, regent and head of government) of the Austrasian kingdom. Pepin had occupied much Frisian territory; and accordingly Willibrord went first to him and gained his protection, before beginning his preaching to the Frisians.

A manuscript which is now in the Bibliothèque Nationale in Paris, which was discovered in the Charterhouse at Treves, contains a calendar which belonged to Willibrord, and in the margin of the November page, opposite the commemoration of the feasts of St. Cecilia (*see* November 22) and St. Clement (*see* November 23), there is a note, presumably in his own handwriting: "In the name of the Lord. Clement-Willibrord in the year 690 after the Incarnation of Christ crossed the seas into the land of the Franks, and in the name of God, in the year 695 after the Incarnation of the Lord, he, though unworthy, was ordained bishop in Rome by the apostolic lord Sergius the Pope. Now truly, in the name of God, in this 728th year after the Incarnation of our Lord Jesus Christ, he lives, in God's name, happily." This corrects Bede's statement that he was consecrated bishop in 696, and it confirms what Bede says, writing while the other is still alive, of his great age.

Pepin gave Willibrord for his episcopal see the fortified town of Utrecht, which he had recaptured; and we are told that there he not only built a new church but also restored an ancient one, dedicated to St. Martin. Whether this was a Roman church, built while they occupied "Trajectum ad Rhenum, Ultrajectum," or a later foundation by the Franks, we do not know.

Willibrord's long years as bishop of the Frisians were not easy. Although he won many for the Christian faith, great numbers persisted in their paganism, and he and his English and Irish fellow-missioners faced many dangers. This is illustrated by the story told by Alcuin (though he is not a wholly reliable source) of how they landed on the island of Heligoland in the North Sea, regarded by the heathen as a sacred place, and knowingly defied local laws by killing animals for food and baptizing a convert in the sacred spring, and how on the orders of Radbod one of their company was sacrificed to the local god to appease him. And Willibrord's efforts to convert the Danes and other peoples to the north met with little success.

His long life was one of unremitting effort to spread the gospel of Christ. He had plainly learned much from the Irish, and one lesson had been a willing acceptance of perpetual exile for the love of God.

The Formation of a Missionary

"When, then, this most blessed youth had lived until his twentieth year, wholly occupied in sacred studies and the pursuit of virtue, he longed for a yet stricter life and to go into exile. And since he heard of the great learning which flourished in Ireland, and was inspired by what he was told of the life of certain holy men, and especially of that most pious father and bishop Ecgbert, always called 'the Saint,' and also of Wicbert, that venerable man and priest of God, both of whom had left their homes and their land and their kin for love of Heaven, their true native land, Willibrord went to Ireland, and there, empty of all that the world can give and full of God, he partook each day of the sweetest fruits of divine contemplation. This holy young man longed to follow the way of life which his abbot and brethren in Ireland showed to him as he lived among them, and like the wise bee he drew nectar from the sweet flowers of their sanctity and stored honey in the hive of his heart. There for twelve years the future preacher to many peoples gathered learning among the greatest teachers of holy living and sacred science, till he had grown to perfect manhood and had attained to Christ's own full age."

    Alcuin: Life of St. Willibrord

Acta Sanctorum, November, vol, iii.
Bede: *Ecclesiastical History of the English Peoples.*
H. A. Wilson, ed.: *The Calendar of Willibrord* (Henry Bradshaw Society, 55, 1918).

Godfrey of Amiens
Bishop

died 1115

AS WAS THE MEDIEVAL CUSTOM, to our minds today deplorable, Godfrey was sent to his monastery, Mont-Saint-Quentin, at the age of five, and thereafter spent his whole life in religion. From Mont-Saint-Quentin he was sent to serve as abbot of Nogent, which he found in a ruinous and disorderly state; and his achievements as a restorer and reformer of the house were great.

If we feel that his character, perhaps because of his narrow and exclusively monastic training, was excessively rigid, that he was too much the implacable disciplinarian, we shall do well to consider the objects of his severity: the ostentatious luxury of the rich affronting and embittering the wretched and destitute, the carelessness and irreligion of bad monks, an abbess neglectful and cruel toward her subjects. Lax times need strong leaders; and Godfrey was never more severe with others than with himself. Even as bishop of Amiens, he lived in the greatest simplicity and was a model of observance.

St. Godfrey was, too, human enough to be much discouraged in his later years by his own personal unpopularity, and by frequent resistance to his rule and reforms. He was attracted by the lonely austerity of the Grande Chartreuse, and retired there, a move which seems to have been very popular with some of his clergy and people. But, true to his life-long standards, he obeyed his archbishop's letters of recall, and came back to serve the diocese again in Amiens, where, less than a year after thus having sacrificed his own will and the peace he had longed for, he died.

The Religious Life

"From ancient times there have been many holy men who have seen what an exile this life is, and have longed with all their hearts for the lasting joys of that city upon high. They gave away their every possession, they spurned all this world's passing joys, and they followed after that poor man, Christ, so that they might be made rich with His riches. They took upon them His bondage, which alone makes free, and out of their great love for Him they relinquished their own liberty. And still in our day their example is of worth; so that we see some in contemplative houses, dying to the world, others living according to different rules of religion, and yet others doing God's work in the solitude of hermits' cells."

From Godfrey's foundation charter, 1105, for a Namur monastery

Acta Sanctorum, November vol. iii.
PL, 162, coll. 735-48.

Benignus
Bishop

died 467

WHAT WE KNOW TODAY OF ST. BENIGNUS we owe to the devotion and learning of the Irish Franciscan, Michael O'Clery, who in Dublin in 1629 copied his *Life* from earlier Irish sources now wholly lost, and of the Belgian Bollandist Grosjean, who edited the unique manuscript of O'Clery's work, now in Brussels.

When St. Patrick (*see* March 17) kept his first Easter in Ireland in 433, Benignus, still a child, was with him. He and his parents had been baptized by Patrick, and the boy had refused to part from him. His Irish name "Benen," had been Latinized as "Benignus"; and he became Patrick's constant companion for the rest of his life. He had many great gifts; among them, he was a wonderful singer, and he was called "Patrick's psalmist." But, above all, he seems to have been distinguished for the sweetness and simplicity of his nature, one of those to whom God gives the faculty of loving Him above all, and of imparting that divine love to every creature with whom they come in contact.

He evangelized Clare, Kerry, and parts of Connaught; and he succeeded Patrick himself as the second bishop of Armagh. His name, like that of Patrick, became later in the Middle Ages involved in the complex evolution of the Glastonbury legend, as we can see, for example, in the writings of John of Tynemouth; but today the historians assure us that the apostle of Ireland and his dear companion had in fact no connection with Glastonbury, which only long after their time established its contacts, enduring though they became, with Ireland and its saints.

Another Christ

"So much, then, for the marvels which Benignus accomplished, though we have only related few out of the many. If you wanted to have all of them told, either he would have to come back to life, or an angel of the Lord would have to show what signs and wonders God performed for Benignus' sake; and through such matters his powers were shown. And he was famous for his frugality, his integrity, his constancy in prayer, his reverence, for his joy in fulfilling the commandments of God, for his unswerving and yet humble spirit. He was quick to forgive, and most generous. His mind and his soul were like a holy burse, made to contain the body and blood of Christ. His words and his instructions brought salvation to people and to churches, wherever he went. For fear of him the devil did not dare to infest any district which he had looked on; for only to see his face was enough to drive discord away from any assembly of men."

The Epilogue to the Irish Life of St. Benignus

Acta Sanctorum, November, vol. iv.

Andrew Avellino
Theatine Clerk Regular

died 1608

LITTLE SERVICE IS DONE TO ST. ANDREW AVELLINO by the hysterically laudatory early biographies which were produced by members of his own congregation; but in modern times several more sober and discriminating studies of him have appeared. He was born in 1521, ordained in 1545, and was then active, as a secular priest, in Naples. It would seem that at this time he was a thoroughgoing clerical careerist, much in demand in the ecclesiastical courts for his skill in canon law and in pleading. Then he underwent a change of heart, abandoned his ambitions, and joined the congregation of clerks regular called Theatines under Cajetan (*see* August 7). He himself gave differing reasons for this transformation later in life: one of them is reproduced below.

Among the Theatines he held many important offices; and he became one of those most active in the Italian Counter-Reformation. He was a famous spiritual director, with, like St. Francis de Sales (*see* January 29), great capacities for understanding the religious problems of ordinary men and women. Also like Francis, he conducted a vast correspondence; and he was very successful with those whose position in life militated against their religious aspirations. We are told that this is especially evident in the unpublished *Treatise on Contempt of the World*, addressed to Donna Maria of Portugal, princess of Parma.

Himself granted many supernatural favors in prayer, he could direct others like him; or he could unmask frauds, such as the notorious Juliana de Marco. Charles Borromeo (*see* November 4)

SAINT LAWRENCE GIVING THE TREASURES OF THE CHURCH TO THE POOR
Bernardo Strozzi
University of Miami, Joe and Emily Lowe Art Gallery, Coral Gables, Florida

See September 5

SAINT FRANCIS RECEIVING THE STIGMATA
Jan Van Eyck
John G. Johnson Collection, Philadelphia

See September 17

SAINT MATTHEW
Simone Martini
National Gallery of Art, Washington, D.C.

See September 21

SAINT THOMAS OF VILLANOVA GIVING ALMS TO THE POOR
Juan de Valdes Leal
El Paso Museum of Art, El Paso, Texas

See September 22

SAINT SIMON
Simone Martini
National Gallery of Art, Washington, D.C.

See October 28

SAINT ANDREW THE APOSTLE
Follower of Pietro Lorenzetti
Museum of Art, Science, and Industry, Bridgeport, Connecticut

See November 30

SAINT LUCY
Attributed to Lorenzo Costa
The High Museum of Art, Atlanta, Georgia

See December 13

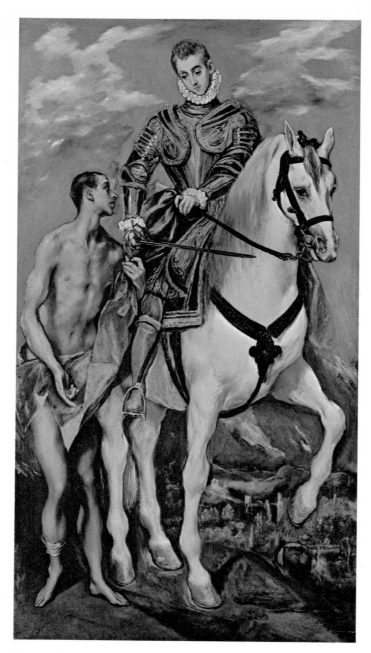

SAINT MARTIN AND THE BEGGAR
El Greco
National Gallery of Art, Washington, D.C.

See November 11

specially asked for him to be assigned to the archdiocese of Milan, where he founded a Theatine house, and formed a close and lasting friendship with the archbishop.

The Lips that Lie Kill the Soul

"When we told Andrew that these were all law-books, just published, he raised his eyes to heaven and wagged his head, saying: 'O, doctors of law are liars!' So I answered him: 'Father, why can't we doctors of law be saved too?' He said to me: 'The lips that lie kill the soul,' and he went on: 'I'll tell you something that once happened to me, when I was a secular priest. I was defending the case of a friend of mine, a priest, in the archbishop's chancery in Naples, and I told a lie to win my case. That night, when I returned to my room, I opened my Bible, and that passage in Wisdom caught my eye: *The lips that lie kill the soul*; and I asked myself why, just to help other people, I was murdering my own soul?' "

From the evidence of Thomas Pelliciono at the process of 1615

G. de Luca, art.: "André Avellin" (Dictionnaire de spiritualite, 1, coll. 551–54).
R. Lechat: *La "conversion" de S. André Avellin* (AB, 41, 1923, pp. 139–48).

Martin
Bishop

died about 400

OUR CHIEF AUTHORITY for the life of St. Martin of Tours is the short biography by his disciple, Sulpicius Severus, which was already completed before Martin's death.

Martin has come to be regarded as a soldier-saint, and as a patron of soldiers, partly because of his iconography, since the most popular representation of him from early times illustrates his best-known legend, and shows him, armed and mounted, cutting his cloak in two with his sword so as to clothe a poor beggar (who later reveals himself as Christ). But he could with equal justice be called the patron of conscientious objectors to military service.

The incident above is said to have occurred when he was performing his last service in France. He had been born in what is now Szombathely in Hungary, the son of pagans; his father was a serving officer in the imperial armies who had risen from the ranks. He had been transferred to Pavia, where Martin was brought up, and he in his turn was drafted for service. He was at this time a catechumen, receiving instruction in the faith but not yet baptized, and we are told that he lived more like a monk than a soldier. He decided that the bearing of arms was not compatible with the Christian profession, and while campaigning in France applied for release from his engagement. The case came to the notice of the emperor himself, who was leading his troops there, and he angrily accused Martin of cowardice. Martin replied that if the emperor chose, he would face the enemy the next morning single-handed, but as a soldier of Christ, not with a sword. He was for a time imprisoned, but then allowed, as he had asked, to go free.

Such pacifism did indeed characterize the rest of his life. Prisoners, pagans, and heretics were spared death at his entreaties; and Pope St. Siricius sided with him and condemned the action of the Emperor Maximus and Bishop Ithacius of Ossanova, when they put to death the heretic Priscillian and some of his followers after Martin had appealed for clemency for them. Even so, he was able to avert the bloody persecution of Priscillian's adherents in Spain which the emperor had planned.

After the young man had been released from the army, he lived in solitude, and then founded the first religious community in Gaul, a settlement of hermits at Ligugé. He was strongly attracted to the eremitical life; but in 372 he was elected by popular acclaim as bishop of Tours, much against his own will, and that of some of the neighboring bishops, who thought that he did not cut the fine figure a bishop should. Later he founded a second monastery, at Marmoutier, and he retired to its solitude whenever he could.

He was marked by his great spiritual powers; and he was gifted with discernment of spirits, with vision and with prophecy. Veneration of him was widespread even before his death, and soon thereafter it spread throughout the West. When Augustine (*see* May 28) first came to Canterbury, and Willibrord (*see* November 7) arrived in Utrecht, they found in both these then pagan cities ruined churches formerly dedicated to him.

A Vision of Pseudo-Christ

"On a certain day, in the false light of early morning, while Martin was praying in his cell, there appeared before him one clothed in a royal robe, crowned with a diadem of jewels and gold, shod with golden shoes, smiling serenely, joyful of countenance, like nothing less than the devil. When Martin first looked at him he felt only a numbness, and both of them kept a long silence. The devil spoke first: 'Confess him, Martin,' he said, 'whom you see. I am Christ, and, coming down to earth, I wished to show myself to you before anyone else.' When Martin still was silent and gave no reply, the devil was bold enough to repeat his blasphemous claim: 'Martin, why do you doubt what you see? I am Christ!' But he to whom the Spirit had revealed that this was not God but the devil answered: 'Jesus did not say that He would come again in purple and a crown. I shall not believe that Christ has come unless I see Him clothed and made as He was when He suffered, and showing me the marks of the Cross.' And when he heard this the other vanished like smoke, filling the cell with an evil stench, and showing in this way beyond any doubt that he was indeed the devil. This story, as I have told it here, I heard from Martin's own lips, lest anyone should think it a mere fable."

From Sulpicius Severus' Life *of St. Martin*

Sulpicius Severus: *De vita beati Martini liber unus* (PL, 20, coll. 159–84).

Nilus "the Ascetic"
Abbot

died 430

THE TRADITIONAL LIFE OF ST. NILUS is derived from the "Narrations" attributed to him; and this was popularized by the tenth-century Synaxary of Constantinople. But recent scholarship has been able to show that there may be confusion between him and another Nilus, "of Sinai," and that, in any case, the "Narrations" are little more than a pious novel, that the work is no kind of autobiography, and that the story told in it, picturesque and edifying though it be, has no foundation in fact.

The truth seems to be that he was born in Galatia, lived in Constantinople, and studied there under St. John Chrysostom (*see* January 27), for whom in his letters he shows great filial affection. He entered regular monastic life, and served as a novice master and a superior; but he seems never to have been ordained priest. He maintained a vast correspondence, not only with churchmen, and showed himself a gifted and perceptive spiritual director. In addition to his letters, other genuine works which survive are: a sermon on Luke 22:36, an instruction to the monk Eulogius on the desire for perfection, and a set of short *pensées*, rather than a treatise, *On Prayer*. There are also other writings on monastic living. A number of apparently genuine works are now lost.

It has been alleged in the past that Pelagianism had its origins in the spirituality of the Eastern Churches, and that one of its fathers was Nilus; but his authentic writings do not support this. On grace, on prayer, on the sacraments, his teaching is unimpeachably orthodox.

For him, a disciple of John Chrysostom, the monastic life is true *philosophia*, the reforming of one's life accompanied by an ever-deepening knowledge of "Him who is." This will be best found in solitary places, but true solitude of the spirit is found better in cenobitic than in eremitical living. Obedience and the common life help to raise men to Christ's stature. The knowledge and contemplation of God were among the gifts which Adam lost; and for Nilus the spiritual life will lead us back to that lost likeness to God. This will be achieved only by incessant warfare against the devil and the vices, and by constant, immediate prayer.

Difficulties in Prayer

"Sometimes it happens that we struggle to achieve pure prayer, and yet we cannot; and on the other hand at times with no effort on our part the soul suddenly falls into such a state of prayer. In the first case, our human weakness is the cause, but the second is caused by divine grace, calling us to return to the soul's former purity. Yet it is true that in either case, grace teaches us not to attribute our powers of prayer to ourselves, but to see who is their true giver. When, then, we seek to purify our prayer and we cannot, but are surrounded by darkness, then let us weep and entreat God that He may dispel this dark night of battle, and send His light into our souls."

Treatise to Eulogius, *chapter 30*

Epistolon Biblia D (PG, 79, coll., 81–582).
Logos pros Eulogion Monachon (*ibid.*, coll., 1093–1140).
Peri Proseuches (*ibid.*, coll., 1165–1200).
M. Th. Disdier, art.: "Nil l'ascète" (DTC, 11, coll. 661–74).

Stanislaus Kostka
Jesuit Novice

died 1568

WHEN, AT THE END OF THE LAST CENTURY, the Bollandists undertook the task of editing and publishing the life of St. Stanislaus Kostka, which had been prepared to advance the cause for his canonization (he was beatified less than forty years after his death), they listed over a hundred books and articles about him which had appeared in print between 1568 and 1640. Yet Stanislaus was only eighteen when he died, and had lived little more than a year as a novice in religious life.

We might well ask how one so young made such an impression on the Catholics of the Counter-Reformation, and particularly in his native country, Poland, of which he is one of the patrons; it was hardly, even, his extraordinary love of our Blessed Lady (he was convinced that she appeared to him in a vision when he was seriously ill, and told him to join the Jesuits), for this was an age of widespread renewal of devotion to Mary in the Church. It was perhaps his spirit of fortitude and generosity in opposing his politically powerful and influential father, a senator of Poland. When finally Stanislaus took the religious habit at the age of seventeen, his father wrote to him threatening that he would procure the banishment of the Jesuits from Poland, and vilifying his son "for putting on a contemptible dress and following a profession unworthy of his birth."

A saint is one who rejects the values of the world in response to the vision of God granted him in Christ; who, when called, takes seriously Christ's injunction, "He who does not hate father and mother, yes, and his own life also, for my sake, cannot be my disciple." It is a hard lesson for Christians to learn, that there must come a moment when they must choose between God and some earthly good they hold most dear. It is in such a moment that we can gain strength and courage from a young man like Stanislaus Kostka.

His parents were determined that Stanislaus should be educated according to the prescriptions of the new learning for gentlemen of breeding and substance. For several years he was privately tutored in the family castle of Rostkovo; but at the age of fourteen he was sent with his brother Paul under the care of a tutor to the Jesuit college in Vienna. In those days he communicated every Sunday and holy day, and, in spite of his brother's bullying, continued his youthful practices of prayer and penance.

The following year, when he had recovered from an illness, he presented himself to Fr. Maggi, the Jesuit provincial in Vienna, as a candidate for the Society. But he refused to receive him; he knew that Stanislaus' father would never give his consent. Stanislaus therefore set out for Dillingen in Upper Germany, where Peter Canisius (*see* April 27) was at that time provincial, a journey of three hundred and fifty miles. He went on foot and alone, dressed in peasant garb, so that his brother and his tutor, who set off in pursuit as soon as his flight was discovered, failed to find him.

Canisius kept him for three weeks in the role of servant to the college students, and having thus made trial of his humility and obedience, he sent him to Rome, where he was admitted into the Society by its general, Francis Borgia (*see* October 10).

His life in the novitiate was extraordinary only for his unfeigned simplicity and the remarkable love that he showed for Christ in the Eucharist. He was often seen in a kind of ecstasy at Mass, and particularly after receiving Holy Communion.

After less than a year as a novice, he fell sick of a fever. His novice master, joking with him about his physical weakness, said to him: "Man of little heart, are you giving up under so slight an ailment?" "I am indeed a man of little heart," replied Stanislaus, "but it is not at all a slight matter, for I shall die of it." He then asked for the last sacraments, and sought pardon of all the brethren. He died on the feast of the Assumption of Our Lady, after confiding to his confessor that he could see her, surrounded by many angels.

Preferring Christ to all Things

"I count all things as loss in return for the high privilege of knowing Jesus Christ my Lord. For love of him I have suffered the loss of all things, and count them as nothing, so that I might gain Christ and be found in him...that I may know him, and the power of his resurrection, and the fellowship of his sufferings, being made like him in his death."

Philippians 3:7-10

A. Arndt, ed.: *Vita et Miracula S. Stanislai Kostkae, conscripta a Padre Urbano Ubaldini, S. J.* (AB, 9, pp. 360–78; 11, pp. 416–67; 13, pp. 122–56; 14, pp. 295–318; 15, pp. 285–315; 16, pp. 253–96).

Lawrence O'Toole
Archbishop

died 1180

IN THE LIFE of St. Lawrence O'Toole the last thousand years of Ireland's tragic history is epitomized. He had a hard and cruel childhood, for he was a victim of the wars between the various regional kings and chieftains, in the constant civil strife which had left the country a prey to her invaders, first the Danes and then the Anglo-Normans. A son of the chief of the Murrays of County Kildare, he had been given as a hostage to his father's enemy, Dermot McMurrough, king of Leinster, and used very ill by him. But these misfortunes turned the boy's mind to God, and determined him to be His servant. He was only twenty-five when he became superior ("abbot," perhaps, but this was a monastery of the ancient Irish discipline, little comparable with Benedictine monasticism) of Glendalough, there living a life of extreme asceticism and solitude, as had so many Irish saints before him.

But the cares of the world soon intruded. He had to maintain the monastery and its domains against the robbers who roamed the countryside in lawless bands, he had to care for the people in times of famine, and those of his own brethren who resisted the reforms in monastic observance which he instituted gave him little quiet. After much resistance on his part, he consented to become the monastery's bishop (again, according to the old Celtic ways), and he was still in his early thirties when he succeeded to the see of Dublin. His predecessor, Gregory, had still been regarded as "bishop of the foreigners" (the Danish colony), had been consecrated in London, and had professed canonical obedience to the archbishops of Canterbury; but Lawrence, named as archbishop, was instituted by Gelasius of Armagh, the Irish primate, and the see of Dublin was integrated with the Irish Church.

From now on Lawrence was, inevitably, one of his country's leaders; but his constant journeyings and negotiations in no way mitigated his own austere life. But he was a realist, and moved with the times. Seeing that the clergy of his cathedral must have a rule, he imposed on them that of the regular canons of Arrouaise as being best designed to promote holiness and discipline, and himself took their habit, lived in community with them, and observed the rule.

His old enemy, Dermot McMurrough, gave the country no peace, and when he was driven into exile he persuaded King Henry II of England to give him aid. Henry was glad to do this as part of his grand plan which, had it succeeded, would have established a "united kingdom" of England, Wales, and Ireland, a great part of the French territories, and, probably, also Scotland. Henry saw himself as the founder of a "pax Normannica," and, in trying to achieve this, the ruin and the suffering he brought to Ireland and to all his other domains was incalculable. For his designs upon Ireland he claimed papal authority; whether he had this, whether it was based upon forgeries, still is disputed. But the Irish bishops whom Henry convened at Cashel in 1172 saw no reason to contest this authority; and during these negotiations Lawrence emerged as the country's chief spokesman with its new masters.

He was in England in 1175, arranging a truce between Henry and the high king of Ireland, Rory O'Connor; and on this journey he went to Canterbury to pray at the shrine of Henry's chief adversary, St. Thomas Becket (*see* December 29), martyred there five years before. In 1179 he led the Irish delegation to the Third Lateran Council; but before they left England, Henry, still very mindful of what Thomas' opposition had cost him, made the Irish bishops swear to do nothing at the Holy See to cause him harm in Ireland. This oath did not prevent Lawrence from telling Pope Alexander III what Ireland needed: peace, stable government, and a Church free to care for the peoples' souls. Alexander sent him back to Dublin with all he asked for, and legatine powers as well.

When, in 1180, Lawrence came back to England again on behalf of Rory O'Connor, Henry, afraid of the consequences if he were to do violence to the archbishop, but determined not to tolerate another "turbulent priest," compromised by forbidding him to return to Ireland. Lawrence followed the king to Normandy and persuaded him to relent; but he died in the abbey of Eu before he could go home to his people.

The resemblances between the characters and careers of Lawrence O'Toole and Thomas Becket are mostly fortuitous; but they had in common a deep love of the people of God entrusted to their care. They were both good shepherds, willing to give their lives for their sheep.

A Bishop's Concern for his People

"Blessed Lawrence bitterly lamented the fate of his people, who would be left defenseless by his death, and in his native tongue he said: 'O, my people, simple and foolish, what will you do now? Who is going to patch up your quarrels? Who will cure your ills?' His love made him long to be dissolved and be with Christ; yet that same love made him fear for his brethren, that oppressed people, and, perhaps, made him long to remain still among them. But the God in whom he had trusted decreed that now he should receive the reward of his labors with no more delay; and so, on the following day, as the eve of the Sabbath approached, the soul of this holy man entered into eternal rest."

From an early Life *of St. Lawrence*

C. Plummer: *Vie et miracles de S. Laurent* (AB, 33, 1914, pp. 121-86).

Albert the Great
Bishop and Doctor of the Church

died 1280

St. Albert, born in Germany in 1206, went as a youth to study in Padua; and in 1222 Jordan of Saxony (*see* February 15) reported having admitted him there to the Dominican Order. By 1228 he was teaching, first in Cologne, then in many other German houses, thereafter in Paris and then again at the Order's international center for higher studies in Cologne, where Thomas Aquinas (*see* March 7) was one of his pupils. In 1254 he became German prior provincial, and defended in Rome the mendicant Orders against the attacks upon them in the universities (their real offense was their intellectual pre-eminence).

At Rome he was made "master of the sacred palace," the pope's theological consultant, a post traditionally occupied by a Dominican, and, in 1260, bishop of Regensburg. This last appointment was against his own wishes and the desire of his religious superiors; he occupied it for only two years, before returning to his teaching. He took part in the Council of Lyons, despite his own great grief at the death, on his way to the Council, of Thomas Aquinas; and his last public act was to defend the dead Thomas' writings before hostile elements in the University of Paris. By this time he was himself complaining that his powers were failing.

This was the close of a career which had been marked by Albert's universal, all-embracing genius, and by a generosity truly Christ-like and supernatural. As a young man, he reminds us of that other great mind, Goethe, which Germany gave to the world. Passionately interested in the natural sciences, he saw that they could only advance through the systematic classification of reliable evidence. Writing in *Of the Vegetable Species*, considered the masterpiece of his scientific works, he shows himself a true man of science: "What I report here on the different kinds of plant life is based partly on my own observations, partly on what others have said, but only after I have been satisfied that their own results came from careful observation." Mammals, fish, insects, birds, man—he reverenced and studied every form of life.

His penetrating intellect, his capacity for systematization, are as evident in his theology. At a time when the rediscovery of Aristotle by the Western world was having an impact on men's thinking as great, and as confusing, as that of Marx and Freud in our own century, Albert saw that the Greek's metaphysical system could be used to construct a Christian theological system. In such problems as universals, causality, the experimental knowledge of God, he tried to apply and advance Aristotle's teaching. And he never thought it other than an honor that in his own time his reputation was completely overshadowed by that of his pupil Thomas, using the methods which Albert had taught him. The greatness of teachers can be measured by their pupils, and by their attitude toward one another; Albert and Thomas saw in each other great minds, wholly illumined by a love of Eternal Wisdom.

Though, in the manner of the Middle Ages, many works have been attributed to Albert which he never wrote (we now know, for instance, that *De Adhaerendo Deo* is by John of Kastl), and though much that he is said to have written seems to be lost (including his commentary on the entire Bible), what remains of his genuine writings represents an immense achievement, and every word shows us a man holy as he was learned. We are told that in his early days in Italy he was in despair over his own stupidity and lack of memory, and determined to abandon his studies. The Church may still be thankful that God guided him otherwise.

True Love of God

"Our love of God is true and perfect when the soul with all its forces fervently pours itself out upon God, seeking in Him no advantage, temporal or eternal, but is affected toward Him only for His innate goodness, sanctity, perfection, and blessedness. For the delicate soul abhors, as it were, to love God for profit or reward; just as God with all His force pours out Himself upon the soul of man, never expecting any profit from it, but desiring to communicate to it His own natural blessedness. But if I love God because He is good to me, and for the special reason that He may communicate His happiness to me, then I am convicted of loving Him naturally and imperfectly."

From St. Albert's Paradise of the Soul

H. Wilms, trans. A. English and P. Hereford: *Albert the Great* (London, 1933). *The Paradise of the Soul*, trans. "N.N." (London, 1682).

Edmund Rich
Archbishop

died 1240

TODAY, WHEN WE condemn the identification of the Church and its hierarchy in any country with a single political system or creed, believing that this limits the Church's capacity for witnessing to God and His kingdom, the history of medieval times in countries like England seems to us deplorable. The Church's leaders were great statesmen, much of whose time was spent in the enforcement of law and in litigation. Many of them, like Thomas Wolsey, in their pursuit and exercise of secular power, seemed to forget that they were ministers of Christ. Men like Wilfrid (*see* October 12) and Thomas of Canterbury (*see* December 29) brought about their own ruin by preferring the cause of the Church to that of the State.

But such a point of view ignores what was then the true state of affairs, regrettable though that may have been. If the magnates of the Church held aloof from politics, they left the Church and its people defenseless before the greed of irreligious lay potentates. The career of St. Edmund, archbishop of Canterbury, illustrates this well.

Edmund Rich (this was his family name—he is also known, from his birthplace, as "of Abingdon," and from his highest office as "of Canterbury") had made his name as a university teacher, as an ascetic and a master of the spiritual life. He studied in Paris, and returned to Oxford soon after 1200 with the master's degree,

840

that is, with a university's license to accept pupils and teach. Roger Bacon, the Dominican, who was his devoted pupil at Oxford, says that he was the first man there to give systematic lectures on Aristotle. Later, he taught theology publicly, and he seems to have moved to Salisbury when he was appointed prebendary there, and to have taught in the cathedral school.

But in 1233 he was elected archbishop. The see had been vacant for several years, while a candidate was sought who would be equally acceptable to Rome, to the English Crown, and to the Benedictine monastic community at Canterbury, which a modern historian has described as "the most touchy and cantankerous in England." The Crown's candidate was rejected, as it was not at that time the Holy See's policy to allow Canterbury to be a civil service appointment; Rome's own preferred man was unsuitable as a curialist and a notorious pluralist; and the chapter's own candidate was manifestly weak, prior of their monastery, chosen by them for his weakness. So, in the end, they decided for a scholar and a holy man and chose Edmund.

But, from the moment of his election, he was immersed in the troublesome affairs of the State. It was above all because of his ability to assert his personality and his principles that he was able to support the king, Henry III, through the greatest crisis of his reign, making peace between him and his rebellious barons, establishing security in the Welsh marches and in Ireland, averting civil war and reorganizing the government. All this he was able to do partly because he was known not to be an interested party, and to have at heart nothing but peace and the peoples' wellbeing.

He seems to have known little but trouble throughout his episcopate. Everywhere in his province he found clergy and religious resistant to his authority and desires for reform; and his greatest cross was his own monks at Canterbury. He truly wished to be to them a father in God (though the system whereby monastic cathedral churches like Canterbury, Norwich, and Durham were ruled by a prior, whom any archbishop or bishop, were he secular priest or member of another religious order, could, if he wished, supersede as "abbot" in dignity and authority, had built-in disaster). But instead he and his monks were involved in constant litigation, in England and at Rome, and matters were not improved when in the course of one of their disputes the monks were discovered to have forged documents to support their case. And, on the other hand, bishops like the saintly Grosseteste reproached Edmund with being too lenient and too disposed to settle for peace.

There is some mystery about Edmund's death, which took place near Pontigny, in France, where he is today buried. We do not know if he was there in exile, like other archbishops before and after him, because of disputes with the throne, or if he was merely overtaken by sickness on his way to Rome on business. Today scholars incline more to the second opinion.

But even if we discard the older view of him as a potential Thomas Becket (*see* December 29), still he has every title for consideration as a holy man; and this is best evidenced by his treatise *The Mirror of Holy Church*. This was originally a series of lectures on "the ascent of the soul to God," preached (in French) to an English audience of young students in a monastery, perhaps at Oxford, perhaps at Salisbury, perhaps at Canterbury; we do not know. But its tender solicitude for his hearers, his compassionate understanding of their spiritual and emotional problems, marks him as a great director. It is from the *Mirror* that we can see how true were Edmund's dying words: "Lord, I have believed in you, preached you, taught you; and you are my witness that here on earth I have sought nothing else but you."

Knowing God through His Creatures

"You ought to recognize and think of God's goodness and His sweetness and His beauty. To do this you should consider well the great beauty and the great goodness and the great sweetness which there is in earthly creatures. How many things there are which delight our earthly eyes by their beauty, and our taste by their sweetness, and our touch by their smoothness, and so all our other senses! See then how great goodness, sweetness and beauty there must be in a spiritual being which is everlasting, when there is so much beauty and sweetness and goodness in a thing which exists today and tomorrow will have passed away."

From St. Edmund's The Mirror of Holy Church

E. Colledge: *The Mediaeval Mystics of England* (New York, 1961).
C. E. Lawrence: *St. Edmund of Abingdon* (Oxford, 1960).

Roque Gonzalez
Martyr

died 1628

THE STORY OF THE JESUIT "REDUCTIONS," or settlements of converted Indians in Paraguay and Uruguay in the seventeenth and
eighteenth centuries, has often been told by historians and travel-
lers, and always in glowing terms. More recently, the shameful
manner of their destruction in 1768, as a prelude to the suppres-
sion of the Society of Jesus, has been set out in dramatic form by
Hochwälder in his play, *The Strong are Lonely*.

The Reductions represent a specific missionary project, devised
by the Spanish Jesuits in South America to defeat the cruelty
and rapaciousness of Spanish colonial adventurers and traders,
who either corrupted or enslaved the Indians with whom they
dealt and bartered. The Jesuits sought and obtained the support
of the colonial power to keep all white men, except government
officials, out of the settlements, and they set about making the
inhabitants self-sufficient, teaching them first all the basic agricultural and artisan skills, and laying plans for progressive education.

It is not too much to say that the extraordinarily difficult beginnings of the Paraguay Reductions owed more to Blessed Roque
Gonzalez than to any other individual priest. He also has the distinction of being the first native-born martyr of Latin America.

He was born in Asunción, the capital of Paraguay, in 1576,
of a well-known Spanish colonial family, his brother being appointed governor of the city in 1614. Several witnesses at the
process for Roque's beatification, initiated at Asunción five

months after his death, speak of the extraordinary example of virtue which he set as a boy. His companions never dared to swear or indulge in immoral talk in his presence; and if his elders did so, he would ask them to stop. He was frequently discovered on his knees in prayer in unlikely corners. That this behavior had nothing to do with childish piety, his later career of hardship and heroism proves.

Though he wished to give himself entirely to God, he felt completely unworthy of the priesthood. It was only at the urgent insistence of his bishop that he reluctantly consented to be ordained. After ten years' work as a diocesan priest, the bishop of Asunción appointed him his vicar-general, an obvious first step to higher ecclesiastical honors. He avoided all this by joining the Society of Jesus.

After only a few months of novitiate, he embarked on the twenty years of work with the Indians which was to be crowned with martyrdom. In 1611 he took charge of the first Reduction to be opened, St. Ignatius, on the River Paraguay. After three years' experience with the Indians here, he spent the remainder of his life travelling into territory as yet unknown to the Spaniards, in order to found new Reductions, seven altogether, in fifteen years. The hardship and dangers of his life during these pioneering years were emphasized by the lieutenant-governor of Corrientes, the man in charge of the investigations into Blessed Roque's murder. He was, he said, "able to appreciate how much the life which Fr. Roque led must have cost him—the hunger, the cold, the exhaustion from his journeys on foot, the swimming across rivers, the wading through morasses, not to speak of the plague of insects and the discomforts which no man but a true apostle, who was holy like the said Father, could have sustained with such endurance."

What sustained him was his great charity. The native witness whose evidence is preserved for us declared that "all the Christians among my countrymen loved the Father and sorrowed for his death, because he was the father of all; and it was so that he was styled by all the Indians of the Paraná."

While on one of his exploratory expeditions along the Uruguay and Rio Grande, he discovered that the leader of opposition to Christian teaching was a certain witchdoctor, called Nezú, who claimed to have supernatural powers. Realizing what a threat Roque Gonzalez was to his position, Nezú blackmailed one of the local chiefs to plot his murder. He and a band of his tribesmen surprised Fr. Gonzalez outside his church in the recently-founded Reduction of All Saints at Caaró. With him suffered a fellow priest and Jesuit, Blessed Alonzo Rodriguez. And two days afterwards, on November 17, 1628, a third missionary, Blessed Juan del Castillo, was murdered at the behest of the same Nezú.

Eyewitnesses, seven or eight in number, testified that when those who had taken part in these murders were rounded up and taken into custody, "their hands became swollen and covered with blisters as if they had been burned in contact with fire."

Christian Perseverance

"We suffer every kind of affliction, but we are not over-whelmed; we are often in uncertainty, but never in despair; we are persecuted, but never abandoned. We carry about in our bodies the death of Jesus, so that the life of Jesus may show forth as well in our bodies. While we live, we are always being given up to death for Jesus' sake, so that the life of Jesus may be shown forth in our mortal flesh."

2 Corinthians 4:8-11

J. M. Blanco: *Historia documentada de la vida y gloriosa muerte de los padres Gonzalez, Alonzo Rodriguez, y Juan del Castillo, S. J.* (Buenos Aires, 1929).
H. Thurston, art.: "The First Beatified Martyr of Spanish America" (Catholic Historical Review, 20, January 1935, pp. 371-83).

Odo of Cluny
Abbot

died 942

OF THE ABBOTS and monks associated with the Cluny reform of
Benedictine observance, St. Odo's name is best remembered. He
was one of the first monks of Cluny, he became its second abbot,
and by the end of his life the reforms which he had sponsored had
been adopted by many monasteries, within France and beyond
its borders.

He was the son of a Frankish knight, and was brought up in
two great households, those of the count of Anjou and the duke
of Aquitaine, William, later to become the founder of Cluny. But
he early showed strong attraction to the life of prayer, and at the
age of nineteen he became a cleric and a canon of the cathedral
of Tours, a sinecure which enabled him to study theology at Paris
for four years. On his return to Tours and to promotion, he became
convinced that the life he was living was no road to perfection;
and so he resigned his benefices, and in his thirtieth year entered
the monastery of Baume.

In the next year Cluny was founded; Odo transferred there,
and the abbot made him head of the monastic school. He succeeded St. Berno as second abbot, and found that he had inherited
no easy situation. Berno's splendid buildings, not yet completed,
had put the abbey heavily in debt; and many of the community
had become resentful and rebellious under his harsh rule. Odo
shouldered these burdens manfully, and was able during his rule
to attract many rich benefactors to endow the monastery. But
he was no easier with his subjects than his predecessor had been.
Berno had intended this new foundation to avoid the sloth and

laxity he had seen in other monasteries, to restore the primitive obedience, to exercise absolute authority, and to maintain the highest standards of spirituality and of learning. In all this Odo followed him; but it is a great tribute to his personality that he could draw young men of great qualities into his monastery, and keep them there, tractable under so strict a regime.

Firm he was, but not unbending, and one of his early biographers tells how he was once met at the door of a house where he planned a visitation with threats of physical violence. He talked to the monks quietly and reasonably, went away, returned three days later as if arriving for the first time, and found every door open to him.

Pope Leo VII called him to Rome on several occasions to negotiate between different armed forces contending for control of the city; and he showed much statesmanship in carrying out such tasks. He was in every respect a masterly character, well fitted to command, in his own violent and unruly age; but his power was spiritual in its sources, and wholly directed toward the service of God. The reform of Cluny owes much to his personal qualities of sanctity and scholarship, and its enduring contribution to religious life is his greatest memorial.

Love and Forgiveness

"This is the woman of whom Luke writes: 'For there was in the city a certain sinful woman, whose many sins were forgiven because she loved greatly,' and of whom Mark says: 'Jesus, rising early on the morning of the Sabbath from the dead, appeared first to Mary Magdalene, out of whom he had driven seven devils.' The loving mercy of God to repentant sinners is shown by the perfection attained by her who had merited not only the washing away of her misdeeds, but also to be made consort of the apostles, when they received the news of the Resurrection of the Lord."

Odo: Sermon in Honor of St. Mary Magdalene

PL, 133.

Elizabeth of Hungary
Franciscan Tertiary

died 1231

ST. ELIZABETH, daughter of the king of Hungary, as a small child was betrothed to and brought up with Louis (*see* September 11), heir to Count Herman of Thuringia. When she was only fourteen years old, the young couple married; they knew no more than six years of life together, but they were wonderfully happy years, blessed with three children.

When Louis died of plague on his way to the Sixth Crusade, Elizabeth is said to have been almost out of her mind with grief; and though thereafter she showed great submission to the divine will, we sense that life was then over for her, and the rest only patient waiting for release from a world which held no joys for her. Soon after her husband's burial she entered the Franciscan Third Order, and devoted herself to her children and to the poor and unfortunate.

From this time onward, the dominant force in her life seems to have been her spiritual director, Conrad of Marburg, and it is hard to disagree with those modern biographers of Elizabeth who suggest that he, from doubtless worthy motives, set about systematically destroying her personality, as is recorded for us, with sorrow and indignation, by her serving women after her death. But Conrad did not succeed; she yielded him submission and obedience, and still retained her own judgment and vision.

She was only twenty-four years old when she died, welcoming her end as a blessing. She is a saint for all those who find the griefs of bereavement insupportable; let them turn, as she did, to God, and He will help them to carry this heavy burden.

The Christian Attitude to Death

"When, with all things made ready, she [Elizabeth] was hastening to her last wedding day, she was filled with joy, for she knew of the coming of her heavenly Bridegroom. The news came in the likeness of a little bird, which, as her own earthly life was passing away, sang to her so sweetly that she too rejoiced to know of the blessedness which awaited her, lying as she was in her death throes, and in her body she felt no pain, and gently she fell asleep in the Lord, as it were into a peaceful slumber."

From an anonymous thirteenth-century Life

D. Henniges, ed.: *Vita Sanctae Elizabeth, Langraviae Thuringiae* (Archivum Franciscanum Historicum, 2, 1909, pp. 240–68).

Ambrose Traversari
Abbot

died 1439

AMBROSE entered the Camaldolese monastery in Florence at the age of fourteen, and lived and worked there for thirty years, becoming a great classical scholar and humanist. In 1431 he was made abbot general, with papal mandate to reform the congregation, an undertaking in which he was not altogether successful. In 1434 Pope Eugenius IV took refuge in Florence from the civil troubles of Rome, and made Ambrose one of his entourage, sending him to Basle to defend the Holy See against a partly hostile Council.

But it was during the Council of Florence that Ambrose came into his own. From the first, he was marked as the right spokesman for the Latins by his learning, his devotion to the pope, and his admirable spoken Greek. Eugene sent him to Venice to receive the Greek emperor, John VII Palaeologus and his brother Joseph, the patriarch of Constantinople. The emperor said that Ambrose was the Latins' best Greek scholar; and he and the great Bessarion, a Greek equally gifted, were entrusted with the drafting and presentation of *Laetentur coeli*, the short-lived agreement between East and West on such topics as "Filioque" and the papal plenitude of power. Unlike Bessarion, Ambrose was spared the spectacle of the collapse of the long-hoped for union and the widening of the rift; a few months after the conclusion of the Council he died.

He was a shrewd and close observer of the Florence scene, with great gifts as a diplomat; but perhaps his greatest gift in these negotiations was his undoubted charity, founded on knowledge, toward the Greeks and their cause. He was always generous in his estimate of others, Latin or Greek, and many of the Eastern delegation recognized him as a well-wisher and treated him as a friend.

Though Ambrose has never been officially beatified, there has always been a popular cultus among the people of Florence and the Camaldolese; and in these days of ecumenism, when the Catholic Church longs for reunion with her separated Oriental brethren and for all that that might bring about for the kingdom of God, he is very much a saint of the times.

Prayer for Unity

"That all may be one, even as you, Father, in me and I in you; that they also may be one in us, that the world may believe that you have sent me. And the glory that you have given me I have given them, that they may be one, even as we are one: I in them and you in me; that they may be perfected in unity, and that the world may know that you have sent me, and that you have loved them, even as you have loved me."

John 17:21-23

A. Dini-Traversari: *Ambrogio Traversari e i suoi tempi* (Florence, 1912).
J. Gill: *Personalities of the Council of Florence* (Oxford, 1964).
Tou makariou Ioannou tou Eukrata Leimon (PG, 87.3, coll. 2847-3112).

Albert of Louvain
Martyr

died 1192

St. Albert's sad history shows him an unwilling victim of the political interests which too often in the Middle Ages were allowed to treat the Church, her possessions, and her people as pawns in a game of power. He was the son of Duke Geoffrey III of Brabant, the brother of Duke Henry I; and he was the family's nominee for the rich bishopric of Liège, in the contest for it, one of many, between them and the rival ducal house of Hainault. Though he had been given a clerical education, he had for a time considered abandoning his status as a clerk and taking up arms, but soon he reverted to his profession in the Church. He was in his middle twenties when the see of Liége fell vacant, and he was elected to it, rather than the rival Hainault candidate, though the chroniclers suggest to us that the election was accompanied with a great show of military power by his relatives. The election was disputed, and the emperor, Henry VI, pronounced against both parties and instituted a candidate of his own, seemingly a simoniac and a man of unworthy life.

Albert's family were ready to wage war for his title to the bishopric, but he, concerned for his people, refused to allow this. He went in disguise to Rome to appeal, and Pope Celestine III pronounced in his favor; but, in fear of the emperor, the archbishop of Cologne would not ordain and consecrate him. Meanwhile, the emperor was swearing to exterminate Albert and his supporters. Albert remained in exile at Rheims, still hoping for peace and justice; but he was assassinated there, a deed for which later the

853

emperor had to do penance, while his creature, Lothaire, the rival bishop, was excommunicated and went into hiding.

The chroniclers' stories show us Albert as a truly noble man, bearing his griefs in resignation, caring always for others and never for himself.

A Saint at a Wedding Party

"They were lodged in one of the city's inns, and a citizen, a nobleman, gave a splendid wedding party to which everyone, citizens and strangers, was invited. All were expected to contribute to the entertainment, and the host pressed Albert and his companions to do so, asking if any of them could sing or play an instrument. His companions brought Albert forward, disguised as their servant, saying that he was a singer; and he, clad in shapeless garments, his face sweaty and begrimed, unrecognizable as the old Albert, handsome, dignified, well born, well bred, took the instrument which their host offered him, and like another David began to play and sing the song, *Young man, rejoice now in your youth.* Indeed his own youth was not long gone, for he was between twenty-five and thirty years of age, in the prime of his manhood and wisdom. Skilfully he plucked the strings and charmed the ears of his audience, a singer sweeter than Orpheus himself. All the wedding guests applauded him, but he was filled with sorrow, remembering the days of his own happiness; he refused the gift they offered him, and pretending that he had to go back to work for his masters, he returned to the inn where he could be alone."

A passage from The Life of Albert, Bishop of Liège

C. Heller, ed.: *Vita Alberti Episcopi Leodiensis* (Monumenta Germaniae Historica, Scriptores, 25, Hanover, 1880, pp. 135–68).

Cecilia
Martyr

died 2d or 3rd century

MANY OF THE details of the legend of St. Cecilia are so beautiful and so picturesque that there have been those who have resisted the contentions of scholars, during this last century, that almost all that we have been told about her has no basis in fact. Yet we must today concede, however reluctantly, that this is so.

For example, most informed people would surely know that she is regarded as the patroness of musicians because of her own gifts in their art; but this story rests upon a medieval misinterpretation of a passage in her *Passio* (the story of her martyrdom), which, correctly translated, reads: "The day came on which the bridal chamber was prepared, but, while they played upon musical instruments, she in her heart sang only to the Lord, saying 'May my heart and body remain unstained, that I may not be ruined.' " But this was misconstrued into meaning that Cecilia sang this prayer aloud, accompanying herself on musical instruments.

But even if the *Passio* had said this, it would be no evidence, for scholars are now agreed that it is unhistorical, of no value as evidence, and largely a fabrication from earlier sources dealing with other saints, made to provide a growing legend with what could pass for genuine documents. The story of her being forcibly wedded to a young man, and of persuading him, then his brothers, to take vows of virginity as she had done, seems to have been borrowed from Victor of Vita's history of the Vandal persecution in North Africa, where we read of two slaves, Martianus and Maxima, forcibly married although she had vowed her virginity to God. Martianus, and, later, his three brothers, follow her example; and they all take religious vows.

All visitors to the church of St. Cecilia in Trastevere are still told that this was Cecilia's private house, that during her three-day agony after she had been tormented there she willed it to the pope and asked that it be turned into a church, and that the marble statue by Maderna, showing the saint lying as if asleep, represents, as the sculptor's inscription claims, the exact appearance of her incorrupt body as it was rediscovered in the year 1599. But all these, the experts now assure us, are likewise fictions.

With what, then, are we left? We can be certain that from very early times veneration was paid to a Roman virgin-martyr called Cecilia. This is attested by the presence in the canon of the Roman Mass of her name among the women martyrs commemorated in the prayer "Nobis quoque peccatoribus," as also by the naming of her feast in the Gelasian and Gregorian Sacramentaries; and we know that on November 22, 545, Pope Vigilius was taken by surprise and captured in her church in Trastevere while celebrating the Mass of her day. All this points to a great veneration, long before spurious legends began to collect around her name, for one who had vowed her chaste body to the Lord, and had sealed the vow by giving her own life for God.

The Companions of the Lamb

"And I saw a Lamb who stood upon Mount Sion, and with him there were a hundred and forty-four thousand, having his name and the name of his Father written on their foreheads. And I heard a voice from heaven like the noise of many waters and the voice of great thunder; and the voice which I heard was like the voice of harpers, playing upon their harps. And they sang what sounded like a new song before the throne, and no one could sing this song except the hundred and forty-four thousand who were purchased from the earth. These are they who were not defiled with women; for they are virgins. And they follow the Lamb wherever he goes. They were purchased from among men, the first fruits to God and to the Lamb. And in their mouths there was found no lie, for they are without spot before the throne of God."

Revelation 14:1-5

H. Delehaye: *Étude sur le légendier romain* (Brussels, 1936).
L. Duchesne: *Le Liber Pontificalis, I* (Paris, 1955).

Clement I
Pope and Martyr

died about 99

OF ST. PETER'S two immediate successors as bishop of Rome, Linus and Cletus, we know nothing but their names; but we are much better informed about Cletus' successor, Clement. Irenaeus, writing in the last quarter of the second century, says that he had been a disciple of the apostles themselves, and was deeply imbued with their teaching. We know this also from another, most important source, Clement's own "Epistle to the Corinthians," from which we derive a very clear picture of the state of the Church at that time, both in Rome and in Corinth, of Clement's own moral stature and authority, and, most of all, of the unique place which the Roman Church enjoyed among the other Christian communities.

St. Clement, informed of the distressing state of affairs in Corinth, tells the Corinthian Christians in his Epistle to remember how Paul himself had reprehended their lawless and factious ways. Now, once again, there is schism among them; and, he implies, he has heard that they have driven out their lawfully-appointed ecclesiastical superiors. This is an intolerable state of affairs, for it inflicts a wound upon the Church, not only in Corinth but everywhere. "Your schism has perverted many, has thrown many into despair, has caused all of us to grieve." He laments their jealousies, ill-will, quarrellings and dissension; and he recalls to them their duty to maintain charity and peace, the true marks of the Church for which Peter and Paul, and, after them, immense multitudes in Rome have shed their blood.

In all this, Clement writes as a father, having authority over the Corinthians and ready to exercise it. He is sending legates to them whom he names; and they are to return to him as soon as possible with satisfactory assurances that his admonitions have been obeyed, and that the right rule of the Church there has been restored. But Clement is not merely peremptory: the tone of his long letter is truly fatherly, written in deep love for Christ and for those children of the Church which Christ has founded and entrusted to apostolic rulers for the good care and guidance of her children.

In this letter we see Clement clearly for what he is. Deeply versed in the Scriptures of both Testaments (though we do not know if he was of pagan or of Jewish ancestry), most strongly influenced by Pauline teaching, especially as it concerns the Church as the mystical body of Christ, learned and eloquent, he paints for us an inspiring self-portrait of a man great and powerful in the office divinely conferred upon him, gentle and loving in his exercise of it.

We do not know how Clement died, but it is reasonable to assume that like his three predecessors and so many of his successors in the next centuries, he was put to death. Few of the early popes ruled for longer than ten or twelve years, and to succeed to the see of Peter was to live in the certainty of an early and violent death. Such men walked daily in the company of Christ and His apostles; and of none of them was this more true than of Clement.

Prayer for the Church

"Lord, let your countenance shine on us for good in peace, that we may be protected by your strong hand and delivered from all sin by your uplifted arm, and deliver us from those who hate us unjustly. Give concord and peace to us and all the inhabitants of earth, as you gave it to our fathers, when they invoked you reverently in faith and truth, so that we may be saved, and grant that we may be obedient to your almighty and excellent name, and to our rulers and governors on earth. You, Lord, have given the authority of the Kingdom to them

through your all-powerful and unspeakable might, that we,
acknowledging the glory and honor given them by you, may
be subject to them, and in no way resist your will."

St. Clement's "Epistle to the Corinthians," chap. 60, 1

F. X. Glimm, ed. and trans.: *The Letter of St. Clement of Rome to the Corinthians*
(*The Fathers of the Church: The Apostolic Fathers,* New York, 1947).

John of the Cross
Doctor of the Church

died 1591

THE SPIRITUAL TEACHING of St. John of the Cross, as we have it in his four great mystical treatises, *The Ascent of Mount Carmel, The Dark Night of the Soul, The Spiritual Canticle,* and *The Living Flame of Love,* seems so sublime and esoteric as to have no relevance for any except those, and they are comparatively few, who are authentically called to the contemplative way of life in silence and solitude.

Yet when the Church celebrates in her liturgy the feast of the man who is now universally recognized as one of the most erudite and practiced teachers of the theology of the divine union ever given by God to His people, it is not his own extraordinary graces in prayer or the profundities of his mystical theology which she lauds. She speaks instead of his spirit of total self-renunciation and his truly remarkable love of Christ's Cross. And there is no Christian who is not called, by virtue of his baptism, to the same forgetfulness of self and the same love of the suffering Christ. It is appropriate that today so many should know of John of the Cross primarily through the *Crucifixion* of Salvador Dali. It was after one of his deepest mystical experiences that John sketched for posterity his crucified Lord overshadowing the world with love and compassion—the world that John knew, the men and women who so need God's love offered to them in Christ's suffering and death. "He loved me, and delivered Himself for me."

John, who was born at Fontiveros in Old Castile in 1542, took the habit of the Carmelite friars at Medina at the age of twenty-one. Immediately after his profession, permission was granted

861

to him to follow the primitive Carmelite rule in all its austerity, ignoring the many mitigations approved in the course of time and accepted in all friaries at this period.

After his studies, and his ordination to the priesthood in 1567, he felt a great desire to withdraw into complete solitude. But he met the great Teresa of Avila (*see* October 15), who had already begun the reform of women Carmelites, and she told him that God was calling him to a special holiness in the Order of Mount Carmel. Teresa asked him to assist her in the work of reform which the general of the Order had authorized. Presently with two companions he established the first monastery of discalced friars, under Teresa's directions, in a small and dilapidated house at Duruelo.

The holiness of John, and the fervor he inspired, soon spread; and Teresa was able, within three years, to establish four more discalced monasteries. And when she herself was commanded to take over as prioress of the unreformed house of the Incarnation at Avila, John became spiritual director.

But by now troubles were occurring between the reformed and unreformed convents and members of the Order, and John found himself in the thick of the fray. In 1577 he was ordered to return to his original, unreformed friary at Medina. When he refused to comply with his provincial's order, on the ground that he was responsible for the work of reform directly to the Holy See, he was removed by force from Avila and imprisoned in Toledo for nine months. At times he was treated with brutality, the object being to persuade him to abandon the reform; and during all this time he was not once allowed to say Mass, or to change his clothes.

Eventually he managed to escape, by what seem to be miraculous means, and he returned to the work of reform in more peaceful circumstances, a separate province for the discalced being formed in 1580.

But his sufferings were not yet over. After the death of St. Teresa, a dispute arose among the discalced themselves; some of them wished for complete separation from the brethren of the mitigated rule. Others, like John, followed a more moderate policy. His defense of the moderates at a chapter in 1591 led to his being stripped of the office of prior, and he was sent to the small and remote friary of La Peñuela. Even here he was not safe from the attacks and vilification of his brethren. Though seriously sick, he was ordered to leave La Peñuela. The journey aggravated his condition, and he died within three months, at the early age of forty-nine.

In the literary world, John of the Cross is reckoned as one of the greatest of Spanish poets. Critics have written of the passionate ardor of his poems, of their eloquence and their exquisite form. "The Spirit of God has passed through his poetry, beautifying and sanctifying it." His systematic treatises on mystical theology consist of line-by-line commentaries on his own poems, perhaps the most successful combination of the theoretical and practical (his poems represent his immediate attempts to record his mystical experience) in the history of the Church's spirituality. Yet through all his theological and scholastic systematization (he depends much for his teaching on St. Thomas Aquinas—see March 7) he never loses sight of his true concern, the ineffable love of God which is given to man through assimilations to the crucified Christ.

Ways of Attaining the Perfect Love of God

"Keep a strict control over your tongue and your thoughts; keep your affections constantly fixed on God. Feed your spirit on nothing except God. Cast out concern for all things; have peace and recollection in your heart. Maintain spiritual tranquillity in loving attentiveness to God, and, if it is necessary to speak, let it be with the same peace and tranquillity. Think constantly on eternal life, and on this truth, that they who are the humblest and poorest in spirit, and count themselves the least, shall enjoy the highest glory in God. Rejoice habitually in God; for He is your health. Know that it is good to suffer in any way for Him who is good."

Maxims of St. John of the Cross

E. Allison Peers, trans.: *The Complete Works of St. John of the Cross* (3 vols. in one, Westminster, Md., 1964).
Fr. Bruno: *St. John of the Cross* (New York, 1932).

Moses
Martyr

died 251

IN EVERY AGE of persecution there will be those who stand fast, ready to give their lives, but others who will weaken and then repent their inconstancy. The problem presented by such contrite apostates, the *lapsi,* and the attitude of St. Cyprian toward them, has already been described (*see* September 16). Cyprian's letters of encouragement to the Roman clergy at a time when they were living under the double trial of pagan persecution and grievous internal schism are our chief source of knowledge of the part played in these times by St. Moses.

His name suggests that he may have been of Jewish or African birth; but he was a Christian priest in Rome at the time of the Decian persecution and the beginning of the Novatian heresy and schism. During the persecution, Pope St. Fabian was martyred on January 20, A.D. 250, and for more than a year it was impossible to elect his successor. During this time, Moses, himself already in prison with many of his brother priests, seems to have acted as their leader, pursuing a policy of resolute defiance to their persecutors and of rigid maintenance of the Church's ancient disciplines until such time as a lawfully elected pope might wish to give other orders, especially on the question of the *lapsi.* This meant that in Rome, as in Africa, such apostates could be reconciled, but only after long canonical penances, unless they were in immediate danger of death. But there was great unrule; many lapsed Christians were claiming, often fraudulently, that those going to martyrdom had offered their deaths for their immediate reconciliation, and there were others maintaining that the Church had no power to absolve such apostasy.

During the year and more that the Holy See was vacant, Novatian seems to have taken it upon himself to act as spokesman for the Roman clergy in their dealings with other Churches, and to have urged changes in discipline, because of which Moses withdrew from communion with him. This we learn from the martyred Fabian's successor, Pope St. Cornelius; and it was Cornelius' election which brought the strife with Novatian to a head, and caused him to set himself up as an anti-pope.

In all his dealings, Moses received the approval and encouragement of Cyprian, who, writing to the clergy of Rome in 250, urging firmness and order upon them, says that he has received letters from Moses and his group "full of the strength of the gospel and the discipline of God's law." In the same year he wrote personally to Moses and some of his brethren, praising their courage and steadfastness in all these troubles. Their reply to this letter shows that they and many others are in prison, where they have been for long. Cyprian's letter has brought them comfort and strength, as they await martyrdom; and they rejoice to know of his own resoluteness in maintaining the Church's rule. From other letters we know that Cyprian is making the letters of this heroic band available to all who wish to copy and circulate them, so that the universal Church may know of their witness.

In late 251 or 252, writing to Antonian of Numidia, Cyprian speaks of Moses' death. Tradition says that he died, in prison, of the frightful sufferings entailed by imprisonment; and he has always been reckoned a martyr for the faith.

Encouragement to Persevere in Following Christ

"Truly those of you are blessed who have followed this path of glory, who have departed from this world, have finished their journey with courage and with faith, and now have received the embrace and the kiss of a Lord who rejoices at their coming. But your glory is no less, you who still do battle, you who are ready to follow where your great companions have gone, you, firm in a faith which cannot be changed or shaken, who show to God each day afresh the spectacle of your virtues. Your struggle is longer; and your crown will be the fairer."

Cyprian: Letter 37

L. Bayard, ed. and trans.: *Saint Cyprien: Correspondance* (2 vols., Paris, 1945–61).
Sister Rose Bernard Donna, trans.: *Saint Cyprian: Letters* (Washington, D.C., 1964).

Leonard Casanova of Port Maurice
Franciscan Friar of the Strict Reform

died 1751

PORT MAURICE, where St. Leonard Casanova was born in 1676, was then a part of the republic of Genoa. His father was the captain of a merchant ship; but in Rome there was a rich uncle to whom Leonard was sent for his education, first with private tutors, then at the Gregorian University. The uncle intended him for the practice of medicine, and when he learned that his nephew intended to join the Franciscans, he turned him out of the house. Leonard entered the monastery at Ponticelli at the age of twenty-one, and in 1703 he was ordained priest.

After several attempts to establish new houses (one in his home town, Port Maurice, where he met with vigorous resistance) dedicated, as was Ponticelli, to the "strict reform," he succeeded in Florence, where he became guardian, or superior, in 1715. In the nearby mountains, at Incontro, he also founded a retreat house, saying that he wished to make this "a novitiate for Paradise," with an even stricter regime.

He was in great demand as a missionary, especially in Rome, and at the age of sixty, in 1736, he was called there to become guardian of St. Bonaventure's; but after a year he was freed from this office, so that he could give all his time to apostolic work. In this he was able to penetrate every circle. He was director to the saintly Clementina Sobieski, wife of the Stuart pretender whom his adherents called "James III," and her son, Cardinal Henry Stuart, was after Leonard's death active in promoting his cause. By contrast, he was able to do great work among the wretched criminals condemned to the galleys, and he himself tells the story of the English ship moored in the Tiber whose crew sent for him to seek reconciliation with the Church after they had attended in Rome a mission service of his whose very words they could not understand.

He was sixty-eight years of age when he was sent on a mission to the island of Corsica, where he labored for six months to recall the inhabitants from their lawlessness and license, with, he feared, little success; and it was this last undertaking which helped to shorten his life. From the day when he, a young layman, had met two friars of the Strict Observance in the streets of Rome, and had discerned in their demeanor that total dedication to the work of God for which he longed himself, he had spent his whole life in the service and the preaching of the word.

The Presence of God

"Consider, as the faith teaches you, how God is in every place. God with His immensity fills Himself heaven and earth, and He is found in all His creatures, each one of which is nearer, closer, liker to God than it is to itself. God is at your right hand, God is at your left hand, God is above you, God is within you. You live in God, you move in God, you breathe in God, you are gathered up and lost in His vast embrace. God watches you always, He sees the depths of your heart, He knows what are your loves, your thoughts, He hears your words, perceives your needs, knows your name, takes account of your deeds, your thinking, your wishes. My soul does not need to go to heaven to find God."

A passage from The Way to Paradise

La Via del Paradiso del V.P.Leonardo da Porto Maurizio (Venice, 1803).
D. Devas: *St. Leonard of Port-Maurice* (London, 1920).

Bernardino of Fossa
Observant Friar Minor

died 1503

BLESSED BERNARDINO AMICI was born at Fossa, near Aquila, in 1420. He studied law, and graduated with the doctorate, at Perugia, but soon afterwards, at the age of twenty-five, he joined the house of Observant Franciscans in that city.

He gained a great reputation as a preacher of outstanding abilities; and he showed also great administrative abilities informed by a wonderful spirit of charity and prudence. He was given the unenviable task of acting as visitor for his Order in Dalmatia and Bosnia, where he found much dissension between the different national and language groups among the friars. Nonetheless, by his own personal abilities and example he succeeded in welding these disharmonious elements into a single and united province.

These rare qualities commended him to the Holy See, and twice he was to have been made bishop of Aquila; but on both occasions he was able to decline the see, so that he could continue working for the people and his Order as a simple friar.

His sanctity is well attested; his reputation as a scholar might be further enhanced, if his many historical works still unedited were published.

The Marks of Charity

"For though he was afflicted by a grave sickness, he received as a grace from the Lord that his habit was redolent of a wonderful fragrance, betraying no trace of his daily sufferings. By that the Lord wished us to know that there were in him so many marks of charity that he merited to be called by all the blossoming rose of love, a love which so shone from him that when he served as vicar of our province, it was not only the brethren who were his subjects, but poor laymen too, and everyone else he had dealings with, whom he consoled with fatherly affection. He showed to all such generous compassion, correcting them, exhorting them, giving them his own example of the true light, to abandon their strivings for the deceits of this world and to follow in the steps of their Maker, that he was rightly esteemed a true son of Francis."

From the Life *by his nephew Anthony Amici*

Acta Sanctorum, November, vol. iii.

Catherine Labouré
Sister of Charity of St. Vincent de Paul

died 1876

ST. CATHERINE LABOURÉ was the ninth child of a small farmer in Burgundy. She did not go to school, and though later she learned to read and write (though never to spell correctly), her lack of education may have helped to produce in her a certain inarticulacy. But that was not the only cause; those who knew her best in religion afterwards said that they had found her "down to earth and unemotional," "somewhat insignificant," "cold if not without feeling." That was her nature, and she chose what may truly be called "a life hidden in Mary." Few less likely recipients can be imagined for the extraordinary revelations which, we may believe, were granted to her.

After a good deal of opposition from her widowed father (to cure her of her notions he at one point sent her to work as a waitress in his brother's eating house in Paris, from which she ran away), she joined the Sisters of St. Vincent de Paul at Châtillon-sur-Seine. After her postulancy there, she went to a Paris house, and there, shortly after her arrival, began the famous series of apparitions of Our Lady.

These apparitions are commemorated in the "Miraculous Medal," now a devotion practiced throughout the world, and in the invocation "O Mary conceived without sin, pray for us who have recourse to thee"; and Catherine said that she received Our Lady's promise that whoever wore the medal "will receive great graces." Since 1830, countless people have claimed that these promises have been verified for them. Probably the most celebrated case, and one which did much to promote the devotion, was that of the rich young Jew, Alphonse Ratisbonne, who consented as an ill-tempered jest to accept a medal, and was, he claimed, given a vision of Our Lady in the church of Sant' Andrea della Frate in Rome. Another fruit of Catherine's experiences has been the foundation of the Association of the Children of Mary; and the devotional life of the world-wide Legion of Mary also owes much to her inspiration.

The Motherhood of Mary

"This maternity of Mary in the order of grace began with the consent which she gave in faith at the Annunciation and which she sustained without wavering beneath the Cross. This maternity will last without interruption until the eternal fulfillment of all the elect. For, taken up to heaven, she did not lay aside this saving role, but by her manifold acts of intercession continues to win for us gifts of eternal salvation."

The Second Vatican Council's *Constitution on the Church*, (*no. 62*)

E. Cassinari, trans. anon.: *Life of Blessed Catherine Labouré* (London, 1934).
E. Crapez, ed. and trans. anon.: *Venerable Sister Catherine Labouré* (London, 1920).

Denis Berthelot and Redemptus da Cunha
Martyrs

died 1638

IT WAS BY many strange turns of fortune that Blessed Denis and Blessed Redemptus came to die together for the faith in Sumatra. Denis was born Peter Berthelot in Honfleur in Normandy, into a family with the sea in its blood. As a young man he went to the East Indies, entered the service of the Portuguese in Malacca, and, as a pilot and highly accomplished cartographer (a set of very detailed and beautiful maps of various maritime countries in the Far East, signed by him, are preserved in the British Museum in London) he took part in numerous expeditions.

In 1635, when he was thirty-five, he met the prior of the house of Discalced Carmelites in Goa, and joined their community, taking the religious name of "Dionysius of the Nativity." Soon afterwards, the Portuguese asked for his services as pilot to an embassy which was being sent to the kingdom of Sumatra. The Carmelites agreed to this, and had him ordained priest so that he could also act as chaplain to the expedition. He was accompanied by "Redemptus of the Cross," Thomas Rodriguez da Cunha, a Portuguese who had been a soldier of fortune in India before becoming a Carmelite lay brother.

We may well imagine some of the motives which had led these two men to turn from the slaughter and the ruthless exploitation of the native peoples and their territories which marked the establishment in the East of British India and the other great European colonial empires, and to seek in the religious life a Christ-like way of bringing men to God. For that way they gave their lives.

As soon as the expedition landed its members were arrested and imprisoned. With others, Denis and Redemptus, who refused to apostatize, were cruelly put to death.

Teaching Christianity by Example

"It does not seem to me at all that the Christian Faith has up to now been shown and preached to the barbarians in such a way that they are obliged to profess it or else to be in sin. They cannot be obliged to believe unless the Faith is exhibited to them with logical persuasion; but I hear of no wonders or signs worked among them, nor even of the good example of lives lived according to religion. On the contrary, I hear of many scandals and atrocious crimes and much irreligion. How can men say that pagans are obliged to believe, when they are not being taught the Christian religion as it should be taught, through holiness?"

Francis de Vitoria, O.P.: De Indis, II

J. do Sacramento: *Chronica de Carmelitas Descalços,* ii (Lisbon, 1721).
P. Gontier: *Vie admirable de Pierre Berthelot* (Paris, 1917).

Andrew
Apostle

died 1st century

AMONG THE STORIES of the martyrdoms of the apostles, current in the Church from a very early date, one of the most moving is the "Passion of St. Andrew the Apostle," versions of which are extant in Ethiopian, Coptic, and other Oriental languages, as well as in Greek and Latin.

According to the legend, Andrew was preaching and teaching in Achaia, a Roman province of Asia Minor. There, in the city of Patras, he was brought before the proconsul Aegeates, accused of teaching a foolish and superstitious religion, since Jesus its leader had been crucified. Andrew was offered his freedom if he would renounce this foolishness; if not, he would be put to death. To this he replied: "Christ commanded never to give up preaching His word and leading to penitence those who stray, in season and out of season." He was then scourged, and crucified, not, however, by being nailed to a cross; instead, he was fastened by ropes, in order that he might suffer the longer. When he set eyes on the cross on which he was to die, he addressed these words to it: "Hail, holy and life-giving cross; you must now receive with joy the disciple of Him who once hung upon you. I come to you with a glad heart, for I know your secret, which gives life."

So Andrew was raised on his cross, and found it a convenient pulpit from which to preach. All that day and through the night the citizens of Patras came to hear him. On the next day, many

of them went to the court of Aegeates, proclaiming that Andrew
was a just man, innocent of any wickedness, one very dear to God,
a wise man who knew how to speak good things. Very reluctantly,
the proconsul yielded to their wishes, and went in person to set
Andrew free and bring him down from his cross. While Aegeates
was still afar off, Andrew began to pray to our Lord in a loud voice,
that he might be permitted to remain on the cross. And even as
he prayed, the Lord Jesus Christ received his spirit.

The agreement among the earliest Roman and Greek calendars
in assigning the martyrdom of Andrew to the same date, November
30, is certainly evidence for the fact of his martyrdom, though
many scholars repudiate all claims for the *Passio's* authenticity.
But even if such critics are wrong, the importance of the story
must take second place to what we know of the apostle from the
New Testament itself.

Andrew was the brother of Peter; they were partners with
Zebedee and his sons, James and John, in a fishing business on
the Sea of Galilee. We learn from John's Gospel that Andrew and
another (unnamed), disciples of John the Baptist, were with their
master when Jesus passed by. The Baptist said to them: "Behold
the Lamb of God!" Andrew and his companion immediately followed Jesus, were invited to join Him at the house where He was
living, "and they stayed with Him that day." The first thing Andrew did after this was to tell his brother: "We have found the
Messiah," and to bring him to Jesus (John 1:35–42).

Andrew, then, was Christ's first disciple, the first apostle to
recognize Him as the Messiah. He is a living reminder to us that
the Christian gospel and way of life involve first of all and essentially a reference to Christ's personal invitation: "Come and see."
It is perhaps because Andrew was the first to desire and to accept
the invitation that he is usually named first after Peter in the
apostolic catalogues; and in the prayer after the Our Father in
the Roman Canon of the Mass, he is specially named with Peter
and Paul.

St. Andrew is the patron saint of Russia and of Scotland.

Love of the Cross

"O sweetest cross, which I have desired so long, loved so well and sought so unceasingly, now at last you are made ready for my thirsting soul. It is from the Lord's own body that you have received your grace. Take me away from the world of men, and bring me into the presence of my Master. Let Him receive me from your arms; for it was by your means that He redeemed me."

Roman Breviary: Second Nocturn at Matins for the Feast of St. Andrew

John 1:35-42; Mark 1:14-20.
M. Bonnet, art.: "Martyrium Sancti Apostoli Andreae" (AB, 13, 1894, pp. 353-78).

Saints for December

A heart tenderly attached to the saints will give vent to its feelings in the language of hyperbole, just as an enthusiastic lover will call his future bride his adorable queen, without any intention of worshipping her as a goddess.

CARDINAL GIBBONS
The Faith of Our Fathers, 13

Edmund Campion
Martyr

died 1581

IN SIXTEENTH-CENTURY Europe, it took brave as well as intelligent men to see precisely how the foundations of the Catholic faith were being threatened, and on what points a stand needed to be taken. Nowhere was this more true than in England, where, after the Wars of the Roses, the need for strong government seemed far more important than theological hair-splitting between the temporal and spiritual power of the papacy vis-à-vis the king's authority. We know how long it took men of the caliber of Thomas More and John Fisher (*see* July 9) to decide that Henry VIII's declaration that he, not the pope, was the spiritual head of the Church in England was, in fact, a repudiation of faith in Christ. They alone and very few others, notably the Carthusian martyrs (*see* May 11) and the Augustinian John Stone (*see* May 12) stood out against the king. The rest, clergy and laity alike, accepted the fait accompli.

The principle that the ruler of the country dictated the religion of the country was similarly accepted in the return to the faith under Mary Tudor, and again when Elizabeth I reverted to her father's policies. Only a handful of men like Cardinal Allen, who saw that priests were needed to combat the new heresy and organized their training abroad, recognized that unless drastic action were taken, England would slip quietly away from the faith.

So it was that Allen persuaded Pope Gregory XIII to ask the Jesuits to lead a mission into England to support the activities of the seminary priests already working there in secret, and in the face of a growing impetus of violent opposition from the government. In 1580 Blessed Edmund Campion and Ralph Emerson landed at Dover, to begin the work which, Edmund was to say, was "of God; it cannot be withstood."

Campion, whose brilliant scholastic promise had been emphasized when he was appointed a fellow of St. John's College, Oxford, at the early age of seventeen, had attracted the special notice of Queen Elizabeth. He also enjoyed the marked patronage of courtiers like the earl of Leicester and prominent statesmen such as Robert Cecil, who looked to men of Campion's quality to establish the new ways of the Queen's religion in quiet order and decency at the universities of Oxford and Cambridge. So he was ordained deacon, in the Protestant rite, in 1568. But his study of the Fathers began to sow in his mind and heart the seeds of doubt. One of his closest friends, Gregory Martin, who had left Oxford to become tutor to the family of the duke of Norfolk, had already gone into voluntary exile for religion's sake; and soon Edmund himself began to be suspected of "Popish" sympathies. Gregory Martin wrote to him from Douai, where he had begun his work on the Catholic version of the Scriptures, begging him to declare himself openly and leave Oxford.

This he did in 1569; but he did not go immediately to Douai. By now it was clear to his friends that he was openly Catholic. He retired to Ireland, where he remained for a couple of years before the persecution consequent on Pius V's excommunication of Queen Elizabeth erupted. Then he became a fugitive, and finally made his way to Douai. For two years he studied theology and taught rhetoric there; and he also decided that he wished to become a Jesuit. After being accepted into the Society of Jesus in Rome, he went to Prague in 1574 to make his novitiate; and there he remained, studying and teaching, until 1580, being ordained priest in 1578.

When he received the call to go on the English mission, he seems soon to have become convinced that God was offering him the gift of martyrdom. When he stayed at Rheims for a time on his way home, he said to Cardinal Allen: "As for me, all is over. I

have made a free oblation of myself to His divine majesty, both
for life and death; and I hope He will give me grace and force
to perform. For this is all I desire."

The English government, with its efficient spy system, was of
course apprised of this Jesuit mission, the main purpose of which
was to restore the Mass and to reconcile the people of England to
their old allegiance to the Church. The government met this
"threat" by re-affirming the principle that it was high treason to
reconcile anyone or to be reconciled to the Catholic faith, and
imposed severe fines and imprisonment as the punishment for
hearing Mass. So the government sought to ruin financially and
to outlaw the Catholic community.

Campion, with Robert Persons, immediately set to work in
London by addressing a secret conference of leading Catholic
laymen and a few priests. They declared that it was not possible
for Catholics to compromise by attending the statutory Protestant
services. (It has been estimated that for a family of four adults
to live a regular Catholic life at this time would have cost in fines
well over a million dollars a year, granted that they were fortunate
enough to keep out of prison.) Next, Campion and Persons decided
that they would set down the purpose and aims of the Jesuit
mission, addressed to the queen's privy council, for clandestine
copying and distribution. Campion's apologia, which became
known as his "Brag," was so successful in putting fresh heart
into the persecuted Catholics that it set a new pattern of theological controversy. In between the secret missionary journeys
which he made throughout the country, he composed his "Ten
reasons for the confidence with which Edmund Campion offered
his adversaries to dispute on behalf of the faith." This, with the
maximum of difficulty, was printed, and copies were secretly
set out on the benches of the church of St. Mary in Oxford. It
included such provocative sentences as "There will come, Elizabeth, the day that will show thee clearly which have loved thee,
the Society of Jesus or the offspring of Luther."

The mission could not last. The government intensified its
searches, and Campion was finally arrested, after saying Mass

secretly at Lyford Grange, a house near Oxford, through the agency of a government spy who was able to pose as a Catholic. Great publicity was given to his capture and his first interrogation. Then there followed his four months' torture in the Tower of London (one can still see there the site of his cell, called "Little Ease" because it was impossible for a man to stand upright in it, or to lie at full length), and the conferences held when he was dreadfully weakened by long hours on the rack. Eventually he was condemned for treason, on perjured evidence. When asked if there were any cause why sentence of death should not be pronounced on him, he said: "In condemning us, you condemn all your own ancestors, all the ancient priests, bishops, and kings, all that was once the glory of England, the island of saints."

On the scaffold, when it was demanded that he should ask the queen's forgiveness, he replied: "Wherein have I offended her? In this I am innocent. This is my last speech; in this give me credit. I have and do pray for her."

The Price of Restoring the Faith

"Be it known to you that we have made a league, all the Jesuits in the world, whose succession and multitude must overreach all the practices of England, cheerfully to carry the cross you shall lay upon us, and never to despair of your recovery, while we have a man left to enjoy your Tyburn, or to be racked with your torments, or consumed with your prisons. The expense is reckoned, the enterprise is begun; it is of God, it cannot be withstood. So the faith was planted: so it must be restored."

From Campion's "Brag"

E. Waugh: *Edmund Campion* (New York, 1946).

John Ruysbroek
Augustinian Canon Regular

died 1381

THOUGH BLESSED JOHN RUYSBROEK lived and died in the obscurity which he sought, though he wrote in a Dutch which few but his own countrymen could or can understand, still he has, ever since his own days, been a potent influence upon those who, like him, have sought to know what is God's essence. Such great saints as John of the Cross (*see* November 24) knew him in Latin translations, which do little justice to the purity of his own language in expressing his thought, and do not always faithfully render that thought.

He was born in 1293 at Ruysbroek near Brussels, and went to be educated by his uncle, John Hinckaert, and by Francis van Coudenberg, who were canons of the collegiate church of St. Gudule in the city. He seems to have spent many years in pastoral work there, and in assiduous study, and he first came to notice as a vigorous opponent of the heresies of the mysterious "Bloemardinne," of whom we know little, except that she seems to have taught the false tenets of "the Brethren of the Free Spirit." It is evident that Ruysbroek's earliest and greatest work, *The Spiritual Espousals,* is in part occasioned by this campaign; though it is in no way polemic in nature, it sets out to oppose the "Brethren's" false teaching about "deification" and quietism with true doctrine about how man can, not by nature but by grace, become like to God, and what is the true nature of the rest in God which, in that likeness, the soul will find.

Ruysbroek is very far from being the simple, unlettered man some of his early biographers would have us believe; he is a master of sacred science, with extraordinary capacities for synthesis, for devotional writing, for conveying his own sublime experiences of divine wisdom.

When he was in his middle years and his uncle already an old man, the three companions withdrew from Brussels, and sought in the nearby forests a solitary place where they could live in prayer and contemplation. They settled at Groenendael, which presently was established as a house of canons regular. We know that many came to consult him there, and that he had contacts with contemplative houses and movements in the Low Countries and in Germany. His works were in constant demand; one of them, *The Kingdom of Lovers*, was copied by a scribe at Groenendael and transmitted to the Carthusians at Herne, even though its author had forbidden its publication as too difficult for the general public. When, to his perturbation, Ruysbroek found that the Herne Charterhouse had read it and was puzzled by it, he wrote for them a simpler exposition of his teaching, *The Little Book of Enlightenment*; and another of his shorter works, *The Book of the Sparkling Stone* (sometimes called *The Treatise of Perfection of the Sons of God*) is a minor masterpiece comparable with the *Espousals*.

Ruysbroek's spiritual insights helped him to synthesize Augustine's teaching on man's reflection of the divine nature with what he had learned, chiefly from pseudo-Denis, about *regiratio*, the eternal cycle of drawing close to God and then receding from Him through which the soul moves. His teachings gave the complete answer to false quietism, with their exposition of the soul's threefold life of action, and of contemplation, and of union with and rest in God. Blessed John is always insistent that the chief means to this three-fold life is the "common way," the sacramental life of grace.

Seeking and Finding Union with God

"For when we proceed out of ourselves into darkness, into a state unfathomable and without manner, then always there shines the single ray of the brightness of God, and there we find our foundation, and it draws us out of ourselves, and we are beyond being, and sunk deep in love. And this sinking-down in love must always of necessity lead us on to the exercise, without manner, of love; for love can never be idle, but at all times it longs to see and taste all the immeasurable riches hidden in its depths. This is a hunger that can never be sated; the more it has, the more it lacks, and ever it swims against the stream. We cannot leave it, we cannot have it; we cannot forsake it, we cannot attain it, we cannot speak of it nor can we conceal it, for it is beyond reason and understanding, far exalted above all created being. And so it is unattainable and indescribable; but if we look into our innermost selves, there we feel the Spirit of God driving and forcing us in the impatience of love. And we must look above ourselves, and there we feel the Spirit of God drawing us out of ourselves into His being, and annihilating us, there, in that love beyond being where we are one with Him, that love we possess more deeply and more fully than any other thing."

The Book of the Sparkling Stone

E. Colledge, trans.: *The Spiritual Espousals* (New York, 1953).

E. Colledge, ed. and trans.: *Mediaeval Netherlands Religious Literature* (New York, 1965).

E. Colledge, art.: "Ruysbroek, Jan van, Bl." (NCE, 12, pp. 763–65).

Francis Xavier
Jesuit Missionary

died 1552

EARLY IN 1552, St. Francis Xavier wrote to Ignatius Loyola (*see* July 31), his friend and superior general, the last of his missionary letters of information. In the course of it he said: "My true Father, just now when I landed in Malacca from Japan, I received a letter from your holy charity; and God our Lord knows how consoled my soul was to have news of your life and health. And among other consoling words in your letter I read the concluding ones: 'All yours without the possibility of at any time forgetting you, Ignatius.' And these words I read, as I now write them, with tears, recalling the old days, and the great love I always bore you and still have for you."

Xavier owed his apostolic and missionary vocation and endeavor, under God, to Ignatius. Like his superior, he came from the north of Spain. The castle of Xavier is not far from Pamplona where Ignatius received the wound which changed the course of his (and Xavier's) life. At the age of eighteen, he was sent to complete his education at the University of Paris, where he met Ignatius for the first time. He took the degree of Master of Arts in 1530, and began to teach philosophy at Beauvais, a college.

It would appear that he had before him a highly promising academic or ecclesiastical career; and it was some time before he succumbed to the persuasion of Ignatius, who tirelessly repeated to him: "Master Francis, what profit is it to a man if he gain the whole world, and lose his soul?" Finally, he made the *Spiritual Exercises* under the direction of Ignatius, and joined the little group who together vowed poverty, chastity, and apostolic service, according to the directions of the pope, at Montmartre in 1534.

With his companions, Xavier was ordained priest in Venice three years later, and had his first taste of preaching and evangelizing in the university towns of northern Italy. With Ignatius and the rest of the infant Society of Jesus he worked in Italy until 1540, when Ignatius, at the request of the Portuguese king, sent Xavier and Simon Rodriguez on the first Jesuit missionary expedition to the East Indies.

Delayed in Lisbon for eight months, they lodged at a hospital in order to attend to the physical and spiritual needs of the sick. With this as base, they catechized throughout the city, spending Sundays and holidays preaching and hearing confessions at the court of John III. Xavier eventually sailed with the Portuguese fleet; but the king detained Rodriguez, to continue their work in Lisbon. So it was that Xavier arrived at Goa in 1541, thirteen months after leaving Lisbon, having instructed and catechized the crews of all five ships on the voyage and looked after the many sick.

As with St. Paul, so with Xavier: it is impossible without a map, or in a few words, to describe his incredible missionary journeys. Xavier's main problem as a missioner in Goa was the usual one, the scandal caused by the greed and licentiousness of the nominal Christians working in the colony for their own profit. He turned his attention first to these Europeans, shaming them into marrying their native concubines, teaching and exhorting their children, and caring for the afflicted, especially the many lepers.

It was from Goa that he first embarked to preach along the Paravas' fishery coast, where there were many who had over the centuries retained vestiges of Christianity. Wherever he went, he lived with the poorest people, sharing their food and rough accommodation. Very often he had no time to sleep or even to say his breviary; but he was filled always with God's presence and joy. Speaking obliquely of himself, he wrote: "I am accustomed often to hear one laboring in this vineyard cry out to God: 'O my God, do not give me so much joy in this life; or if in your mercy you are determined to heap it upon me, take me altogether to yourself.' "

Ceylon, the Moluccan islands, the straits of Malacca, Japan: all were evangelized by Xavier in ten short years. Mission stations were set up, and more and more Jesuits began to arrive from Europe to work with and to be guided by him. In 1548 he established a novitiate and a house of studies in Goa, where there was soon a flourishing college. He learned enough Japanese to preach to simple folk, to instruct, and to baptize, and to establish stations for those who were to follow him.

China at this time was closed to all foreigners, but Xavier hoped to land there secretly with one other Jesuit and a young Chinese servant. They came ashore on Sancian, an island near the mouth of the river Canton, in August, 1552. There he provided himself with an interpreter, and negotiated with a Chinese merchant to land him by night at some port of the Canton province. But before his plans could fructify, he fell sick of a violent fever, with no possibility of medical help. After two weeks of suffering, he died on December 3. He was only forty-six, but his immense labors had inevitably taken their toll.

O God I Love Thee

"My God, I love thee; not because
I hope for heav'n thereby,
Nor yet because who love thee not
Are lost eternally.

Thou, o my Jesus, thou didst me
Upon the Cross embrace;
For me didst bear the nails and spear
And manifold disgrace,

And grief and torments numberless,
And sweat of agony;
Yea death itself, and all for one
Who was thy enemy.

Then why, most loving Jesu Christ,
Should I not love thee well,
Not for the sake of winning heav'n
Or of escaping hell;

Not for the hope of gaining aught,
Not seeking a reward;
But as thyself hast loved me,
O ever-loving Lord.

So do I love thee, and will love,
Who such a love hast show'd,
Only because thou art my King,
Because thou art my God."

    St. Francis Xavier: O Deus ego amo te, *trans. E. Caswall*

J. Brodrick: *St. Francis Xavier* (London, 1956).

Peter Chrysologus
Archbishop and Doctor of the Church

died about 450

St. Peter Chrysologus, "of the golden words," was born in Italy, at Imola, and there educated and ordained deacon by the bishop Cornelius. The legend is that Cornelius, accompanied by Peter, went to Rome to seek ratification from Pope St. Sixtus III of the city of Ravenna's choice of a new archbishop, but that the pope, who had already been warned in a vision, refused the city's candidate and chose instead the young deacon Peter.

After some first difficulties, he was gladly accepted by the citizens of Ravenna, and by the dowager empress and her son the emperor, Valentinian II, whose imperial seat Ravenna was; and we also know of the high esteem in which he was held by Pope St. Leo the Great.

Peter was much occupied in the repression of paganism and in the reconciliation of heretics. He had a great love of pastoral work, and won fame as a preacher, partly because, contrary to the customs of those days, he was, as those of his genuine homilies which survive show, an outstanding exponent of the five-minute sermon. He never tired of preaching devotion to Christ in the Eucharist, and, again unusually for his times, was a great advocate of frequent communion. But he is remembered today, more than for any other quality, for his passionate care for the peace and unity of the Church.

Peace

"My dearest brothers and sisters, the Evangelist says: 'Blessed are the peaceable, for they will be called the sons of God.'

Justly do the Christian virtues flourish in a man who possesses the singlemindedness of Christian peace, nor shall anyone be called 'a son of God' unless he be first called 'peaceable.' My dearest ones, it is peace which takes away our servitude and gives us the title of free-born men, it is peace which gives us a new standing before God, in whose eyes slaves become sons and serfs beloved children. Peace among brothers is the will of God, it is the joy of Christ, the perfection of holiness, the rule of justice, the teacher of wisdom, the guardian of morality, and a way of life praiseworthy in all things. Peace is the object of every prayer, easy to ask for, easy to pursue, and the total fulfillment of every wish. Peace is the mother of love, the bond of concord, and the open sign of a pure mind asking for itself of God what is His will."

Peter Chrysologus: Sermon 53

Vita S. Petri Chrysologi (PL, 52, coll. 13-20).
Sermones (*ibid.*, coll. 188-680).

John Almond
Martyr

died 1612

WHEN BLESSED JOHN ALMOND in 1601 was completing his theological studies in Rome, he was called upon "publicly to sustain theses of universal divinity, which he did with great applause." It is recorded that his defense was so magnificent that the great Cardinal Baronius came to him and publicly embraced him.

When this priest and scholar was next engaged in public debate, it was in England in 1612; and his disputant was the bishop of London, Dr. King. The chief difference was that John was on trial for his life.

Born in Allerton, near Liverpool, about 1577, John Almond was almost certainly a cradle-Catholic. When he was eight years old he went to Ireland, doubtless to be educated at one of the religious houses still remaining there. We know nothing more of his early life; but when he arrived in Rome (he was just twenty), he was already a tonsured cleric. After four years of study, he was ordained in 1601, and left for England the following year.

The Catholic Church in England was in very sore straits at the time. Not only was the Elizabethan security system highly organized against Catholics, and especially priests, but quarrels and divisions had broken out among the priests themselves, and these the government was anxious to foment. Amidst the greatest difficulties and the closest possible secrecy, Almond worked for five years, eluding the pursuivants by constant changing of his clothing and his name. A report sent to Rome at the time says of him that "the great success of his apostolate spread abroad, and the king's ministers, filled with rage and hatred, set upon this saintly priest." We know that he was captured and imprisoned at this time, in 1607; but he was either released, or managed to escape. We hear of him next in Staffordshire, where he signed a petition, sent to the Holy See, for a bishop to be appointed for English Catholics.

Bishop Challoner, in his *Memoirs of Missionary Priests,* provides us with this description of Almond's character and apostolate: "He exercised a holy life with all sincerity and a singular good content to those that knew him, and worthily deserved a good opinion both of his learning and sanctity of life; a reprover of sin, a good example to follow; of an ingenious and acute understanding, sharp and apprehensive in his conceits and answers, yet complete with modesty. Full of courage, and ready to suffer for Christ that suffered for him. In his conversation mild, learned and persuasive, and worthy to be remembered of those that did converse with him."

His interrogation by the bishop of London, when he was captured again in 1612, certainly bears out Challoner's praise of his "ingenious and acute understanding." Almond himself recorded the debate, which so impressed his interrogator that he visited Almond in prison in order to continue their discussion. A fellow priest, one who knew and worked with Almond, later wrote that the interrogator, Bishop King, was converted on his death bed, and died with a prayer to the martyr on his lips.

John was at last brought to trial for being a priest, though no evidence was forthcoming. "For being a priest they sentenced him, as a traitor to king and country, to be hanged, drawn and quartered alive." "Almond himself," says an eye witness, "was overjoyed, for he burned with longing to suffer for the love of Jesus Christ."

When the hangman put the rope around his neck, he blessed himself, saying, in Latin, "Into your hands, O Lord, I commend my spirit. Redeem me, Lord God of truth. Jesus, Jesus, Jesus, be to me a Savior."

A Penitent's Prayer to a Martyr

"O happy Almond . . . in thy blood, even in thy blood did I wash my hands; it was I that did further thy death. Be thou, o blessed saint, who now seest and hearest me . . . out of thine angelic charity, as propitious to pray for the remitting of that crying sin, as I am ready to acknowledge the sin; and let thy blood not resemble the blood of Abel, which cried for revenge against his brother, but rather the blood of Christ, which prayed for pardon against His crucifiers."

Prayer attributed to Bishop King

W. J. Steele: *Blessed John Almond, Martyr of Liverpool* (London, 1962).

Nicholas of Bari
Bishop

died about 342

THERE ARE FEW saints in all the calendar who have been paid wider or greater honors than Nicholas; yet we can be sure of very little about him, except that he was bishop of Myra in the province of Lycia in Asia Minor, in which province he seems to have been born, and that, dying in Myra, he was buried there. We have no trustworthy evidence for even the more credible of the innumerable legends associated with his name: that he suffered in the Diocletian persecution, for example, or that he was present at the Council of Nicea.

Yet these legends repay our study, for they witness to enduring Christian values and to men's veneration of them. Thus, he is the kindly spirit who on the eve of his feast, December 5, secretly rewards good children, the "Sinte Klaas" of popular Dutch tales who, transferred to Christmas Eve, has become "Santa Claus." The hagiographers tell us that this story originated in the much older and very beautiful legend of how Nicholas, as a rich young layman, full of grief to hear that his ruined neighbor proposed to introduce his daughters, whom he could not support, to a life of prostitution, secretly endowed each of the three girls with a bag of gold as her dowry.

In the West, one constantly-repeated story is that of the three children, murdered by an innkeeper and pickled in brine, then miraculously restored to life by the prayers of the saint. This too, we are told, is a distortion of the earliest form, in which the bishop, knowing that the tyrant of Myra has accepted a bribe to condemn to death three innocent men, rescues them, and when, later, three imperial officers who had been witnesses of this and were themselves in the same plight invoked his help, he appeared in a dream to the Emperor Constantine and ordered him to release them.

Then there is the narrative, especially beloved of medieval painters, of how a witch (in some versions identified with the goddess Diana, jealous of the worship paid to Christ in Nicholas' cathedral) tricks sailors into carrying a destructive charm to place in the cathedral by stealth. Here, undoubtedly, we have an elaboration of earlier allusions to Nicholas' fight to suppress paganism in his diocese.

Patron of children, of sailors, of the ill-used and oppressed, Nicholas' legendary figure became the center of the aspirations and the cries for help of peoples robbed of justice, lacking humane treatment, living lives of danger and hardship. Today we may laugh, not altogether kindly, at the financial acumen shown by the city of Bari in despoiling the Saracen invaders of Myra of Nicholas' relics under the noses of their Venetian rivals; but Christian pilgrims of every age, to Myra or to Bari, have believed that in Bishop Nicholas they have found a kind and powerful intercessor before God's throne.

The Legend of the Witch's Charm

"Once some sailors came from far-off lands to blessed Nicholas to be strengthened by his healing benediction. Those at home had given them pious offerings to bring with them, and among them was a glass vessel containing oil, which a certain woman, feigning great devotion, had put into their hands, asking them for the good of her soul to anoint with this oil, which, she said, was the sort used for lights to adorn churches, the walls of Nicholas' cathedral. But his prophetic spirit enabled the man of God to discern that this was an evil wile of the devil, no holy work at all, and he ordered the sailors, so soon as they had received his blessing, to sail back on the course they had come by and to throw into the sea the object they had been given. They were able to tell what would have happened if they had anointed the church's walls with this oil . . . for when they threw the vessel into the sea, a fearful fire began to spread upon the waves in every direction; and had they not obeyed the order of the man of God and sailed away with all speed, there is little doubt that the sailors themselves would have been burned up by this devilish deceit."

From a Vita Sancti Nycholai

De S. Nicolao Myrensi (AB, 2, 1883, pp. 143–56).
C. W. Jones: *The Saint Nicholas Liturgy and its Literary Relationships* (Berkeley and Los Angeles, 1963).

Ambrose
Bishop and Doctor of the Church

died 397

THE PART PLAYED by St. Ambrose in the lives of Augustine (*see* August 28) and his mother, Monica (*see* May 4), has already been described; and he would merit the eternal recollection of the Church, if for nothing else, for having helped to bring Augustine to the sacrament of baptism. But they were very different men, and their careers had been quite unalike. According to the custom of their age, to us strange, Ambrose, like Augustine, was not baptized in his infancy or youth; but he had always responded to his mother's holy influence, and as a child and a young man was filled with a very pure love of God. Though he had been born in Gaul, where his father was on government service, his mother, early widowed, took him to Rome, where he received an excellent education in sacred and secular subjects.

He himself entered the imperial service, and was in Milan, occupied with the government of Emilia and Liguria, when he had to help to supervise the election to the vacant bishopric of the city. The lawful bishop, St. Denis, had died in exile, and an Arian pretender to the see, who had been grievously oppressing the orthodox Christians, had also just died, leaving the way open for the nomination of a Christian successor. But the proceedings were factious and disorderly, and were only brought to an end when the people, prompted, no doubt, by the piety, eloquence and fervor of the young Ambrose, were moved to declare with one voice that he should be their new bishop. His protests were unavailing; he was compelled to receive baptism and all the necessary orders, and to take charge as the bishop of Milan.

The rest of his life showed how well his people had chosen. He became a great leader of the Church, at a time when she was sorely needing great leaders. Paganism still had not disappeared, and everywhere the Christians were encountering a new danger in the usurpations and oppressions of the Arians. Against them and their protectors Ambrose fought valiantly. Justina, the mother of the Emperor Valentinian II, herself an Arian, tried to overbear the bishop and restore her co-religionists, to their position of favor in Milan, but without success. Valentinian and his successor, Theodosius, accepted Ambrose's rulings and guidance in all matters which concerned the Church.

Augustine had been attracted to Ambrose, despite himself, by his wonderful eloquence. Ambrose had a deep love of classical Latin literature, and especially of the poet Virgil; and all his writings which have survived show him as a master of the Latin tongue. But he excelled as a Scripture scholar, and in the West was equalled by only Augustine himself as an expositor of the "senses" of the Bible, of the deeper meanings hidden beneath the merely literal sense. He was also a most talented letter-writer, an occupation which, he confesses, he loved; and it is from his letters that we gain much of our knowledge of the man and his mind.

For Ambrose, the Church is all. She is God's promise of life to His people, the chosen instrument of their salvation, and, outside the Church, there can be neither salvation nor life. To separate oneself, as the Arians had done, from the Church, to deny the authority of the see of Peter, to deflect from the apostolic faith which the Roman Church had preserved in utter purity, is to cut oneself off from God and be deprived of His Holy Spirit; and this Ambrose never wearied of proclaiming.

One other gift of Ambrose must not be forgotten: he was one of the greatest Latin hymn-writers of all ages. When we discount the apocryphal stories (such as that which tells of how he and Augustine spontaneously composed and recited the *Te Deum* on the occasion of Augustine's baptism), when we disregard the hymns falsely attributed to his pen, still we are left with a small body of undoubtedly authentic poems which will be sung, in Latin or in translations, so long as the Church on earth still lifts up its voice in the praise of God.

Christmas Hymn

"O come, Redeemer of the earth,
Show to the world thy virgin birth!
Let age to age the wonder tell;
Such birth, O God, beseems thee well.

No earthly father thou dost own;
By God's o'ershadowing alone
The Word made flesh to man is come,
The fair fruit of a mother's womb.

A maiden pure and undefiled
Is by the Spirit great with child;
Like standard fair, her virtues tell
'Tis God within her deigns to dwell.

Forth from His chamber cometh He,
The court and bower of chastity;
Henceforth in two-fold substance one,
A giant glad His course to run.

From God the Father He proceeds,
To God the Father back He speeds;
Runs out His course to death and hell,
Returns on God's high throne to dwell."

> *Ambrose:* "Veni, redemptor gentium"; *translation by the compilers of the* Historical Edition of Hymns, Ancient and Modern

PL, 14–17.
A. Largent, art.: "Ambroise" (DTC, 1, coll. 942–51).

Romaric
Abbot

died 653

St. Romaric is one of those who inherited and strengthened the great monastic traditions brought to the European continent by the Irish missionaries of the sixth and seventh centuries who left their own country to bring to other lands the learning and the holiness for which the monasteries of Ireland were pre-eminent in the West.

In 591 Columban was sent by Comgall on such an enterprise. He was fearless in his attacks upon the state of affairs he found in France, degenerate clergy, an immoral court and many corrupt local customs; in the end he was driven out, and settled and died at Bobbio in Italy. But still he had been able to achieve much among the Franks; and, especially, he left behind him one of the greatest and most enduring of the Irish monasteries, at Luxeuil, which he had built on the site of a Roman fort.

Columban's fortunes, and those of his successors, were deeply involved in the constant strife between the several kingdoms of the Merovingian dynasty founded by Clovis. One of the dominating figures of the epoch was Brunehilde, a Visigothic princess from Spain who had married Sigebert, king of Austrasia, in the eastern part of the empire. So many different accounts of her have come down to us, from her supporters and her enemies, that it is hard to assess her true character; but it is evident that she was an able and ruthless despot, who after her husband's death ruled the kingdom as regent for her son, grandsons, and greatgrandsons, until she was violently overthrown and put to death. Columban had incurred her enmity, and it was for this that he had had to leave the lands of the Franks.

The father of Romaric had also been one of her political opponents, and had lost both life and lands; but his son had nonetheless made his way in the world, and become a rich and powerful member of the court of Clotaire II. Then he met with Amatus, one of Columban's spiritual sons, who encouraged him to abandon his possessions, to leave the world, and to enter Luxeuil. Later, Romaric accompanied Amatus when a new foundation, a daughter house, was made at Remiremont; of this house Amatus was the first abbot and Romaric the second.

At the end of his life, Romaric was held in such veneration for his sanctity that he was able to impose a peaceful settlement of the differences between King Dagobert of Austrasia and those who were threatening his throne. This shows well how the Church had gained prestige and influence in a short period, and how Columban and his successors had labored to teach Christian principles and life to men until then dedicated to violence and lawlessness. The Church which we in the West have inherited has been built, under God, by many different cultures and nations, and in it few influences have been more potent than that of the Irish saints who, in the words of an Anglo-Saxon chronicler, left their home country "because they wished to dwell in strange lands for the love of God."

The Master Becomes the Servant

"In the course of time he [Romaric] came to be regarded as one of King Clotaire's first courtiers; but God, whose ways men cannot speak of, seeing His warrior fighting so valiantly, but for the spoils of this dark world, willed him to battle in the armies of light. So He brought to him that holy man Amatus, whom He called from his solitary dwelling. No more was needed. When he had found Romaric, he urged him to humble himself, to give his possessions to the poor, to lay up his treasure in heaven, and to direct his life to more perfect ends. When Romaric heard his words, he seemed to be wholly filled with these godly aspirations. Much of his fortune he brought with him as a gift to Luxeuil, much he had already used to give his serfs their freedom; and so he took upon himself to serve humility and obedience for Christ's sake. Many of his former slaves took the tonsure with him, and he who formerly was their mighty master made himself their servant now."

From an early Life

B. Krusch, ed.: *Vita Sancti Romarici Confessoris atque Abbatis* (Monumenta Germaniae Historica, Scriptores Rerum Merovingicarum, 4, Hanover and Leipzig, 1902, pp. 221–25).

Peter Fourier
Canon Regular of St. Augustine

died 1640

ST. PETER FOURIER was born in Lorraine in 1565; after his university studies, he taught for a short while, until at the age of twenty, he joined the Augustinian canons regular of Chaumousey. After further studies he became procurator, and was also in charge of the parish church served by the house. It was a lax and undisciplined one, and its members ridiculed his efforts to recall them to any sense of their religious responsibilities. He persisted, and was then offered charge of one of the abbey's distant parishes, a well-known device for getting rid of troublesome and over-zealous members of a community. He accepted this, and went to Mattaincourt, a village in the Vosges, where he worked for thirty years.

On arrival he found an appalling state of affairs, the district riddled with Calvinism, and many of his own people sunk in depravity. He set about putting things to rights; and an early diagnosis was that children ceased to come to Mass and receive the sacraments because they were not properly educated, in the faith or in general subjects, in their homes or elsewhere. Free education must be available, and this he set about providing. The boys' school he first opened was a failure (he was never to realize his ambitions in this field, partly because Rome then considered that teaching secular subjects was not fit work for priests); but he persisted with a girls' school, helped by a small band of women volunteers. He had many original ideas, on pedagogy as on other topics. He insisted that Protestant children be received if they applied, and, more than that, kindly treated by their teachers and their schoolmates. Later, when he began to conduct missions, he always stressed that if his hearers wanted to recall Protestant districts to the faith, they must begin by reforming themselves.

The new institute of nuns which he formed was given papal approbation in 1616 as Augustinian canonesses regular, when they were allowed to take a fourth vow, that of dedicating themselves to the cause of free education. He reformed houses of canons in Lorraine, and united them into one congregation, of which he became superior; but his wish for them to undertake work similar to that of his nuns was not in his lifetime fulfilled.

All that we read of Peter conveys to us the attraction of a sincere and dedicated realist, seeing problems for what they are, going to work to solve them in the first place by his own efforts and example.

A Servant of the People of God

"When he buried the dead, instead of the candles which used to be offered he accepted bread and wine, which were then distributed at the church door for the dead person's intention. It was easy for him to put the wellbeing of God's people before his own interests. For them, his body was all heart, his heart all fire, a fire which burned to console the wretched; and he had a special compassion for merchants and tradesmen who had fallen on hard times through bad business or theft. Love makes men wise; and he had the idea of starting a fund to put such people on their feet again; he called it 'St. Epure's Burse,' and into it he used to put gifts, pious legacies, fines, and other such acquisitions. If a man were in debt and in risk of being disgraced, he would receive from the burse the means of starting in business again, on condition that if he prospered he would repay the loan."

From Jean Bedel's Life of St. Peter Fourier

Jean Bedel: *La Vie du Très-Révérend Père Pierre Fourier* (Mirecourt, 1869).

Gregory III
Pope

died 741

HINDSIGHT MAY SUGGEST to us today that the endowing of the
Church in Italy with great territories, and the emergence of the
popes as temporal as well as spiritual rulers, did western Christianity untold harm. Yet the careers of popes such as St. Gregory III
show us that men in his historical situation had to choose between
governing with a strong hand, by force of arms if necessary, and
abandoning their peoples to those who would have enslaved them
and abolished the practice of the faith of the Roman Church.

St. Gregory III succeeded Gregory II under dramatic circumstances. He was a young Syrian, well known in Rome, above all
for his holiness of life, who was among the many clerics attending
the obsequies of the dead pope; and the people acclaimed him,
demanded that he be made pope, and installed him in the See of
Peter, virtually by force.

At once he inherited his predecessor's woes. The first of these
was the determined attack which by Byzantine emperor, Leo III,
the "Isaurian," was organizing against the papacy. The outward marks and the occasion of this attack was the "Iconoclastic,"
"image-breaking" controversy. The emperor claimed that the veneration given to holy images and pictures was in itself a form of
idolatry, that it led to much superstition, and that it was the chief
obstacle to the conversion of great numbers of Moslems and
Jews. Accordingly, he was having all such images in the East
destroyed, wherever his word prevailed, and he sent emissaries
to Rome demanding that the same be done there, and that a general council be called to impose his rules upon the universal

Church. But it is plain that iconoclasm was the mere pretext for this hostility, and that what Leo really desired was the transfer of the central power of the Church from Rome to Byzantium, where it would be exercised by the puppet patriarchs of Constantinople, taking orders from the emperor. At one point Leo became so deluded that he claimed that he could, and would, rule as emperor and pope in one.

Against this kind of onslaught Gregory had no option but to resist. This he did manfully, insisting that piety and true doctrine alone inspired the veneration of images, and that those who considered it idolatry were themselves promoting false doctrine. As a silent witness to this, he restored and adorned with sacred images the "Confession" in St. Peter's, as fragments of inscriptions still testify.

Gregory was most active in promoting the apostolates of St. Boniface (*see* June 5) and St. Willibald among the pagan Saxons. His letters to Boniface and the Saxons show him to be a truly apostolic man, as anxious to make the name of Christ known among the Gentiles as to preserve the Church in its more ancient homes.

The end of his life was darkened by a new threat to the Italian territories for which he was responsible, the territories of the Lombards, the Germanic people who had settled in northern Italy. Gregory did all he could to put the city of Rome into a state in which it could be defended, and he appealed for help to the Franks; but when the danger was at its height he died, and was buried in St. Peter's in a chapel he had built.

He was venerated by the Romans for the qualities they had discerned in him when they had chosen him as pope: his holiness, his learning, his militant love for the Church, and his compassion for all those in need of his protection.

The Duty of Bishops

"The practices and doctrines of the heathens, of Britons who come to you, of false, heretical and adulterous priests wheresoever they may come from, you are to reject, prohibit, and cast away from you. The people entrusted to you by God you are to instruct with kindly admonition and turn them absolutely away from sacrifices to the dead. According to the teaching of our afore-mentioned fellow-priest (Boniface), make haste so to hold fast the Catholic and apostolic faith . . . that in the day of the coming of Christ Jesus you may be worthy to stand before His judgement seat, saying: 'Lo, here are we with the children thou hast given us; we have not lost a single one of them.'"

Gregory to the Saxon bishops

E. Emerton, ed. and trans.: *The Letters of Saint Boniface* (New York, 1940).

Peter Tecelano of Siena
Franciscan Tertiary

died 1289

"HAPPY MEN HAVE NO HISTORY"; and had it not been for the veneration paid to Peter Tecelano as a saint whose prayers went very swiftly to God, we might today know nothing of him. What we do know tells us of a simple, God-fearing, God-loving man, who found in honest labor and in the service of other men a life of complete happiness.

He was a comb-maker, a skilled craftsman, in Siena. Some, though not all the authorities hold that he is the "Peter Pettinagno," "Comb-maker," to the efficacy of whose prayers Dante alludes in the thirteenth canto of his *Purgatorio*. He had known a marriage of great happiness; but he and his wife had no children, and her death left him alone in the world. He went on working and earning his bread; but he joined the Third Order of the Franciscans, and presently the Franciscan guardian allowed him to live and work in a cell close to their infirmary. There he spent long hours each day at his trade (like so many manual workers, he found in the constant occupation of his hands a release for his mind into prayer); and whatever time and money he had to spare went to the care of those less fortunate than himself. He was most regular in his visits to the sick in the Della Scala hospital; for the rest, he lived a life withdrawn, humble, very devoted to the virtue of silence; and those who knew him tell of the many hours of contemplative prayer which, each day, this busily-employed man found time for.

He was indeed one of those for whom Christ thanked His Father, to whom secrets are revealed which are hidden from the great and wise ones of this earth. The secret which Peter learned was of the content and peace and happiness which God alone can give.

Christ is All to All Men

"I saw Him clothed in flesh as man. He came from the east.
I saw Him bathed in blood that ran. He came from the west.
I saw the multitude He brought. He came from the south.
I saw the world, how it cared nought. He came from the north.

I came from the wedding as a sweet spouse, who has led his
   bride within.
I came from the fight as a valiant knight, who shall every
   battle win.
I came from the market as a rich merchant, who has bought
   the human race.
I came from an unknown land like a holy pilgrim who has
   wandered in many a place."

English, anonymous, fourteenth century

B. Mazzara: *Leggendario Francescano* (Venice, 1721). Archivum Franciscanum Historicum, 14, 1921.

Edburga
Abbess

died 751

WE ARE TOLD that St. Edburga was herself of the royal house of Kent; and she succeeded two Kentish princesses as the third abbess of Minster Thanet. The site of this abbey, in the northeastern corner of Kent, had evidently been chosen for its seclusion, far from other habitations and close to the sea shore; but those who built it could not have foreseen how utterly defenseless it would be, once Danish pirates began invading the Thames estuary and the surrounding territories. Edburga herself was spared these horrors, but soon after her death occurred the first of two disastrous Danish attacks, in one of which the abbess and all her sisters were burned alive as their house was put to the flames. The monastery rapidly declined, and in the early eleventh century it was totally abandoned.

These events are typical of the dreadful ruin which the Church in England suffered in this epoch, the ruin which King Alfred lamented when he recalled the learning, the godliness, and the splendor of the monastic houses before the Danish wars began. Alfred contrasted it with the total decay of religious life and of education which he found when he succeeded to the throne of Wessex. In former times, England had been especially notable for its great numbers of holy and learned women; one of them, the missionary abbess St. Lioba (*see* September 28) has been mentioned. Another such was Edburga, of whom we know most through her

913

friendship and correspondence with the great missionary, St. Boniface (*see* June 5).

Boniface evidently had her whole confidence. When she wanted an account of a recent vision of the after life, said to have been granted to an English monk, it is to Boniface, as a reliable source, that she applies for information. On the other hand, it is plain that he received many benefits, spiritual and temporal, from her. In one letter he thanks her for a gift of books, and in another asks for a splendid copy of the Epistles of St. Peter to be made (he sends her the necessary materials for this), so that he may by this impress upon his converts the worth and the sacredness of the Scriptures. It would seem that at Thanet Edburga or her predecessors had established a notable writing-school. Later, a few years only before her death and his martyrdom, he is writing to her to ask for her prayers. He tells her of the hardships of his life, and, above all, of his anxieties for the pagans whom he is seeking to convert, and for whom, too, he begs her to pray.

So to be honored with this great man's friendship and trust is itself a measure of the abbess' own qualities, and of how women like her, dedicated to the service of God in seclusion, could and can help those who are out in the world preaching His kingdom.

A Missionary Asks for Prayers

"Pray, therefore, the merciful defender of our lives, the only refuge of the afflicted, the Lamb of God who has taken away the sins of the world, to keep us safe from harm with His sheltering right hand as we go among the dens of such wolves; that where there should be the lovely feet of those who bear the torch of gospel peace, there may not be the dark and wandering footsteps of apostates, but that when our loins are girded the Father all-merciful may put blazing torches in our hands to enlighten the hearts of the Gentiles to the vision of the gospel of the glory of Christ. And I pray also that you may be pleased to make intercession for those heathen who have been given into our charge by the Apostolic See, that the Savior of the world may see fit to rescue them from the worship of idols and join them to the sons of the only Catholic

Mother Church, to the praise and glory of His name whose will it is that all men shall be saved and shall come to the knowledge of the truth."

From A letter of St. Boniface to St. Edburga (trans. Ephraim Emerton)

J. Capgrave: *Nova Legenda Angliae* (Wynkyn de Worde, 1517).
E. Emerton, ed. and trans.: *The Letters of Saint Boniface* (New York, 1940).

Lucy
Martyr

died third century

THERE CAN BE LITTLE DOUBT that Lucy existed, that she lived in Syracuse in Sicily, and that she died there for the Christian faith. She may well, like so many Sicilians, have been of partly Greek stock; the legends are unanimous in giving her mother a Greek name, Eutychia. She is commemorated in the canons both of the Roman and the Ambrosian (Milan) Mass, itself evidence that veneration of her was of great antiquity; and that veneration has always been widespread, among Greeks and Latins alike.

Perhaps because of her name and its suggested association with "light," she has been invoked as one whose prayers will help those with failing or diseased sight. This may be the genesis of the commonest form of her legend, in which, betrothed against her will to a young pagan, she disfigures herself (or prays to be disfigured) by the tearing out of her eyes. In the gruesome fashion of the Middle Ages, she is commonly represented by painters holding a dish with her eyes lying on it. The historians now tell us that this whole legend is a mere fiction, of which nothing, except her martyr's death, can be shown to be true of the real Lucy.

But in the persistence and the popularity of her cult, we see the great reverence in which the Church has always held and still holds those who vow their virginity to God and live for love of Him spotless lives, as did Christ and His blessed Mother, and those also who seal with their blood their self-dedication to Him. Constantly, in the cruel and barbaric times in which Lucy lived, we find the martyrs' persecutors and judges amazed and awed to see

916

such constancy and fearlessness not only in grown men but in tender women and girls, ready to fight like soldiers for their forbidden faith. Such a tender warrior was Lucy; and for this alone, all that we know of her, she deserves her place in the Church's liturgies and prayers.

Love Conquers All

"How sweet the cross! how painless falls the steel!
Are these brief pangs all that of death I feel?
A thousandfold such wounds my love shall heal.
Love carries me through all, love conquers pain;
O let me die indeed, but die without a stain."

Quid Tyranne, Quid Minaris *(trans. D. T. Morgan)*

H. Delehaye: *Les légendes hagiographiques* (Brussels, 1927).

Venantius Fortunatus
Bishop

died about 605

THERE ARE MANY holy men and women in the Church's calendar who, after leading deeply sinful and worldly lives, were suddenly converted from sinner to saint. Not so frequently commemorated are the less vivid characters who are pulled along over the years by the power of grace from a limited kind of worldliness into a solid sort of sanctity which appears unremarkable. St. Venantius Fortunatus is one of these. He has attracted attention more for his poetry than for his holiness. And because a good deal of his poetry reveals worldly tastes and qualities, his slow but steady growth in holiness has frequently gone unnoticed, sometimes has even been denied. But it can fairly be maintained that through his ever deepening grasp of the truths of faith which his poems reveal, and his deep love and respect for saints like Radegunde and Gregory of Tours, he did eventually, especially in his short term as bishop of Poitiers, reveal in an especial manner the holiness of Christ.

This is specially evident in his series of meditations, written toward the end of his long life, on the petitions of the "Our Father." Dilating on the phrase, "our daily bread," he writes: "It seems to imply that every day, if it is possible, we should reverently take communion of His Body; for since He, our life, is our nourishment, we make ourselves strangers if we are slow to approach the Eucharist."

Born at Treviso about 535, he received his first schooling in the monastery at Aquileia. It was there that he acquired the knowl-

918

edge of the Bible, particularly of the Pauline epistles, which gives such strength and form to his religious poems. Though he never claimed to be a theologian, it is clear enough that in the monastery, where, two centuries before, St. Jerome (*see* September 30) had gathered his ascetic circle, Venantius became thoroughly acquainted with Jerome's translations and commentaries.

His schooling finished, he resisted the suggestion of Paul, bishop of Aquileia, that he should become a novice in the monastery. Instead, he took up residence in Ravenna, where he continued to study the classical Latin poets. At the age of thirty, he left Ravenna for Tours, to give thanks at the shrine of St. Martin (*see* November 11), to whose intercession he attributed the cure of an eye ailment. (Of this journey, one of Venantius' biographers somewhat waspishly remarks that "it was not so much a pilgrimage as a tourist-trip.") From Tours he went to Poitiers, where he returned to his Scriptural studies, and was ordained priest.

Here, for most of the years remaining to him, he acted as general agent and estate manager for the convent of the Holy Cross, and became firm friends with its foundress, Radegunde, and with Agnes, who later became abbess. For the latter he wrote his longest poem, in praise of virginity, which contains many beautiful and memorable passages.

The Church through the ages has profited most from Venantius' relations with the convent of the Holy Cross, through the great hymns he wrote there, the *Vexilla Regis*, still recited in the Roman Breviary at Vespers during Passiontide, and the *Pange Lingua Gloriosi* ("Sing, my tongue, the glorious battle"), which is sung during the Adoration of the Cross in the Good Friday liturgy. These, and another splendid poem, *Crux benedicta*, were composed for an occasion when a relic of the true Cross was presented to the convent. These hymns mark Venantius as one of the finest of medieval Latin poets.

Radegunde died in 587, and Agnes not long afterwards. Venantius lived on to be consecrated bishop of Poitiers in 600.

The Cross: Emblem of Christ the King

"The royal banners forward go,
The Cross shines forth in mystic glow,
When He in flesh, our flesh who made,
Our sentence bore, our ransom paid.

His feet and hands outstretching there,
He willed the piercing nails to bear,
For us and our redemption's sake
A victim of Himself to make.

There whilst He hung, His sacred side
By soldier's spear was opened wide,
To cleanse us in the precious flood
Of water mingled with His blood.

Fulfilled is now what David told
In true prophetic song of old,
How God the heathens' King should be
For God is reigning from the tree.

O tree of glory, tree most fair,
Ordained these holy limbs to bear,
How bright in royal hue it stood,
The purple of a Savior's blood!

Upon its arms, like balance true,
He weighed the price for sinners due,
The price which none but He could pay,
And spoiled the spoiler of his prey.

To Thee, eternal Three in One,
Let homage meet by all be done,
As by the Cross Thou dost restore
To rule and guide us evermore!"

The hymn Vexilla Regis, *by Venantius Fortunatus (trans. Neale)*

P. Godet, art.: "Fortunat" (DTC, 6, coll. 611–14).

Nino
Virgin

died 4th century

RUFINUS OF AQUILEIA, who died in 410, translated Eusebius' *Ecclesiastical History,* and added to it portions, one of which contains his account of the virgin, Nino, and of her share in the conversion of Georgia. Rufinus says that this was recounted to him by Bacurius, a Georgian king whom he had met in the Holy Land.

Georgia in Transcaucasia, on the shores of the Black Sea, had as its focal point the east Georgian kingdom of Iberia. Its people, ethnically and linguistically distinct from their neighbors, were Christianized at the end of the third century, and ancient tradition attributes this to the witness and apostolate of St. Nino. The version of her story given by Rufinus is the oldest and purest, free from the many later Georgian and Armenian accretions, which developed into a whole cycle of legends of no historical value whatever.

As told by Rufinus, the story has several curious features. Apart from the name of Bacurius, there is no single indigenous name of person or place given, not even that of the virgin who converted the land (she acquired the appellation "Nino" later in Georgia, and the Roman Martyrology called her "Christiana," "the Christian woman," because it did not know her name). Nor are there any dates. Nonetheless, the Bollandist Peeters was satisfied with the historical content of Rufinus' story.

It tells that she was a Roman captive, taken as a slave to pagan Georgia, who there edified all the inhabitants by her chaste life and her constancy in prayer. Her prayers obtained the miraculous cure of a dying child. The queen of the land, sick, sought her out, and was also cured. She and the king received instruction and baptism, and Nino was given license to preach and teach. It was only then that the king sent to the emperor for bishops and priests to continue and extend her work.

It is the antiquity and persistence of this tradition, and the lasting devotion of the Georgian people to this mysterious woman evangelist, which most encourage us to remember her among the many who have obeyed the Lord's command to make His word known among all nations.

Conversion through a Miracle

"Now there was a young boy of noble birth who was very sick, and his mother took him from door to door, to see if perchance she might find some skilled in healing, and helpful in his trouble. They all diligently enquired into his sickness, but none could cure the child, and the physicians told the woman that her boy could never be healed. The woman was a bitter heathen, hating the Christian faith, and hindering others from going to consult Nino; but, being in despair, she came and fell down before Nino, entreating her to heal the lad. Nino said: 'That healing art which is of man I do not know; but my God whom I serve, Christ, can cure this child, though all think his case hopeless.' She placed the sick boy on the cloth on which she always prayed, and began to entreat the Lord, and the child was cured. She gave the astonished and joyful boy back to his mother, who confessed Christ, saying: 'There is no God save Christ whom Nino preaches.'"

From an early Georgian Life

M. and J. O. Wardop, trans.: *Life of St. Nino* (Studia Biblica et Ecclesiastica, v, 1900, pp. 1-66).
P. Peeters: *Lés débuts du christianisme en Georgie* (AB, 50, 1932, pp. 1-58).

Mary Fontanella
Carmelite Nun

died 1717

THERE ARE SAINTS as well as sinners who seem only to be able to do things the hard way; and Blessed Mary Fontanella was one of these. The story of her life in religion reads like a long series of disasters; but each one of these was a disguised blessing, and at every reverse which she met she found a way to renounce yet more of her own will. When she was dying, her sorrowing community asked their superiors to put her under obedience to recover; they were sure that she would obey this, as she had every other command throughout her life.

She came of a noble family of Turin, and, though hers was a deeply Christian home, her parents did not wish her to enter religion. Her first start was a false one; she and a Cistercian convent deceived her mother into allowing her to live there, and she was very unhappy with them. She returned home when her father died, and a little later, after further difficulties, she entered Carmel in Turin, this time with the family's consent.

It seemed at first as if this, too, was a mistake; the separation from her home, the Carmelite life, and, above all, her unsympathetic novice mistress tried her resolution. But she persisted, and in the end prospered.

Even as a little child she had had great devotion to the Passion of Christ and compassion for His physical sufferings; and she dedicated herself to severe, self-inflicted bodily mortifications which to most modern minds will appear grotesque and unhealthy. "Other times, other fashions"; and Mary was very convinced that God wanted these sufferings from her in reparation for the sins of others.

She had further sufferings to endure. She served, first as novice mistress, then as prioress, with extreme reluctance and only at a great sacrifice of her own inclinations; but, perhaps because this cost her so much, she was of outstanding ability as a superior.

Her life of prayer was extraordinary, and marked by many supernatural favors. The first of these was a prolonged "dark night," during the years of which she was convinced that she was worthless and abandoned; but in the end she emerged from this trial into a state of great peace, knowing a very close union with God.

Penance for Sinners

"As I stood with my lips pressed to the feet of the Crucified, I understood from my Jesus that it was His will that I should receive each day the discipline, saying thirty-three times the verse, 'We therefore pray you, help your servants, whom you redeemed with your Precious Blood,' with the intention of paying Him as much honor as He received of dishonor from sinners, and that I should offer up His Precious Blood to His eternal Father, praying Him not to permit the Precious Blood of His beloved Son to have been shed in vain, but that He would permit me to be of help to them, asking Him constantly mercy for them. And at this I offered myself to Him, declaring myself ready not only for this but for all that I had perceived of His will for me."

From Blessed Mary's autobiography

A. di S. Luigi Gonzaga: *Vita della B. Maria degli Angeli* (Rome, 1865).

Olympias
Widow and Deaconess

died 408

THE TWENTIETH CENTURY has been marked by the opening to women of many professions and occupations hitherto regarded as proper only for men; and it is natural that in the West many should now be asking whether women should not be permitted to take an even more active part in the apostolate than what is now permitted to them. Those who would wish for this often point to the revival in non-Catholic Churches of the ancient institution of "deaconesses," and the success it has met. We know that Christ Himself, and, after His Ascension, some of His apostles, were accompanied by such "serving women," who cared for them, and, if they were women of means, provided for them on their missionary journeys. This institution survived longer in the Eastern Churches than in the West, and St. Olympias well represents its best characteristics.

She was the only child of a rich Constantinople family, related to the imperial house. She had inherited a huge fortune, and was married to the emperor's treasurer. He, however, died within a very short time, and she incurred the emperor's displeasure by refusing to consider a second match which he thought suitable. For a time she was deprived of the management of her estates and income; but the emperor was so edified by the patience and humility she displayed over this (she wrote to thank him for relieving her of so many burdens) that he relented.

When St. John Chrysostom (*see* January 27) was summoned to Constantinople to serve as its bishop, he found Olympias already established in a way of life which could not fail to win his approval. Living in an austere seclusion with other religious women, her whole life, and her wealth, were devoted to prayer and the care of the needy and afflicted. The bishop himself, never to be forgotten as their friend by the poor of the city, had to remonstrate with her over her prodigal and indiscriminate alms-giving, pointing out to her that she was helping many able-bodied persons to live an idle life.

When, in 404, John Chrysostom was sent into exile, Olympias, like his other friends, was subjected to cruel persecution. Her nearness to the royal family did not spare her, for it was because of the enmity of the empress Eudoxia that the bishop and his adherents were being attacked. Olympias, who was inconsolable for the sufferings and the banishment of John Chrysostom, refused communion with the schismatic usurper who had followed him; her community of women was dispersed because of this, she was fined a great sum of money, insulted and physically assaulted, and finally herself sent into exile.

It is from this last, unhappy period of their lives that we have the seventeen long and beautiful letters which the exiled bishop wrote to her, preserved in the first instance, without doubt, by Olympias for the consolation they gave her in her deep sorrow. He urges fortitude and resignation upon her, he forbids her to despair, he bids her to join her own sufferings to those of Christ and His saints, he praises the holy and useful life she had led in Constantinople, and he begs her to take proper care of her health. One cannot but be moved by these godly and loving counsels, and by all that they tell us of his own patience and resignation, his grief and concern for those involved in his unjust persecution.

Less than a year after his death, caused by the cruelty of his captors, Olympias followed him to God.

The Lord's Light in the Night of Exile

"So long thy power hath blest me, sure it still
   Will lead me on,

O'er moor and fen, o'er crag and torrent, till
  The night is gone,
And with the morn those angel faces smile
Which I have loved long since, and lost awhile."

    John Henry Newman

Vita Sanctae Olympiadis et Narratio Sergiae de eiusdem Translatione (AB, 15, 1896, pp. 400–423; 16, 1897, pp. 44–51).
St. John Chrysostom: *Epistolae* (PG, 52, coll. 529–791).

Winebald
Abbot

died 761

ST. WINEBALD belonged to the heroic age of the conversion by the Anglo-Saxons of their pagan kinsmen of the Germanic lands of the European continent, that age which produced, besides Boniface (*see* June 5), many other great men and women. Winebald's whole family was outstanding for its sanctity and its devotion, so characteristic of the English Church, to the Holy See; and he as a youth was accompanying his father and brother on pilgrimage to Rome, when the father died in Lucca. The sons continued, but Winebald stayed in Rome, being judged too delicate to go with his brother to the Holy Land. He remained in Rome for seven years, studying; then he returned to England, but only to collect others, and take them back to the Holy City, where they seem to have lived some form of the religious life.

Boniface, on his third visit to the pope, learned to know and esteem his fellow countryman, and he took him back with him to his mission territory in Thuringia. There Winebald was ordained priest, and presently he served under his brother, St. Willibald, bishop of Eichstätt. Winebald and his sister, St. Walburga, to whom after her death so much honor was to be paid in Germany, founded a double monastery at Heidenheim, where they established the observance of the Benedictine Rule.

It is from the *Life* written by Hugeburc, a learned nun of Heidenheim, that we know of Winebald's life and works, of his great holiness, and of the zeal which a lifetime of ill-health did not impede. In Boniface's missionary efforts, and in the sanctity of his assistants such as Winebald, there is a lesson relevant to the needs of the mission territories today. They asked in their homeland for men and women who were saintly and accomplished, so that learning might quickly flourish in the lands newly won for Christ; and they deemed it no waste that many of these should live in contemplative houses, to help that work with their prayers and example.

Devotion to the Mass

"The time was not now far off when that venerable man [Winebald] became so infirm that he could no longer go to the church. But he ordered them to arrange an altar in a room adjoining his, and there, whenever sickness would allow him to do so, he celebrated the sacred mysteries of the Mass. And before this, when ill-health did not prevent it, it was seldom or never that a day passed without his saying Mass."

From Hugeburc's Life

Monumenta Germaniae Historica, Scriptores, 15, pp. 106–17

Urban V
Pope

died 1370

BLESSED URBAN V was one of the seven popes of the "Babylonian Captivity," during the years 1305–78, when the Holy See was in permanent residence at Avignon, in southern France, where today an immense palace stands above the river as an empty monument to that strange episode in the history of the Western Church. It may be that even now we tend to see it too much through Roman eyes, to regard the "Captivity" as an unqualified disaster, to forget the lesson which it taught, that even if Rome cannot do without the papacy, the papacy can, if there be need, do without Rome.

It was Benedict XI who, restricted and opposed by the great Roman families, and powerless to control the lawlessness and brigandry in his own territories, withdrew from Rome to Perugia, where he died; but several of his predecessors had, in fact, spent more time out of Rome than in the city. Benedict's successor, Clement V, a Frenchman, created a French majority in the Sacred College, and lived as pope in France, latterly at Avignon, where he died, having there established a seat which was in theory independent, though in fact much under the influence of the French kings.

Urban V was born William de Grimoard, and at the time of his election he was the abbot of the Benedictine house of St. Victor in Marseilles. He was chosen because of an impasse among the electing cardinals. He was well known as a man of outstanding holiness of life; and from the beginning of his pontificate he carried on the reforms of his predecessor. He was crowned at Avignon with the minimum of pomp (the luxury for which the papal court in France had become notorious was to him detestable). Immediately he began to suppress the widespread immorality, heresy, and sloth among the clergy, to enforce the Church's laws concerning the holding of provincial councils, and to put an end to the disgraceful corruptions of the Roman curia.

In 1367 he overbore the resistance of the cardinals, who did not want to leave France, and returned with them to Rome. He entered the city to fantastic scenes of rejoicing; but when he saw its ruined state he wept. The Vatican palace, where he was to reside, had not even a roof; and we are told that cattle roamed in the basilica of St. Mary Major, cropping the grass that grew between the broken paving stones around the high altar. There, as in Avignon, he showed himself, despite the extreme simplicity of his own life, a great patron of learning and of the arts. He set about restoring the city with immense energy, not always, his critics said, stopping to ask where the money was to come from and by what questionable means it was to be raised.

But three years were enough to make him lose heart. Like his cardinals, he longed for the peace, the security, and the milder climate of France, and he wearied of the endless, violent Roman squabbles. In 1370, despite the warnings of Bridget of Sweden (*see* October 8) and Peter of Aragon that if he departed he would never see Rome again, he returned to Avignon, where he died in December of that year. The final restoration to Rome of the Holy See was achieved under his successor, Gregory XI.

Perhaps Urban was not the man for the times. Beyond doubt, he would have been venerated as a saint had he never become more than an abbot in Marseilles. During his lifetime his sanctity was no match for the worldly forces against which he was committed to fight. The popes had become secular princes, so deeply involved in European power-politics that they could not feed Christ's sheep; and the history of holy men like Urban only serves to emphasize how far the Church of their time had strayed from the commands of her divine master.

A Lament for Desolated Holy Places

"Level, level with the ground
the towers do lie
which with their golden glittering tops
pierced once to the sky.
Where were gates, no gates are now,
the ways unknown
where the press of peers did pass
while her fame far was blown.
Owls do shriek where the sweetest hymns
lately were sung;
toads and serpents hold their dens
where the palmers did throng."

A Lament for Our Lady's Shrine at Walsingham, *anonymous,
sixteenth century, attributed to B. Robert Southwell*

J.-H. Albanes, ed. U. Chevalier: *Actes anciens et documents concernant le bienheureux Urbain V pape* (Paris, 1897).
G. Mollat, trans. J. Love: *The Popes at Avignon, 1305–1378* (London, 1963).

Philogonius
Bishop

died 324

ALL OUR INFORMATION about St. Philogonius comes from a panegyric preached on his feast-day, five days before Christmas,
in 386 by St. John Chrysostom (*see* January 27). From being a lawyer of high repute for his integrity and knowledge, Philogonius became a bishop, and brought the same qualities of probity and fearlessness to leading his people and protecting the purity of Catholic
doctrine, during one of the worst phases of the Arian heresy.

John Chrysostom speaks of him as a great spiritual benefactor;
not to sing his praises on his feast-day would be equivalent to
disobeying the precept, "Honor thy father and thy mother."
Beginning with the text, "The memory of the just is full of praise"
(Prov. 10:7), he exhorts the congregation to rejoice in Philogonius' glory, peace, and tranquillity in heaven, whither the Lord
has conducted him as one endowed not with material blessings,
but with the fruits of the Spirit, love, joy, goodness, peace, and
patience. He praises him especially for his magnanimity, his
greatness of soul, which enabled him to treat in exactly the same
way all who sought his help, rich and poor alike.

"God chose Philogonius for his outstanding moral rectitude; He
plucked him from the midst of the law-courts and raised him to
the episcopacy. He had acted as counsel for so many who had
suffered injury; now he was his people's protector against infernal
enemies. God judged him worthy to be a magistrate in His own
kingdom . . ."

Christ said to Peter: "If you love me, feed my sheep," meaning "He who loves my sheep loves me." Christ said to Peter:

933

"Strengthen your brethren"; and Paul said: "Be imitators of me, as I am of Christ." In all these texts we can recognize that the man who loves Christ truly and faithfully is one who has care for the brethren, and looks out for their salvation. Even such, says Chrysostom, was Philogonius, and especially during the time when his flock was harried by Arian persecution. His reward is in the heavenly Jerusalem, in the company of countless angels.

The Heavenly Jerusalem

"Jerusalem the golden,
  With milk and honey blest,
Beneath thy contemplation
  Sink heart and voice opprest.
I know not, O I know not
  What joys await us there,
What radiancy of glory,
  What bliss beyond compare.

There is the throne of David;
  And there, from care released,
The shout of them that triumph,
  The song of them that feast;
And they who with their Leader
  Have conquer'd in the fight,
For ever and for ever
  Are clad in robes of white.

O sweet and blessèd country,
  The home of God's elect!
O sweet and blessèd country
  That eager hearts expect!
Jesu, in mercy bring us
  To that dear land of rest;
Who art with God the Father
  And Spirit ever blest."

From Bernard of Murels' De Contemptu Mundi (*trans. J. M. Neale*)

John Chrysostom: *In beatum Philogonium* (PG, 48, 747-52).

Thomas
Apostle

died first century

OFTENTIMES IN THE NEW TESTAMENT, in His dealings with His apostles, our Lord is recorded as saying: "O men of little faith, why do you doubt?" Thomas, who "is called Didymus," "the twin," has become, largely through the special attention given to him in the fourth Gospel, the personification of that state of doubt which finds belief in God's power, or His promises in Christ, rather too much for human comprehension. That this, in fact, was not Thomas' state of mind ought to emerge from a prayerful reflection on what St. John has to say about him.

When our Lord received the news of the sickness of Lazarus of Bethany, He said to His disciples: "Let us go into Judea again." They remonstrated with Him: "Master, the Jews have just now been seeking to stone you, and will you go there again?" Eventually it is Thomas who cuts short any further argument by saying to his fellow-disciples: "Let us go too, that we may die with Him" (John 11:1-16).

Again, at the Last Supper, Christ says to His disciples: "I go to prepare a place for you; I will come again and take you to myself, that where I am you may be also. And you know the way where I am going." We can have no doubt that all the apostles were puzzled by this statement; but it is Thomas who with simplicity and directness voices the question in the hearts of them all: "Lord, we do not know where you are going, so how can we know the way?" And Jesus uses Thomas' question to enlighten their minds on His own nature and His relationship with His Father: "I am the way, the truth and the life; no one comes to the Father except by me" (John 14:1-7).

The Lord had also warned the disciples that in a time of great tribulation there would appear false prophets and false Christs, who would, if possible, lead even the elect astray: "Then, if anyone says to you, 'Lo, here is the Christ!', or 'There he is!' do not believe him" (Matt. 24:23-24). So when Thomas is told by the other apostles, in that time of great tribulation after the Crucifixion, "We have seen the Lord," he may well have recalled Christ's own warning (cf. John 20:24-25).

When, at last, the Lord appears again to His disciples, this time with Thomas among them, He turns to him immediately, and picks up the words His apostle had used concerning the sort of assurance he would require: "Unless I can put my finger into the point of the nails . . ." But, as soon as Thomas sets eyes on our Lord, there is no longer room for any hesitation. The Lord's presence brings him out of his darkness into the full light of faith, and he voices his conviction by confessing his Master's divinity. And, for the consolation of every troubled Christian from that day to this, Jesus crowns the faith of the apostles (all of whom, including John himself, did not remember the Lord's prophecy about His resurrection until after the event, and so were all in this sense "doubting Thomases") by promising happiness to all who find it in their hearts to believe fully without seeing what Thomas saw (John 20:26-29).

The apostolic Church appreciated the promise "Blessed are they who have not seen, yet believe," as we learn from the first letter of Peter: "You have never seen him, yet you love him; you do not see him now, yet you believe in him. And if you continue to believe, how your faith will triumph, when you receive its reward, the salvation of your souls" (1 Pet. 1:8-9).

We know nothing further for certain of Thomas after Pentecost. Scholars still continue their researches into the apocryphal Acts of Thomas and the various traditions concerning his preaching and martyrdom in Persia or India. All this is less important than the Scriptural facts about him, and the blessing that our faith has received through his agency.

An Act of Faith in Christ's Presence

"Thy wounds as Thomas saw I do not see,
Yet thee confess my Lord and God to be.
Make me believe thee ever more and more,
In thee my hope, in thee my love to store."

St. Thomas Aquinas: Adoro Te Devote

John 11.5-16; 14.1-6; 20.24-9.

Frances Xavier Cabrini
Foundress of the Missionary Sisters of the Sacred Heart

died 1917

THE EVILS WHICH attend mass emigrations are only too familiar: the low standards of education of those whom poverty forces to leave their homes, their ignorance of the conditions and customs of the lands they go to, their ruthless exploitation when they arrive, too often by their own countrymen already settled there, and the bitter antagonisms they encounter. St. Frances Cabrini was called to work with her nuns among their compatriots in "Little Italy," the appalling New York ghetto created last century by the millions who crossed the Atlantic in search of the fabled prosperity of the New World.

From her infant years, she had had a dream of helping to save pagan souls in China; and when she founded a new congregation, she called herself and her first helpers "missionary sisters" without knowing how and when they would leave Italy. When in the end her call came, from her own diocesan bishop and the then archbishop of New York, to go to the United States, she was disposed to refuse this as too easy an assignment, with little real sacrifice in it. She soon learned how mistaken she was.

Her first inklings of the apostolate which awaited her came on the overcrowded ship in which they sailed, where she was of comfort and help to the sick and bewildered Italians packed in the steerage holds. A cruel disappointment awaited her in New York; nothing of what she had been promised had been done, and her chief lay sponsor and the archbishop were quarrelling. When the archbishop told her to go home again, she replied that it was the

938

Holy See which had sent her, and only the Holy See could recall her. With that, she set to work.

Her achievements belong to history: her orphanages and hospitals, her perilous journeyings in South America, her disregard of every obstacle and difficulty. She had all an Italian's drive and energy and business acumen, and boundless faith and trust in God. "Are we doing this, or is Our Lord?" she would answer to expostulations. And her nuns, fired with her own spirit, made themselves known as intrepid workers for God. When they celebrated their first jubilee in 1914, they received a congratulatory letter from the inmates of Sing Sing prison, where they were regular visitors, and had helped many condemned to death to end their lives in peace.

Three years later Mother Cabrini died in the America which had more than fulfilled all her early dreams of China. Her rapid progress to beatification and canonization was helped by the great devotion of those who had recognized in her a true servant of God's universal Church.

Prayer for Conversions

"Pray much, for the salvation of these people does not depend upon material power, or the vain learning that clouds and blinds the understanding; nor does it depend upon arms, nor upon sterile diplomatic congresses, nor, in fine, upon any human agency. The grace of their salvation can come only from the loving heart of the chief Shepherd, who gathered the apostles and promised grace and blessing to all their successors who remain faithful in union with him who is the foundation rock, the pope."

Mother Cabrini

A Benedictine of Stanbrook Abbey: *Frances Xavier Cabrini, the Saint of the Emigrants* (London, 1944).

Servulus
Beggar

died about 590

ONE SEXAGESIMA SUNDAY in the Basilica of St. Paul in Rome, St. Gregory (*see* March 12) was preaching on the gospel of the day, the parable of the sower. When he came to the phrase "The seed that falls on good ground . . . brings forth fruit in patience" (Luke 8:15), he used, as an illustration of the text, the story of Servulus, a holy man whom many of Gregory's congregation had known, for he was a beggar whose regular station was near the church of St. Clement. The story and the man obviously made a great impression on Gregory; the holy portents accompanying St. Servulus' death, he told the congregation, were a sign of his entry into Paradise, the reward for true Christian patience and charity. For, as Gregory emphasizes, whatever alms he collected were not for himself, but for distribution to the poor. Since Gregory told the story again in his "Dialogues" for the Roman people on the holy men and women of the past, it is well that he be allowed to tell it in his own words here.

The Beggar at the Door of San Clemente

"In one of my homilies on the Gospels, I remember telling you the story of Servulus. I expect that many of you knew him, because he used to be in the portico which leads into the church of Blessed Clement. He was a man poor in this world's goods, but very rich in merit. His body was wasted by long years of suffering. As long as I remember seeing him, and to the end of his life, he was completely paralyzed. To say that

940

he could not stand up hardly describes his condition; he could not even raise himself up on his stretcher to a sitting position, or turn on his side, or lift his hand to his mouth. His mother and his brother looked after him; and he would ask them to distribute among the poor whatever alms had been given him. Though he could not read, he had bought for himself the books of Sacred Scripture; but he used to invite certain religious to his house, and get them to read regularly to him from the Scriptures. In this way he soon became deeply learned in the word of God, although, as I say, he was completely illiterate. It was his practice when in pain always to give thanks to God; he spent whole days and nights singing His praises. When at last the time came for his great patience to be rewarded, his sickness spread inwards to the vital organs. He knew that he was very close to death; and he warned some pilgrims to whom he had given shelter to get up out of bed and to join him in the singing of psalms as a preparation for his end. While they were singing psalms with the dying man, he suddenly silenced them in the midst of their song, crying out in a loud voice: 'Listen! Can you hear how these same praises are ringing out in heaven?' And even as he was inwardly listening to the heavenly music, his soul was freed from his body. At the same moment, so fragrant an odor filled the place that all present were overcome by an indescribable sweetness, which told them plainly that those singing in heaven had received his soul."

From St. Gregory the Great's "Dialogues"

St. Gregory the Great: *Dialogorum Liber IV* (PL, 77, coll. 341–44); *Homiliarum in Evangelia*, XV (*ibid.* 76, coll. 1131–34).

Paula Cerioli
Foundress of the Institute of the Holy Family of Bergamo

died 1865

ON CHRISTMAS EVE, our minds turn to the Holy Family, to the poverty and wretchedness into which our Savior was born, homeless and destitute in Bethlehem. Blessed Paula Cerioli, who died on this day a century ago, found her recompense for her own sad life in caring for the homeless and destitute. Robbed by death of her only natural consolation, her own child, she devoted herself to orphaned children who did not know the love and the care she had lavished on her son.

She was the child of wealthy and noble parents, who, when she was nineteen years old, married her off to a widower forty-one years her senior. His only charm appears to have been his great fortune; her biographers seem to be expressing themselves mildly when they call him "misanthropic and unattractive." She gave birth to three children, only one of whom survived, a boy called Charles who gave early signs of great holiness of life. He died when he was sixteen; the memory of him was to be a potent influence in his mother's life.

After nineteen years of unhappy marriage she was left an extremely rich widow. She withdrew from society, and devoted herself to works of charity, especially to the care of orphans, beginning, in a very practical way, by taking two of them into her own home. Three years after her husband's death her orphans had so increased in numbers that she founded, first an institute to care for girls, then a parallel brothers' congregation for the education of boys. She had more than riches and piety to bring to this undertaking; at a time when rural districts and their workers were depressed and deprived, she saw the necessity of training her children to take a full and fruitful part in agricultural life. Her wisdom was as great as her compassion.

The Justification of Affliction

"It was God alone who in His providence led her soul along the rough ways of this world, not as men would have expected; He, that same God, alone who fired her with a burning desire for the life of the cloister, in His care for her leading her, and trying her by many sufferings, before He made plain to her the road along which He was calling her. It was God alone who guided her to turn the vast wealth which she had inherited to use for the profit of souls and for the works of everlasting salvation. It was God alone who at last changed His servant's life of daily sacrifice, impossible for human judgment to explain, into the healing joy which she brought to so many boys and girls, cruelly robbed of their parents."

Pius XII's promulgation of Paula's beatification

Acta Apostolicae Sedis, xlii, 1950, pp. 290–94.
S. Mattei, art.: "Cerioli, Paola Elisabetta, beata" (BS, 3, coll. 1138–39).

The Nativity

"WHEN OUR LORD AND SAVIOR was born in Bethlehem, as the sacred story of the Gospel witnesses, it was shepherds of that region, watching and keeping guard by night over their flocks, to whom the messenger of the Lord appeared. He came surrounded by a great light, and he announced that the Sun of Justice had risen over the world. This was made known to them by hearing this voice from heaven, but also by the brightness of a light from God. In all the Old Testament, when angels so often appeared to the patriarchs, never do we find them coming in such a light; this privilege was rightly withheld until today, when over the darkness rose that light, the merciful and just Lord, to shine upon those who are true of heart. Nor was this made known upon the authority only of a single angel, for when he had proclaimed this mystery of a new birth, at once a great multitude of the heavenly hosts appeared, singing glory to God and preaching peace to men, showing plainly that by this nativity men were to be turned to the peace of a common faith and hope and love and were to give glory to God by their praises."

Bede: Homily for the Dawn Mass on Christmas Day

"We know in our faith and our belief, through the teaching and the preaching of Holy Church, that the Blessed Trinity made man's nature in their image and likeness. In the same way, we know that when man fell so deep and so wretchedly by sin, there was no other help to restore man than through Him who made

944

man. And He that made man for love, by this same love willed to restore man to the same happiness, and even more. For just as we were made like to the Trinity in our first making, our Maker willed that we should be like to Jesus Christ our Savior, in heaven without end, by virtue of our remaking. Then between these two makings, He willed for love of man and in reverence for him to make Himself as like to man in this mortal life, in our foulness and in our wretchedness, as a man could be without sin."

Julian of Norwich: Revelations, *chapter 10*

"Since by the mystery of the Incarnate Word the eyes of our mind have been illumined by the new lights of your brightness, as we recognize a God made visible, by Him may we be borne into the realm of an invisible love."

Preface for the Christmas Mass

Stephen
The First Martyr

died first century

DURING THE PERSECUTION of Diocletian at Heraclea in Thrace, when the imperial officers came to seize the church and turn out the worshippers, Bishop Philip (*see* October 22) said to them: "The most High does not dwell in houses made with hands, but rather in the hearts of men. As the prophet says: 'Heaven is my throne, and the earth my footstool.' 'What house will you build for me,' says the Lord, 'or what is my place of rest? Has not my hand made all these things?' " (cf. Acts 7:48-50).

Philip was citing from the great sermon of St. Stephen before the high priest and the council at Jerusalem, the most complete description in the New Testament of the salvation history of Israel. In this sermon Stephen recalled God's repeated covenants with His people, through Abraham, Isaac, Jacob, and Moses, and the wise men David and Solomon, and he showed how the whole culminates in Christ, whom the Jews had just rejected, "His betrayers and murderers."

The passion of Stephen and his speech before the Sanhedrin is closely patterned on the events of Christ's trial and His prophesying before the high priest. We recall, too, that the Jews took up stones to cast at Christ, alleging that He was blaspheming. Stephen reminded his hearers also of what the Lord had said: "Jerusalem, Jerusalem, you kill the prophets and stone those who are sent to you" (Matt. 23:34–37). He is aware of being the first of those whom Christ has promised to send to the Jews and who, He prophesied, would be put to death by them.

As he speaks, Stephen is aware of the fulfillment, for him, of our Lord's prophecy before the Sanhedrin that "hereafter the Son of Man shall be sitting on the right hand of the power of God" (Luke 22:69). "Behold," he says, "I see the heavens opened, and the Son of Man standing at the right hand of God."

Like our Lord, as he offers his life for the sake of his persecutors, Stephen prays that they may be forgiven: "Lord, do not hold this sin against them." Again like his Master, who offered up His spirit into the hands of His Father, Stephen offers himself thus: "Lord Jesus, receive my spirit."

Stephen, then, chosen by the apostles as the first deacon, because he was "a man full of faith and the Holy Spirit," is revealed to us as the ideal servant of Christ; and the first fruits of his service is the conversion of Saul (*see* January 25), who "was consenting to his death." Stephen draws for us the bold, clear lines of the preaching of Christ's gospel, and of Christ Himself. So he was chosen out by God to be the Son's first witness; and the Church honors him specially as such, by placing his feast at the heart of the annual commemoration of God becoming man.

The First Martyr

"First of martyrs, thou whose name
   Doth itself a crown proclaim
Not of flowers that fade away,
   Fashion we thy crown today.

First to offer up to Christ
   Life for His life sacrificed
By a death like His to be
   Witness for the Deity.

First to follow where He trod
   Through the deep Red Sea of blood;
First, but after these shall press
   Ranks of martyrs numberless."

   "Hymn for St. Stephen's Day" from Hymns Ancient and Modern

Acts, chapters 6-8.

John
Apostle and Evangelist

died end of first century

FOR MANY YEARS it has been the fashion among biblical exegetes to cast doubt upon the universal tradition that John the apostle was also the evangelist of the fourth Gospel, of the three epistles attributed to him in the canon of Holy Scripture, and of Revelation (the Apocalypse). But despite the many literary and stylistic problems which remain to be solved, most Christians, including many scholars, accept the tradition, reaching back at least to St. Irenaeus (*see* June 28) in the second century, that John the apostle wrote his Gospel and his letters at Ephesus, and Revelation on the island of Patmos.

John, though he worked as a fisherman with his brother James, his father Zebedee, and their partners Peter and Andrew, had connections with the family of the high priest at Jerusalem; he was able to have Peter admitted to the high priest's house on the night when Jesus was betrayed and taken there for interrogation (John 18:15–16). He was, like Peter and Andrew, a disciple of John the Baptist (*see* June 24); he was with Andrew when the Baptist pointed out Jesus, in those words which have been so cherished by Christians through the ages, "Behold the Lamb of God" (John 1:36).

John, "the Theologian," as he soon came to be called in the Church, speaks first in his Gospel of Christ, the eternal God, the omnipotent Creator, the Life-giver, who became a man among us all that we might receive grace from His fullness, might become the sons of the Father by receiving the only begotten Son.

But he is soon telling us of the impact this man made upon him the first time that they met (John 1:37-39). And whenever afterwards he speaks of Jesus, setting down some of His wonderful signs and words ("If they were all written down, the world itself, I think, would not be able to contain the books that should be written" — John 21:25), no matter what mystery He is propounding, no matter what great miracle He is performing, John never forgets, or lets us forget, that Jesus is his true friend, as well as his master, Lord and God; a God who can manifest in human terms care, concern, tenderness. He is "the Word of Life," but "our hands have touched him" (1 John 1:1). He and the Father are one, but He has washed John's feet, the clearest sign of human service, devotedness, love. He forgives sins, and gives His apostles the same ineffable power, but He can stand before Mary Magdalene on Easter Day, and let her think that He is the gardener. And He can confirm Peter, who has denied Him three times, as the keeper of the keys, on the basis of the most radical human question whenever relationship is involved: "Simon, son of John, do you love me?" (John 21:15–17).

This is how John presents his master, Christ our Lord, in his Gospel; and he is anxious that all who read or listen to his message may hear the new commandment Jesus gave, and which John tirelessly preached throughout his long life, "that you love one another as I love you" (John 13:34). We are to understand that eternal life is to know the one true God, and Jesus Christ, whom the Father has sent (John 17:3); but this knowledge, this belief, contains within itself the unifying force of love. So John will say in the last words he wrote for us, for all those who have come, through his Gospel and letters, to understand a little what this knowledge and love means: "Come, Lord Jesus. The grace of our Lord Jesus Christ be with you all. Amen" (Rev. 22:20–21).

Love One Another

"A new commandment I give you: love one another; as I have loved you, you also must love one another. By this love

you have for one another all men will know that you are my
disciples."

John 13:34-35

R. E. Brown, arts.: "John the Apostle" (NCE, 7, pp. 1005–6); "John, Gospel according to" (*ibid.,* pp. 1080–88).

The Holy Innocents
martyred during the infancy of Christ

THE GOSPEL OF ST. MATTHEW is at pains to show that in Christ our Lord we are given a new Moses who has the power to bring the Mosaic Law to its consummation, and to dispense His followers from the spirit, and in many cases, the letter, of its observance. So the evangelist, in writing of the birth and infancy of Christ, selects those traditions which enable him to establish parallels with the infancy of Moses. The birth of both is associated with massacres of Israel's children (Ex. 1:16-22; Matt. 2:13-16); both go down into Egypt (Ex. 3:10; Matt. 2:13-14); in both is fulfilled the prophecy "Out of Egypt have I called my son" (Ex. 12:37-42; Matt. 2:15).

The Gospel narrative, then, for the feast of the Holy Innocents concentrates rather on this vocation of the new Moses, revealed in the events of His infancy. The Roman liturgy, however, particularly in the prayer of the assembly, draws our attention very forcibly to how these innocent children are the first witnesses, in blood, to the Christ, the truth and the life; they are the first fruits from among the redeemed offered to God and to the Lamb, as the first reading in the Mass reminds us (Rev. 14:4). The Church seeks their intercession that God may put to death all evil in us, so that our actions may correspond to the faith we profess.

The feast day must have been established as early as the fifth century in the Latin Church, since it occurs in all the ancient calendars and liturgical books from the sixth century onwards.

It is a feast which has taken hold of popular imagination through many generations, especially in medieval times. In England it was long called "Childermass," and the carol which sings of "Herod the king in his raging, Charged he hath this day, His men of might In his own sight All children young to slay" still retains its popularity.

A Hymn for Innocents' Day

"A hymn for martyrs sweetly sing,
For innocents your praises bring;
Of whom in tears was earth bereaved
Whom heav'n with songs of joy received;
Whose angels see the Father's face,
World without end, and hymn His grace;
And, while they praise their glorious King,
A hymn for martyrs sweetly sing.

A voice from Ramah was there sent,
A voice of weeping and lament,
While Rachel mourn'd her children sore
Whom for the tyrant's sword she bore.
After brief taste of earthly woe
Eternal triumph now they know;
For whom by cruel torments rent,
A voice from Ramah was there sent.

Fear not, o little flock and bless'd
The lion that your life oppress'd;
To heavenly pastures ever new
The heavenly Shepherd leadeth you;
Who, dwelling now on Sion's hill,
The Lamb's own footsteps follow still,
By tyrant there no more distrest,
Fear not, o little flock and bless'd.

And every tear is wiped away
By your dear Father's hands for aye;
Death hath no pow'r to hurt you more;
Your own is life's eternal shore.
And all who, good seed bearing, weep,

In everlasting joy shall reap,
What time they shine in heavenly day,
And every tear is wiped away."

The Venerable Bede's Hymnum Canentes Martyrum *(trans.
J. M. Neale)*

Matthew 2:13–16.
L. Duchesne: *Christian Worship* (London, 1903).

Thomas Becket
Archbishop and Martyr

died 1170

THERE ARE FEW men about whose careers and deaths we are better informed than St. Thomas Becket, chancellor of England and archbishop of Canterbury. There is a vast quantity of contemporary evidence. And many poets and playwrights have found fruitful matter in his life, which answers so completely to the requirements of Aristotle for the subject of tragedy: that it should treat of the rise, fall, and death of a great man, brought about in part by the flaws in his own character.

Yet though we are so well informed, it is very hard to discern what Thomas himself really was like. Here we are primarily concerned with him as a saint; and in this respect, too, we see conflicting elements. His own life was always irreproachably chaste; but what of his thirst for power, his delight in wealth and pomp and glory? Even his enemies admired and respected him, but it would seem that no one in all his life ever loved him. He was all candor and honesty; but though it took a brave man in a moment of great peril to turn on the king's bastard brother and throw his illegitimacy in his teeth, was that the conduct of a holy man? He knowingly and dedicatedly gave his life for the Church and the people of God; but his very prayers were mixed with insulting epithets hurled at his murderers as he fell beneath their blows.

Perhaps the truth is that we expect the saints to be too much of one pattern. Because a Teresa, of Avila or of Lisieux, is given by God total mastery over all that is discordant in her nature, we think that we may expect this of every saint. Thomas was headstrong and wilful, haughty and defiant, scornful of those whose abilities were less than his own, stiffnecked and passionate; but had he not been all these things, he might not have been the man to withstand Henry II and to defend the Church against those determined to despoil her. Nor was it the Church's wealth, vast though that was, which he was protecting; it was her free rule over men's souls for which he fought and died, and that is a principle which will be vital until the end of time.

Martyrdom in Canterbury Cathedral

"Thomas came forward. 'Here am I, no traitor, but a priest ready to suffer in my Redeemer's cause. God forbid that I should flee from your swords or depart from what is just. But do not dare to touch any of my people.' He then retired a few steps and stood by a pillar, with a few monks and clerks by him. 'Reginald, Reginald' he said to FitzUrse, 'is this your return for all that I have done for you?' The knights rushed at him and endeavored to hoist him on the shoulders of William Tracy to carry him outside the church. The first to touch him was FitzUrse. 'Unhand me, Reginald,' exclaimed the archbishop, 'you are my sworn vassal,' and then, struggling with him, 'Unhand me, pander!' He shook himself loose, seized FitzUrse by the mail coat and sent him reeling back. 'I will not leave the church. If you wish to kill me, kill me here.' Then as they delayed to strike, he covered his eyes and bowed his head: 'To God and blessed Mary, St. Denis and St. Alphege I commend myself and my Church'. . . . After the first two blows he was still standing, and FitzStephen heard him say 'Into Thy hands, O Lord, I commend my spirit.' At the third stroke he fell upon his hands and knees, and said in a low voice: 'I accept death for the name of Jesus and for the Church.' Then at the fourth stroke he fell at full length, with his hands outstretched as if in prayer, and his cloak covering his whole body to the feet."

M. D. Knowles' synthesis of the eye-witnesses' accounts

M. D. Knowles: *Archbishop Thomas Becket: a Character Study* (London, 1949).

Margaret Colonna
Virgin

died 1280

BLESSED MARGARET belonged to one of the oldest and most power-ful princely houses of Rome, the Colonnas, still today flourishing. She was the daughter of Prince Odo Colonna, and, early orphaned, she was brought up under the care of her two brothers, one of whom, John, was after her death to write her "First Life."

When in her adolescence the usual suitable marriage was ar-ranged for her, she refused to consider this. Retiring from Rome to a country house in the nearby hill town of Palestrina, she lived there a withdrawn life, devoting herself to work for the sick and the poor.

She founded a convent of nuns, but she seems to have been prevented by sickness from ever herself entering it. Most of her life was a struggle to do the Lord's work despite her own infirmi-ties. She suffered cruelly from cancer for seven years before she died, and in all this time she bore herself not only with patience and resignation but also with gallantry.

While she lived, she received many supernatural graces, in-cluding that of foreknowledge of events; and after her death many miracles were attributed to her intercessions in heaven.

Fortitude in Sickness

"She was suddenly attacked by a tumor, which devoured her skin and flesh and seized upon her very bones, and from it there flowed so much pus mixed with blood that it bathed her entirely, as if it were drawing off the strength of her whole body. But she did not complain, and bore it with great patience until the end of her life. For a long time she concealed her malady even from her brother and her companions, keeping up all her old regime of fasting and vigils and sleeping in her usual hard and narrow bed. When in the end she was forced to reveal her condition to her brother, who had charge of her, he prudently ordered a modification of her austerities. To her great sorrow she had to make this change, but she kept her vigils still with great fervor and much prayer, her spirit seeming always to rise higher as her bodily state afflicted her more cruelly."

From Prince John Colonna's "First Life"

L. Oliger: *B. Margherita Colonna* (Rome, 1935).

Melania
Widow and Abbess

died 439

ST. MELANIA is known as "the Younger" to distinguish her from her grandmother, who as a widow left Rome for Jerusalem and there founded a convent for fifty nuns. They belonged to the Valerii family, who possessed enormous riches and estates throughout the Roman empire.

As a girl, Melania was married by her ambitious family to a boy called Pinian. She already loved God greatly, and wished to dedicate her virginity to him, but Pinian would have none of this; and presently she gave birth to their first child, a girl. A second child soon followed, a boy who lived for only one day; and Melania's own life was in great danger. Pinian was in agony, and vowed to respect his wife's wishes if she lived. She did recover, and he kept his promise, but this greatly displeased her father, who, as long as he lived, insisted that in every respect she comport herself like a rich and fashionable young woman. But the life of luxury and license with which she was surrounded in Rome was deeply distasteful to her, and at her father's death she, her mother, and her husband went to live in retirement in the country. Their villa soon became a center of religious life, and Melania was able to realize some of her wishes: getting rid of the greater part of her fortune, freeing her hordes of slaves, and endowing many charities.

The Gothic invasions caused them to leave Italy for North Africa, where Pinian, now as devoted to God's service as his wife, visited St. Augustine (*see* August 28) at Hippo. From there they went to Jerusalem, and were introduced into the pious circle surrounding St. Jerome (*see* September 30). After fourteen years in the Holy Land, first her mother died, then her husband, whom the Roman Martyrology names together with her as venerated. Then at last Melania was able to do as she had always wished; she founded two monasteries and she herself ruled over one of them.

Her rule was marked, in that age, by its mildness and gentleness; and what we are told of her holy death testifies to the great love in which she was held, not only by her own nuns but by all Jerusalem.

Though her cult was kept alive by the Byzantine and other Churches, in the West she was largely forgotten until modern times, when manuscripts of Greek and Latin versions of her *Life* began to be studied and edited. Since then she has been adopted as patron by the Latin Catholics of many places in the East, including Jerusalem.

Guiding Others with Gentleness and Love

" 'First of all, pray for me; and, if you have any love for me, keep my instructions and my rule. And I would wish you to remember that I have never once rebuked one of you in anger, but always gently, lest I should bring grief to anyone. Never have I allowed any one of you to hold resentment against a sister of hers for as much as a day or a night, but I have always made peace between you, for it is love which perfects our heavenly crown.' "

Melania's dying charge to her nuns—from the Life of St. Melania

Vita Sanctae Melaniae Junioris (AB, 8, 1889, pp. 16-63).
H. Delehaye, ed.: S. *Melaniae iunioris Acta graeca* (AB, 22, 1903, 5-50).

Index

A *general index covering all three volumes of* Following the Saints *begins on page xiii*

Index

iii

General Index

General Index

Picture Credits

Saint Lawrence Giving the Treasures of the Church to the Poor by Bernardo Strozzi; Samuel H. Kress Collection, University of Miami, Joe and Emily Lowe Art Gallery, Coral Gables, Florida.

Saint Francis Receiving the Stigmata by Jan Van Eyck; John G. Johnson Collection, Philadelphia.

Saint Matthew by Simone Martini; Samuel H. Kress Collection, National Gallery of Art, Washington, D.C.

Saint Thomas of Villanova Giving Alms to the Poor by Juan de Valdes Leal; Samuel H. Kress Collection, El Paso Museum of Art, El Paso, Texas.

Saint Simon by Simone Martini; Samuel H. Kress Collection, National Gallery of Art, Washington, D.C.

Saint Andrew by Follower of Pietro Lorenzetti; Kress Study Collection, Museum of Art, Science, and Industry, Bridgeport, Connecticut.

Saint Lucy, attributed to Lorenzo Costa; Samuel H. Kress Collection, The High Museum of Art, Atlanta, Georgia.

Saint Martin and the Beggar by El Greco; The Widener Collection, National Gallery of Art, Washington, D.C.